The Michigan Historical Reprint Series

Reprints from the collection of the University of Michigan University Library

This volume is produced from digital images created through the University of Michigan University Library's preservation reformatting program. The Library seeks to preserve the intellectual content of items in a manner that facilitates and promotes a variety of uses. The digital reformatting process results in an electronic version of the text that can both be accessed online and used to create new print copies. This book and thousands of others can be found in the digital collections of the University of Michigan Library. The University Library also understands and values the utility of print, and makes reprints available through its Scholarly Publishing Office.

For access to the University of Michigan Library's digital collections, please see http://www.lib.umich.edu.

The Scholarly Publishing Office seeks to disseminate high-quality, cost-effective scholarly content through both print and electronic publishing. Information about the Scholarly Publishing Office can be found at http://spo.umdl.umich.edu.

The Scholarly Publishing Office
the University of Michigan
University Library

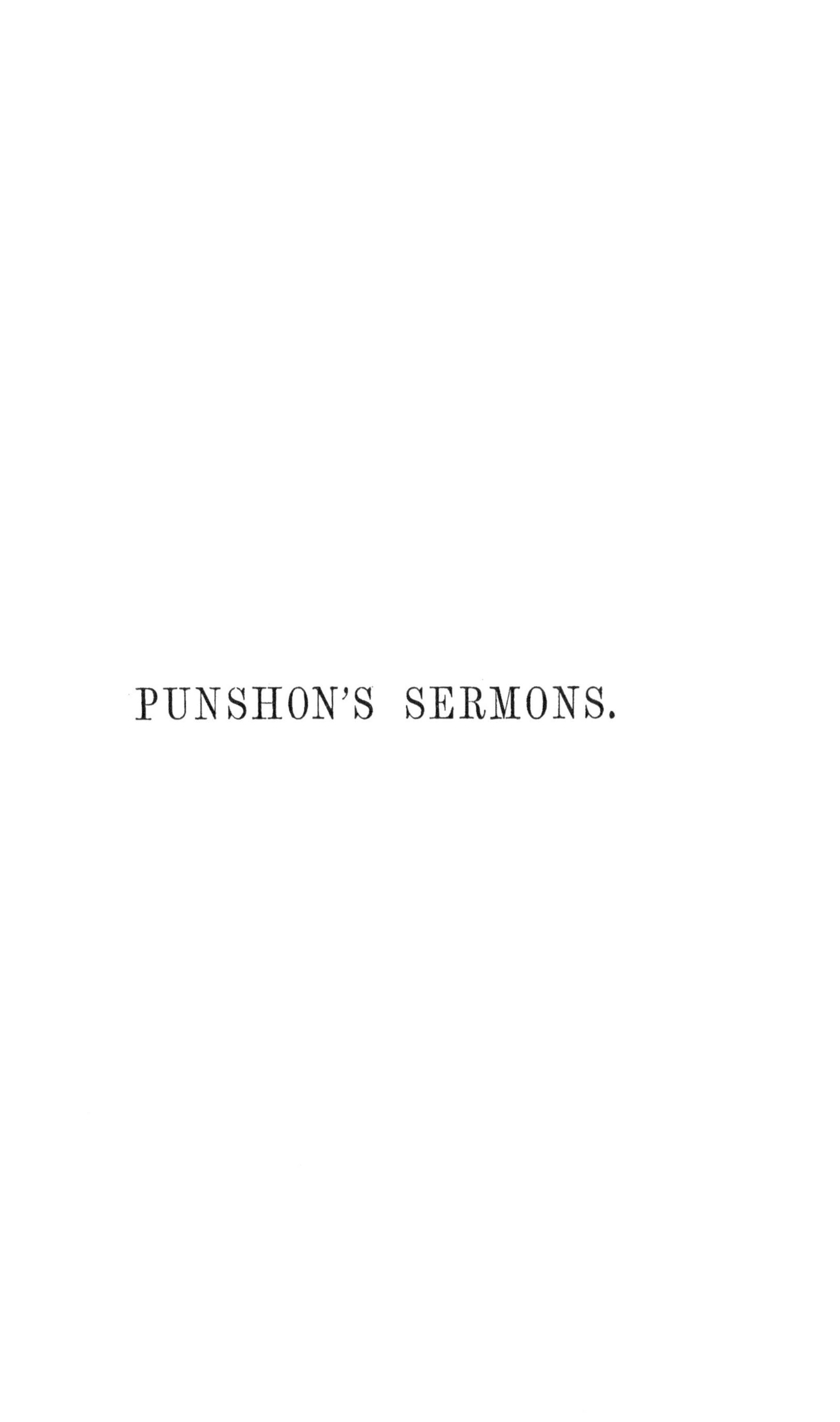

PUNSHON'S SERMONS.

SERMONS

BY

REV. WILLIAM MORLEY PUNSHON.

TO WHICH IS PREFIXED

A PLEA FOR CLASS-MEETINGS,

AND

AN INTRODUCTION BY REV. WILLIAM H. MILBURN.

NEW YORK:
N. TIBBALS & CO., 118 NASSAU STREET.
1860.

W. H. Tinson, Stereotyper.

Geo. Russell & Co., Printers.

CONTENTS.

INTRODUCTION.

On a bright sunshiny morning (and such were strangely frequent in London in the summer of 1857) I drove from my lodgings, Little Ryder street, St. James', two or three miles in a southwesterly direction to Brixton Hill Wesleyan Chapel. The edifice was that day to be dedicated to the worship of Almighty God, and the preacher on the occasion was the Rev. William Morley Punshon. I had heard much of him, and was naturally desirous to listen to one who was called the most eloquent of living Wesleyan preachers.

As I reached the chapel in advance of the time for commencing the service, I entered the vestry, where I was introduced, among others, to the preacher I had come to hear. He seemed a man about five feet ten inches in height, rather inclined to corpulency, for one of his age (not then, I should say, above thirty-four), with by no means a striking or expressive face when in repose, and possessed of a voice rather husky and not at all prepossessing.

His dress was that of all Wesleyan ministers in England, closely approaching the style of the clergy of the established church—the invariable white neck-tie surmounting the uniform of black. The appointed hour arrived, and we entered the chapel.

The prayers of the church of England—excepting the Litany—were read by the superintendent of the circuit from a desk on one side of the chancel. Mr. Punshon then mounted a desk on the other side of the chancel, gave out a hymn, and offered a brief extemporaneous prayer.

His reading was not at all impressive, and I began to wonder whether, indeed, he could be an orator. In truth, I had been so often disappointed that I had almost come to regard a reputation for eloquence as *primâ facie* evidence against a man's possessing it, and I was tempted to think in this case, that I was once more befooled. The preacher took his text and proceeded with the discourse. A brief exegetical introduction was followed by the announcement of the points he meant to treat. The arrangement of the sermon was textual, methodical and Wesleyan. The English take far less latitude in such matters than we. The Wesleyans are Wesleyans indeed, imbued with the spirit and almost adhering to the letter of our Great Founder. Well-nigh every sermon has its three heads, and each head its three subdivisions, and at the conclusion of the third "thirdly," comes a close, searching, and practical application. This style seems to be considered almost indispensable to orthodoxy, and forms a striking contrast to the large, often latitudinarian, and frequently *helter skelter* freedom of style allowed in this country, where all manner of truth, and even untruth, is preached from any text that may be selected, under the plea that the style is "topical."

The form of the English pulpit obliges the preacher to adhere to a pulpit manner. It is modelled upon the shape of the little wooden boxes we see in Roman Catholic churches in this country, affording room for one person only—access to it being gained by a long flight of winding steps, and when you have toiled to the dizzy height, you find yourself overlooking the galleries, and perched, perhaps twenty feet above the floor. Not a little self-control must be practised by the preacher, and he is compelled, whether he will or not, to pay a good deal of attention to the laws of gravitation, and other decorous regulations, or the stern penalty of a tumble may be enforced upon him.

The platform of this country (for our pulpits are nothing more), in its slight elevation above the floor, its nearness to the people, its susceptibility to impression from the audience, and the vantage-ground it affords the preacher for imbuing the hearers with his own sympathies, is a great advance upon the English desk, and a near approach to the *ambo* of the early Church. The difference, as to the standing-ground of the preachers of the two countries, is significant—almost symbolic—of the difference of their styles.

The English seem to fancy, that our method, in its reach after the people, its disloyalty to technical rule, its range of illustration, and its disuse of a strict theological phraseology, as well as in its free adoption of the language of common life, borders upon a reprehensible looseness.

To the American, on the other hand, the close adherence to models, the almost single variation between a dogmatic and hortatory style, and the employment of a limited range of words, not so much Scriptural as conventional, make the English pulpit appear formal. No doubt each could learn something of advantage from the other; and it seemed to me, that Mr. Punshon occupied the enviable position of standing midway between the two, with many of the advantages of both. He is systematic, yet untrammelled, and while technical in his arrangement, he is still free and varied in illustration. Confining himself to the legitimate themes of the pulpit, he at the same time does not despise the use of general literature. His aim seems to be to make men Christians—either to convert them from sin, or to establish them in holiness, not to teach them political economy, to educate them in æsthetics, to afford them brilliant disquisitions in metaphysical science, or to enforce on them the flattering assurance, that the private soul (that is, the essential *me*) is higher and grander than society, state, church, law, or Scripture.

The staple of his discourses, when I heard him, concerned man's spiritual and eternal welfare, and did not consist in flowers, stars, breezes or clouds. I should say that he is better read in the writings of St. Paul and St. John, than in those of the Gnostics, and that he holds the canon of Scripture to be binding upon men, as a rule of faith and practice.

As to politics, I have a suspicion (but I can only state it as a suspicion, for I heard him say nothing on the subject), that he prefers the English Revolution of 1688, to the French Revolution of 1789; and that he holds the powers that be, are ordained of God, and not of the Devil; and therefore, if he taught anything on the subject, that he would teach fealty to the constitution of the land in which he lives, loyalty to the law, obedience to constituted authority, as the duty of every good citizen, and not, that insubordination and revolution are the crowning glories of every regenerate soul. He is liberal, but his liberality is not the equivalent of a contempt for orthodoxy; and while some of his countrymen may esteem him a progressive, I hardly think his progressiveness consists in the recently expounded doctrine of consistency, "be true to yourself to-day—no matter what you said or did yesterday"—that is to say, progress and the weathercock are one and the same thing.

As Mr. Punshon advanced in his discourse on that pleasant June morning, an occasional emphasis, applied with judgment, betokened the practical speaker; and the finish of his sentences betrayed thorough preparation. As he warmed to his work, quickening at the same time the gait of his articulation, you found him gaining a strong hold not only upon your attention, but upon your feelings; and you discovered that underneath the ample and rather loose folds of adipose tissue with which his outer man is invested, there are great stores of electrical power. He possesses that attribute indispensable to the orator, for which we have no better name than *magnetic.* You are rooted as by a spell, and surrender for a time the guidance of your own thoughts. You have dropped the helm of your mind, for a more skillful pilot has for the nonce taken your place at the tiller.

Occasionally, you find the speaker's power over you going to such lengths as to control your respiration, and you breathe as he breathes, or as he gives you liberty. Whoever has known the delicious pain of a long, deep inhalation —half a sigh of relief, half a welcome of the outer world for the time forgotten—while listening to a speaker with such rapt earnestness that every faculty of mind and sense is concentrated in the one act of hearing, has felt what oratory is. He has felt it, but can he describe it? He might as well attempt to describe the thrill of love or rapture. I doubt not, Mr. Punshon has showed many people what oratory is, and made them to know the power of the orator; but I question much if he can teach them the power of his art, or how to analyze and define it. It is not the power of intellect, for I have seen and heard nothing from him extraordinary as an intellectual production. It does not lie in his taste—I am not sure it that would bear the test of rigid criticism. It is not in the exhibition of stores of learning; his life has been too busy and practical, to enable him to gain great stock of lore. It is not in the tricks of a charlatan or the skill of an actor, for Mr. Punshon is a sincere, devout and godly man. The charm of eloquence retreats from the scrutiny of analysis as life retires from the knife of the anatomist.

Before he has reached his major "thirdly," it is all over with your independent consciousness; you have yielded at discretion and are the prisoner of his feeling. I am half inclined to believe that his own intellect is in the same plight, and that memory acts as the warder of the brain, under writ from the lordly soul. You have thrown criticism to the dogs; your ear has exchanged itself for an eye; the bone and flesh of your forehead become delicately thin, as the laminæ of the cornea, and your brain seems endowed with the power of the iris. You enjoy the ecstasy of vision, and as the speaker stops you recover yourself enough to feel that you have had an apocalyptic hour.

It seems to me, that the true measure of eloquence is found, not so much in what is said as in what is suggested; not so much in the speaker's ability to convey to you an idea, as to suffuse you with the glow of a sentiment; not so much in the truth which is uttered, as in the soul behind the truth, of which you become, for the time, a sharer.

Mr. Punshon is much more of an orator than any man I heard in England. In society he is simple, quiet, and genial; his excellent good sense, and unaffected piety deliver him from the snares of egotism, and the foolish weakness of self-conceit. The chalice of praise turns many a great man's head. The goblet which the English public has offered to Mr. Punshon is huge and brimming; but if the contents have affected him, I did not discover it. I have an idea, that he gives close and scrupulous heed to the Apostle's admonition: "Let no man among you think more highly of himself than he ought to think, but let him think soberly, righteously, according as God has dealt to every man the measure of faith."

Mr. Punshon is not as robust as he looks. He is not able to study closely more than three hours at a time, and frequently not more than that out of the twenty-four hours. He prepares himself for the rostrum and pulpit with the most scrupulous and exhaustive care. I should say that the greater part of his sermons and lectures are committed to memory, and delivered almost word for word, as they were beforehand composed. His recollection is, therefore, at once quick and tenacious. This plan, while it insures a higher average of public performance and saves him from many mortifying failures, at the same time shuts him out from the ground of highest power.

"Mr. Punshon was born (I now quote from reliable authority) on the 29th of May, 1824, and successfully passed his examination for the Wesleyan ministry in the year 1845. He is a native of Doncaster, and is related, on the mother's side, to the Morleys of that town, and since of Hull, Sir Isaac Morley being his uncle. The only child of his parents, he early displayed that wonderful memory for which he is now so remarkably distinguished, and a propensity to store it with facts which rarely interest mere boys. At the Doncaster Grammar School, where he was educated, he is said not to have discovered any surprising proficiency; but when still a child he was able to name nearly all the members of the House of Commons, with the places for which they sat, and the color of their politics.

"In early life he associated himself with the Wesleyan Methodists, to which religious body his family belonged; but public affairs continued to be his ruling passion, and the most surprising thing is, that his oratory, instead of adorning the Methodist chapel, should not have been electrifying the chapel of St. Stephen. When his grandfather and uncles removed to their establishment in Hull, he was placed in their counting-house as junior clerk. He may have had talents for business, but his inclination ran in another direction. During the three years that he was supposed to be making out invoices and footing up ledgers, he was absorbed in newspapers; and the only account he cared to keep was of the way in which the representatives of the people voted in Parliament.

"In the debates nobody was better posted up. The temptation of a daily newspaper was irresistible; and while the other clerks were deep in figures, he was culling figures of speech from the orators of the Reformed Parliament—watching the opening genius of Gladstone and Macaulay, noting the maturer excellences of Peel and Palmerston, and marking the finest flights of Shiel and O'Connell for his own. The predilections of a young politician are seldom of much importance; but it so happened that young Punshon's devotion to newspaper studies threw him into the society of three young men who were earnest disciples of the then newly born conservative opinions of Sir Robert Peel and his adherents, and who held weekly meetings to strengthen each other in their political faith. Once a month one of them read a paper to the rest on a given subject; and though not more numerous than the celebrated knights of the thimble in Tooley street, they called themselves "The Menticultural Society." Two of the three survive, one being a Wesleyan minister, and the other a clergyman of the Established Church. In these weekly discourses and monthly lectures, Mr. Punshon first distinguished himself as possessed of those faculties which have made him eminent. Nor did he and his associates confine themselves to politics; for there is in existence a small volume of poetry, which they published conjointly, and to which Mr. Punshon contributed a piece entitled "The Orphan," of considerable promise. About the same time he received, under the ministry of the Rev. Samuel Romilly Hall, those impressions, which resulted in his religious conversion. He then became a Sunday-school teacher, and subsequently a local preacher. He began to preach when he was eighteen years of age, and exhibited much ability in the pulpit. His first attempt was made at Ellerby, near Hull, and it was so successful as to cause the sermon to live in the memory of at least some who heard it, for they talked about it years afterward, when Mr. Punshon visited the place. Under such circumstances there could be little doubt that his vocation was not in the counting-house. But still he was kept in the commercial circle, for from his relatives in Hull he was sent to an uncle at Sunderland, to follow up the pursuit on which he had entered.

"But the books in which he delighted were neither ledger nor day-books. His refined fancy and polished taste made him an ardent admirer of the sublime and beautiful in literature, and at the same time his religious views led him to employ his talents more than ever in the preaching of the

Gospel; and as certain rivers are lost in morasses, we lose sight of his commercial career somewhere among the coal-pits and iron-works of the North.

"During these events he had been bereaved of both parents; and his grandfather, at length convinced that secular business was not his vocation, made liberal arrangements for his being trained for the ministry in the Wesleyan Institution, after a preliminary course of instruction at the house of his uncle, the Rev. Benjamin Clough, at Deptford.

"There, however, he did not long remain; it being found, probably either that his genius was ill-suited to the restraints of an academical course, or that by self-culture, and the help of his ministerial relative, he had attained a proficiency which, with talents such as his, superseded a more formal training. In the spring of 1845 a secession of the parishioners from the Episcopal Church at Morden, Kent, formed the nucleus of a Wesleyan church in that town, and Mr. Punshon was invited to accept the pastoral charge of the seceders. He complied with the request, and under his ministry their numbers so greatly increased that a commodious chapel was erected, and always well filled. It was only for a short time, however, that he remained in this place, for in the autumn of the same year the Conference, under whose jurisdiction the Morden church seems to have come, sent him to Whitehaven, where he resided two years, and attracted large congregations. From thence, in 1847, he was removed to the city of Carlisle, and two years afterward to Newcastle-on-Tyne. In both of these great centres of population Mr. Punshon at once acquired a worthy name, and became a mighty power for good, as well as at Sunderland, Gateshead, Shields, and the other towns of the district, where he never had to preach or lecture to empty, or only partially occupied pews and benches. While stationed at Newcastle, being then in his twenty-fifth year, he married a daughter of Mr. Vicars, of Gateshead, a very estimable and highly accomplished lady, whose premature death in 1858 threw the darkest shadow across Mr. Punshon's path, just when he had been appointed to a Metropolitan circuit, where enlarged usefulness and new honors awaited the gifted and ardent ambassador of Christ; when most unwelcome, the King of Terrors came and took the angel of the pastor's home away to her sister spirits in glory.

"From Newcastle Mr. Punshon was removed in 1851 to Sheffield, and thence to Leeds in 1855. It was while he was at Sheffield that the fame of the preacher became noised abroad; and his services were soon in very frequent request for special sermons, and also for lectures. It was, we believe, in the character of a lecturer that he appeared for the first time in London, some six or seven years ago. We well recollect the circumstance of his standing upon the platform of Exeter Hall to discourse to the members of the Young Men's Christian Association on the Prophet of Horeb. It was not, strictly speaking, a lecture; but an oration of extreme brilliancy, suited in a high degree to captivate the minds and find its way to the affections of a youthful audience; and we never remember to have heard such rapturous applause as that with which the thousands there assembled greeted each glowing period. The whole of the oration was delivered *memoriter*, and with extraordinary fluency; and such was the literal fidelity with which the speaker had followed the manuscript, which was either in his pocket, or at home, that when it shortly afterward appeared in print, it would have been difficult for the most retentive memory of the closest listener to have pointed out a sentence that the lecturer had not uttered. By this single performance Mr. Punshon established a Metropolitan reputation outside his own denomination, which was increased some two or three years afterward by his second lecture in Exeter Hall, before the same Association, on the Immortal Dreamer, John Bunyan; and, more recently still, by that most masterly oration on the Huguenot, which tens of thousands in almost all parts of England have listened to with unbounded delight. With one or two exceptions, perhaps, there is no living minister in this country possessed of so much popular power as Mr. Punshon. It is something wonderful and grand to witness the spell of his genius upon miscellaneous audiences of from three to five thousand people in St. James' Hall, Exeter Hall, or the provincial theatre, who have paid from a shilling to a half crown each for admission. Most people will probably prefer Mr. Punshon in character of a lecturer rather than that of a preacher. In the pulpit he is unquestionably a master, and only second to a very few preachers of the age; but the platform furnishes a better sphere for the display of his varied abilities. In neither capacity does he give the people that which has cost him nothing; for so accurate, and elaborate is almost every sentence, and so appropriate and polished every illustrative simile, that it may be confidently said he writes out and commits to memory every sermon and lecture that he delivers. Whatever he undertakes he does well. Whether it is in the preaching of an ordinary sermon in a Methodist chapel, or in the delivery of an ostensibly popular discourse in some great public building, or as taking part in the meeting of some benevolent or religious association, or as a lecturer, occupying the rostrum before thousands of delighted hearers, he is always earnest, always energetic, always effective.

"In a two hours' discourse upon such a theme as that of the history of France throughout the whole period of the Huguenot persecutions, ordinary and even very superior lecturers would have considered a manuscript indispensable. But, not so Mr. Punshon. A few notes on some small cards held in the hand were all the prompting he required, when we heard him go through his magnificent address. He told that old story of persecution with an inspiring eloquence that made men hold their breath while they listened, or burst forth into a tempest of applause. Vigorous, inventive, and impassioned, he adapted himself to the versatile tastes of his auditory, not by any apparent effort, but by simplicity, and strength, by speaking right out the thoughts that were in him. He roused every passion, touched every emotion, and awakened every sympathy in the hearts of his hearers."

With God's blessing Mr. Punshon has yet, according to the English standard, full thirty of his best years before him. May he have length of days and fullness of power, so that he shall continue to grow in favor with God and man, is the hearty wish of his friend,

W. H. MILBURN.

BROOKLYN, *May* 15*th*, 1860.

PRELIMINARY PLEA.

TABOR; OR, THE CLASS-MEETING.

If any of you, dear friends, had been privileged to witness the scenes which once hallowed the summit of Tabor—if you had seen the Saviour baptized as the King of Glory—if you had "feared as you entered into the cloud"—if you had been a favored listener to that heavenly converse—if you had been thrilled, as Peter was, by the upliftings of wondrous hope and unfoldings of gracious purpose, as "they spake of his decease which he should accomplish at Jerusalem"—who of you could have withheld the deep-felt expression of gladness, "Lord, it is good to be here!"—who of you could have restrained the desire to build, upon that sacred spot, the "tabernacles" of remembrance and of rest?

Dear friends, there is yet an institution in whose observance the humblest Christian talks with his Master, and with his Master's followers—that institution is the "assembling of ourselves together" for the purposes of church communion—there is yet a place upon earth where some relics of that excellent glory linger, where the experiences of that mount of blessing are not all forgotten—that place is a pious and properly conducted Class-Meeting. Many a time has the writer of this brief address felt its salutary influence, to gladden the soul in seasons of intensest trial, to encourage the failing spirit in heavenward progress, to brace and nerve the mind for difficult duty; and, with a grateful recollection of these, its Tabor-pleasures, he commends its advantages to you. "I believed, therefore have I spoken."

We do not claim for the Class-Meeting an essentially divine origin, although it would be difficult to doubt that an overruling Providence presided at its birth, and has kept it in operation until now. The mind, which devoutly remembers that with God there is nothing trivial, will readily acknowledge that when John Wesley, ministering merely to present necessities, and with no foresight of the future, called together at their own request "eight or ten persons in London"—there were in heaven an eye that marked and a love that blessed the deed.

> "A thing is great or little only to a mortal's thinking,
> It is but the littleness of man that seeth no greatness in a trifle."

Mark the tenor of the language which tells of the rise of the "United Societies," which, founded upon scriptural principles, have now expanded into a flourishing church:

"In the latter end of the year 1739, eight or ten persons came to me in London, who appeared to be deeply convinced of sin, and earnestly groaning for redemption. They desired (as did two or three more the next day) that I would spend some time with them in prayer, and advise them how to flee from the wrath to come, which they saw continually hanging over their heads. That we might have more time for this great work, I appointed a day when they might all come together; which from henceforward they did every week, viz., on Thursday, in the evening. To these, and as many more as desired to join with them (for their number increased daily), I gave those advices from time to time which I judged most needful for them; and we also concluded our meetings with prayer suited to their several necessities."

How forcibly does this remind us of the days of Malachi, when "they that feared the Lord *spake often one to another*, and the Lord hearkened and heard—and a Book of remembrance"—*the Lord's class book*—"was written before him for them that feared the Lord, and that thought upon his name!" How vividly does it recall that union in prayer which gives it such a princely power! "If two of you shall *agree* on earth as touching anything that they shall ask, it shall be done for them of my Father which is in heaven." How does it bring before us the exhortations scattered through the whole compass of apostolic writing!

"Bear ye one another's burdens, and so fulfill the law of Christ;"—and especially how accordant is it with the confession of our faults *one* to *another* (not auricular confession to a priest—*that* we abhor), which St. James enjoins. (Jas. v. 16.) If we have not direct Scripture command, we have Scripture permission, approval, and usage; and, while we are content that a Class-Meeting should be considered as prudential rather than authoritative, we hold to the persuasion that it has been a means of grace, which, perhaps beyond all others of a supplemental character, has been signally honored by the blessing of God.

You, as hearers of our ministry, are doubtless aware that membership in one of these Class-Meetings is indispensable to constitute union with Methodism, and that those only, who statedly attend these seasons of Christian fellowship, are "accredited and rightful communicants of our Church." Writing as Methodists, we condemn not other sections of the church universal. It may not be their vocation. They certainly do not prize it as their privilege. For ourselves, however, for the benefit of our own family, we are free to confess an ardent attachment in this matter to the "good ways" of our fathers. The Class-Meeting is storied of old. It is associated with our traditional and sacred records of the master spirits of early Methodism—those large-hearted men "of whom the world was not worthy." It was to them as the blest Elim of palms and fountains to the desert wayfarer; and such is the sanctity of affection with which we regard it, that it compels the prayer, not with bated breath, but with the loud voice of earnest entreaty;—God forbid the day should ever dawn when the Class-Meeting shall cease to be as an organized system of testimony, the badge of membership in the Methodist branch of the Church of Christ.

Let us be guarded here. We do not believe, nor do we affirm, that connection with the Class-Meeting is necessarily an indication of piety, nor of that right state of heart which is acceptable in the sight of God. There may be—there probably are—numbers amongst us of whom we are "in doubt," and over whose defective consistency we mourn. It is not surprising, when there were "carnal walkers" in the Corinthian church, and even a Judas amongst the twelve. But where is there an equal vigilance to prevent the recognition of improper persons as members? In what church in Christendom are there manifested greater fidelity and solemnity in matters of experience and practice? The charge of encouraging mixed fellowship, which has been so injuriously cast upon our ministers, is unwarranted and untrue. That our only requirement is "a desire to flee from the wrath to come," is certain. But what does this mean? How is it manifested? It is not the careless confession, in which there is no heart—nor the emotion of the man, who repents to-night and sins again to-morrow—nor yet the mere feeling of remorse, the Judas-like penitence, which "worketh death." There must be "repentance toward God"—the deep and abiding penitence—the strong conviction of personal guilt and danger—the "broken heart," which is God's chosen sacrifice—the godly sorrow, which chastens the entire character—the whole of the emotions comprehended in the expressive word—*contrition*. None, in the judgment of our church—as embodied in her inimitable Rules—sincerely feel this desire but they who bring forth its "fruits meet for repentance"—the crushing sense of ingratitude—the careful avoidance of evil—the earnest inquiry after good—the submissive search for truth—and the restless anxiety which refuses to be satisfied without the experience of its power. None but these, therefore, are interested in this address. Do not mistake us. We invite you on the assumption—and that assumption is indispensable—and that assumption is *all* that is indispensable—that you are thus desirous to "flee from the wrath to come." We are jealous of accessions that may pollute its purity. The careless, and the profane, and the trifling, and the selfish—alas! that we have such hearers!—our invitation passes by. Dearly as we wish their welfare, *we* dare not invite them, in their present state, amongst us. "They have no part nor lot in the matter." But we believe there are thousands of our hearers in different parts of the land, whose hearts God hath touched—who are hopeful and promising as to religious impression, and who manifest a ceaseless concern for their souls; and it is to them we make our appeal.

Dear friends, those of you that are in such a case, to this membership we invite you. We have watched for you with eager solicitude. We have yearned over you with a pastor's yearning. Upon your spiritual state we have expended many an anxious thought, for your spiritual welfare we have breathed many a fervent prayer. We rejoice to see you in the sanctuary, but we would have you glad us with your presence at our family festivals. We see you standing at the threshold—we wish you to cluster round the hearthstone and to be warmed at the fire. Perhaps you have not adequately considered the advantages of this invaluable fellowship. Will you lend us your attention for awhile to a brief enumeration?

I. *The Class-Meeting induces Self-examination.*—Thoughtlessness is the great sin and inveterate habit of the world. The natural man presents the "remarkable spectacle of a soul afraid of itself, afraid to stay with itself, alone, still and attentive." He may, perhaps, have parleyed sometimes with his immortal spirit, after the manner of some lordly nobleman speaking to an old servant of his house: "Soul, thou hast much goods laid up for many years, take thine ease, eat, drink, and be merry;" or, haply some adventurous one set out with the fixed intention of visiting his heart's secret chambers, but his feelings were like those of one who entered a gloomy and long-deserted mansion. To his disordered imagination strange tremors shook the arras, unearthly echoes sounded from the stair, apparitions met the straining eye-ball upon every landing—

"For over all there hung a cloud of fear,
A sense of mystery the spirit daunted,
And said, as plain as whisper in the ear,
The place is haunted!"

and he retired affrighted, with the big, cold drops upon his brow, and it must be a powerful motive that will tempt him into those chambers again. Nay, the Lord's accusation against his ancient people is chargeable to a great extent upon his people now, "*My people* do not consider." How apt is the Christian, the heir of a nobler life, the professor of a living faith, to neglect the examination of himself! The countless activities of this utilitarian age have been all temptations, to which his busy spirit has been but too prone to yield. The engrossing influence of business, the onward march of intellect, the absorbing strife of politics, even the enterprises of religious philanthropy, have all, in turn, contributed most sadly to hinder the practice of self-communion. The active has banished the reflective; and it is to be feared that there are professors of religion, who strangely reckon all the moments spent upon themselves *as so much wasted time.*

Wordsworth has entered his indignant protest against the intrusion of a railway to disturb the serenities of Grasmere and Rydal. Oh, for some spiritual laureate

—some sweet singer in Israel, to decry the multiplied excitements which tramp and rattle through the offended mind! My friends, the Class-Meeting will "lead you beside these still waters." No right-minded and devotional spirit *dares* enter it without some kind of self inquiry—some examination of himself—"whether he be in the faith." During the week, it may be, when the strife of competition waxed fierce, and the race of human pursuits was going vigorously on, your thoughts were hurried into the midst of them, until they were bewildered even to exhaustion; but now the Class-Meeting is at hand, and the mind retires into its sanctuary, and communes with itself and its God. It is like the court-day of the soul, when the steward conscience takes cognizance of all the tenants, and brings them respectively beneath their Master's eye. How searching that inquiry! How hallowed that communion! "Another week of my probation has fled. What record has it borne? What blessings has it scattered from its wings? What deliverances have I experienced? What battles have I won? What have been my omissions, heart-wanderings, sins? Am I holier, more spiritually-minded? Have I a nobler scorn of the world? a more earnest avarice for heaven? The heart must be the better for inquiries like these, made searchingly, and in the spirit of prayer. Then, perhaps, heavenly thoughts will troop upon us, like the descending visitants of Jacob's dream—and it may be—who knows? that we may 'entertain angels unawares;'

or, better still, some kind-looking stranger may join us on our Emmaus-travel, and make 'our hearts burn within us as he talketh with us by the way.'" These are no trifling blessings, and these the Class Meeting indirectly procures, because it, in some sort, *compels* self-communion, and thus induces a habit which may be as powerful for good as former habits were powerful for evil.

II. *The Class-Meeting produces Gratitude.*—Love—the love of gratitude—is the essence of religion—the first feeling of the regenerate soul. It springs electric in the mind of the believer at his first sight of Jesus. Authority cannot command it. Terror cannot frighten it into existence. All the thousand-fold appliances of worldly wisdom cannot create it. There must be perception of love in God—a sense of his good-will—a view of the crucified as well as of the cross before it be enkindled. "We love him *because* he first loved us." This feeling of gratitude is too deeply grateful for description. Language is but a mockery. Illustration fails. It is beyond a figure, and without a parallel. Who sees not the danger that an emotion like this, if hidden in the breast, should spend itself by its own continuity? Gratitude is not like the mountain avalanche, which gains intensity from repression—it is rather like the fire, which imprisonment extinguishes—or air, which, pure and free, is the refreshing breath of heaven; but, fouled by confinement, is the blast of pestilence and death. Contemplation upon God's boundless love tends naturally to expression. "While I was musing the fire burned, then spake I with my tongue." Now, the Class-Meeting furnishes the most appropriate occasion for this expression of praise. It is large enough to redeem from privacy, and not large enough to exclude the notion of a family, and it would be difficult to find a more legitimate sphere, in which the full heart may utter its thanks, unfold its hopes, and breathe its prayers. Nay, can there be gratitude without this thankful acknowledgment? Is there not enough in the dealings of your heavenly Father to compel it? The grace which loved you from the beginning—the visitations of mercy which have lighted your path—the beams of promise that have shone upon your head—the kind heart that has borne with your wanderings—the beckoning hand which restored you when you went astray—are they not constraining you? If we were permitted to anticipate the objection which the rebel heart sometimes whispers: "I cannot speak," might we not say—Ah! friends, get the love of God shed abroad within you, and it will fill your mouth with arguments. Wondrous is the power of this surpassingly mighty theme. It makes the lips of the stammerer eloquent, and the heart of the diffident bold. Under its inspiring influence, knowledge kindles on the countenance—praise flows from the tongue—and the most timid and retiring are transported into the invitation of the Psalmist, "Come all ye that fear God, and I will *declare* what he hath done for my soul."

III. *The Class-Meeting recognizes brotherhood.*—It is a mighty truth which God has written upon the universe, and stamped enduringly upon the great heart of humanity, that "No man liveth to himself." The world is a vast mass of dependencies. The feeblest woman or the humblest peasant exerts an influence which must be felt in the great brotherhood of mankind. It is a precious appointment of Providence, that it has, in some sense, made our very selfishness benevolent—that it has bound us, at the peril of losing our own enjoyments, to care for the necessities of others—and that it has extracted the most satisfying elements of public happiness from the joys and perils of individual lot. The heart, by a law of its constitution, must have something to which it can attach itself. Its emblems are the summer-tendril and the clasping ivy. It was never formed for the hermitage or the monastery—and you must do violence to all its excellent charities, before it will entirely denude itself of all objects of solicitude and love. The Class-Meeting here comes in to *supply a great want of nature.* It concentrates the feeling of brotherhood—prevents it from being frittered away in vague and sentimental generalities—and gives it a definite object and aim. If the church is the temple, the Class-Meeting is an inner and sacred inclosure. If the church is the populous city, the Class-Meeting is the united family, where love is throned in the heart and confidence nestles in the roof-tree. Every faithful leader will impress upon his flock, and every devoted member will take care to feel, that, while the church at large claims his philanthropic sympathy and effort, to his own fellow-members he is to cherish the closer and deeper feelings of home. Here especially there are no orphans. "Whether one member suffer, all the members suffer with it; or one member be honored, all the members rejoice with it." They are joined as in a commonwealth. "They love as brethren." Why join you not this heavenly communion? Are you not, like the prodigal, in a far country, and, perhaps, if your pride would but confess it, inwardly pining for the "bread enough and to spare" of your Father's house at home? Have you sufficiently considered that in your present state, regarding you as travellers to another world, you are isolated, and—forgive the word—*selfish*—exhibiting a practical denial of all brotherly relationship, by remaining to wrestle with your enemies, and gain your heaven alone?

IV. *The Class-Meeting elicits Sympathy.*—Good sense and rich exprerience are the fruits of intercourse. No man ever yet became either wise or holy by exclusively "communing with his own heart upon his bed." We have heard much lately on the tendency of seclusion to cherish the spirit of piety, and there are not wanting those who would revive in all their severity the monasticisms of past ages. Mistaken men! The sweet flowerets of Divine grace can rarely be acclimated to the damp soil of the convent; they are not like the sensitive mimosa, which shrinks even from the gentlest handling, but rather, like the delicate heart's-ease, grateful for gracious dew-falls, and breathing zephyrs, and the blessed sun, and yet courting the culture and the companionship of man. Christianity is not an imaginative revelry upon great truths—it is an earnest endeavor to exemplify them. It is not contemplative pietism, it is unceasing labor. It is not an alien principle, which has no sympathy with our nature, and is content with its distant and constrained submission—it is an all-pervasive element, shrined in the heart, and influencing benignly the whole of the character. "Knox," says Dr. Chalmers, "did not destroy the old Romish pulpits at the time of the Reformation; he did better: he *preached* in them." Christianity does not annihilate a single passion—does not extinguish a single affection of our nature. It does better. It employs the former for its own noble purposes, and it fixes the latter where they may attach themselves, without fear of idolatry, even upon "things above." The passions of the Christian, therefore, are as strong—the affections of the Christian are as warm—as those of any man. The charities of life, and of love, and of home, flourish as endearingly in the mind of the Christian as anywhere, and he has that intense yearning for sympathy which characterizes universal man. Here again, the Class-Meeting *supplies a great want of nature.* It is composed a band of wayfarers, met for the express purpose of sympathizing with each other in the struggles and perils of their common journey. How often has it opened up a weekly heaven, amid the dull and clouded atmosphere of sinfulness and time! One is sorely tempted. The temptation presses hard upon his spirit, with such mighty fascinations is it clad—in such newer blasphemy does it prompt him to indulge, that he thinks surely *this* is a "temptation that is not common to men." But at the Class that week, a fellow-traveller relates the *bitter* experience of the same suggestions, and the *blest* experience of deliverance from their power; and a new song is put into his mouth, and he goes on his way rejoicing. Another is bowed down beneath the influence of a temptation adjusted with such nicety to his peculiar besetment as to be almost irresistible in its appeals, but the weekly season of fellowship has come, and the words of the faithful leader "are words in season," and One mightier than the leader is there, and a glance at *his* pure countenance—a touch of *his* invigorating hand—and he is nerved for the conflict, and spurns the assaulter away. Another has been stricken with a spiritual paralysis—a wearisome torpor has seized him, a strange indifference has come upon his soul—and, as in the Class-Meeting, he tells his tale of half-heartedness and sin, amid the counsels of the faithful and the prayers of the pious, the glorious presence of the Saviour bursts in light upon the chained one, and in all the strength and nobility of spiritual life, he "walks" afresh "with God."

And who can tell the beneficial influence to the Zionward journeyer, when persons of all ranks, character, and ages, *unite* to testify that "the same Lord over all is rich in mercy unto all them that call upon him?" Perhaps there is an aged pilgrim who for years has walked and fainted not. Many a hill of difficulty has he climbed, many a valley of humiliation has he trodden—he has tales to tell of wary walkings on enchanted ground—of hair-breadth escape out of the net of the Flatterer—aye, and of ravishing prospects for the Delectable mountains and from the elevations of Pisgah; and, while his eye brightens and his voice falters, he tells also that he has never repented his setting forth on pilgrimage, and that the pleasures are sweeter, and the toils less irksome, than when, in youth, he grasped the palmer-staff and strapped on the sandals. Is it nothing to be favored with the testimony of such an one, and to sit under his shadow with delight? to have our rash judgments rebuked by his experience, and our faith confirmed by the ardors of his imperishable hope? There is a young convert there, it may be, who has recently realized a wonderful change, even, "from darkness to light, and from the power of Satan unto God." He has found "peace and joy in believing;" and the new-found gladness that is within him steeps the sky in brighter blue, and decks the earth with bonnier green; and, blushing at his own fervor, he pours forth in the Class-Meeting his ascriptions of praise. The old man hears, and is reminded of the days of his first love—it is like a snatch of the music that used to thrill the soul of yore, and, in a moment, memory has painted the first conviction—the early struggles—the doubt that harassed his young mind—the triumph with which he hailed its departure—and, above all, the eventful moment when joy broke through his swimming eyes as he believingly said, "My Father!" Who sees not the mutual and glorious benefit—the young instructed by the experience of the aged—the aged charmed and quickened by the enthusiasm of the young. And then there is one sympathy on this head which it would be unpardonable in us to omit, and that is the sympathy of prayer. Who can be lonely or despairing, even in this wilderness world, with the consciousness that there are hearts *praying* for him? hearts of those who are animated by similar hopes, and depressed by similar fears, and who are bound by their membership to "make intercession for" the household of faith "according to the will of God?" My friends, if there were no other disadvantage in your present anomalous position as aloof from the church of Christ, than this—that by your separation you deprive yourself of the church's *prayers*—there is a fearfulness in the thought which might well cause you to reflect and tremble. Desolate indeed is the spirit—cursed as the dewless hills of Gilboa—for which no prayer ascends, on whose behalf no knee is bowed to heaven. Rich in his penury is poverty's poorest child, if his portion is the supplication of the faithful! Happy the lonely watcher upon the gallant vessel's deck, if over the waste of waters the wife of his bosom prays! Never is a heart orphaned, or divorced utterly from hope and heaven, if in some extremest corner there rises one yearning spirit's prayer. And if individual prayer can do so much, what must be the effect of many? My friends, we would be almost content to rest the whole matter here, this one advantage would so overwhelmingly constrain your decision. Bold indeed must you be in self-confidence, in infatuation, in SIN, if you refuse to avail yourselves of the sympathy of prayer. Oh! by every motive which your souls will acknowledge as having either sacredness or power, you are adjured, against the evil day, to insure for yourselves the "effectual fervent prayer."

V. *The Class-Meeting confesses Discipleship.*—Every believer is called to *witness* for God. You cannot have forgotten how largely our Saviour impressed upon his immediate disciples the duty of "not being ashamed of him," and of "confessing him in the sight of men." You will also recollect how the Apostle of the Gentiles makes confession to be on a parallel with faith in that memorable passage, "If thou shalt *confess with thy mouth* the Lord Jesus, and believe in thine heart that God hath raised him from the dead, thou shalt be saved. For with the heart man believeth unto righteousness, and with the mouth *confession is made unto salvation.*" Such confession cannot be adequately made either by mere verbal acknowledgment or exemplary obedience, it can only be made by a solemn dedication "to God's people according to his will." Your solitary "witness" of obedience, or of faith, is lost like an invisible atom in the air, it is the *union* of each particle, in itself insignificant, that constitutes the "cloud" of witnesses which the world can see. Ask yourselves, we pray you, whether this is not just the element that is lacking in your religious decision. You are desirous to flee from the wrath to come—you have yielded in some measure to religious influence—you are endeavoring to "square your useful lives below by reason and by grace"—you have even felt at times some emotions of religious joy, and yet you are not permanently happy. Why? Because you have been, pardon the word, traitorous to the grace of God, in that, like Hezekiah of old, you have not "*rendered again* according to the benefit done unto you." Oh, remember how seriously you peril, by your present conduct, the interests of your souls! You are like a venturous traveller, who plunges, unaided and alone, into the tangled thicket, whose every tree may covert a robber. You are like a ship that has voyaged from the fleet, and forsaken the convoy, and if a storm should arise, where are the friendly hands to launch the life-boat, or to rescue the perishing? You are like a soldier, who, confiding in his own prowess, spurns the discipline of the regiment, and passes singly through the armies of the aliens, and if he *should* be surprised and stricken, where are the generous comrades to cover his retreat, or bear him from the field, or "bind up his wounds, pouring in oil and wine?" Nay, friends, for we can hesitate no longer; we must deliver our soul—God REQUIRES this public dedication. He must not only have the enlightened approval of the head, and the loyal allegiance of the heart, but *the cordial embrace of the hand;* and we dare not refrain from the expression of an opinion, founded, we believe, upon the requirements of the law of God, that so long as you keep aloof from his people, and are not united with some branch of his visible church, YOU ARE NOT SAFE—YOU ARE IN DANGER.

We believe in the present state of the antagonist armies of truth and error—*Neutrality* is *Opposition.* "He that is not for us is against us," and the transition is a very natural one to the belief that *connection with some visible branch of the Church of Christ is necessary to salvation.* We neither limit nor specify—God forbid that we should trammel the conscience of any one—but as right-hearted Methodists, Methodists from conviction and preference, we should be guiltily wrong if we dared not recommend our own.

It is not our business, it is not our wish to make proselytes. We would not descend from our elevation, we would not leave our vantage-ground to do it. "We have not so learned Christ." With other churches we have no quarrel. We regard them—all who hold the head—as "houses of the Lord," and heartily do we wish them God speed. "Let there be no strife between our herdmen and theirs." But we differ somewhat in our notions of spiritual agriculture, and haply it is our vocation to reclaim some waste lands that they would not think worth the tillage. You will not blame us, therefore, if while we do not disparage their communion, we prefer our own. Broad principles of philanthropy, however expansive, never root out the love of home. He is a churl, who cannot warm himself at any hearth but his own; and he is only half a man, who is not, after all, loudest in praise of his own ingle nook, and of the comfortable blaze that mantles from his own fire. Upon *you* we have a claim. You are haunted by no scruples as to the validity of our orders, or the purity of our doctrines. By your attendance upon our ministry, you have accorded us your free and generous preference. "If we are not apostles unto others, yet doubtless we are apostles unto you." Be no longer outer court worshippers. Bind yourselves to us by a tenderer tie. Come into our church. Approach the inner shrines of our worship. Attach yourselves to our Class-Meetings, and you will find them to be as the "upper room," renowned for the rushing wind and for the cloven tongues of flame.

Now, dear friends, what is your decision? Bring all your objections, all the thousand excuses which the unwilling heart coins; the fear of man—the inconsistency of professors—the dread of ridicule—the apprehension of falling—the repugnance to *declare* God's dealings with you; weigh them in the balance of the sanctuary, and ask yourselves, I entreat you, in the name of God, and under the impression of his eye, "Shall I deem these apologies sufficient in the article of death, and when the light of eternity shall flash upon the doings of time?"

Dear friends, our task is done. This address has been written in many weaknesses, and in much prayer. Read it in a similar spirit, and ask God in the secrecy of your communion-closet, to teach you his will. Change is the great law of the present state of being. The autograph of decay is graven upon temple, and tower, and time. Our friends have faded and fallen in our sight—"who hath not lost a friend?" Ourselves are dying creatures. He who writes, and you who read, will speedily pass to the judgment. Already the broad shadow of eternity looms upon us; under that shadow meditate and decide. Everything around you seems to urge a recognition of the vast importance of the claim. The wiles of the enemy—the deceitfulnes, never yet fathomed, of the human heart—the perils of the yet untravelled future—the awfulness of wandering onward, agonized and *without a praying friend*—the blessings of Christian communion—the helpfulness of rich and mellow experience—the absolute requirement of God—all, as with the voice of many waters, swell the forcefulness of our last appeal, which we now fling forth upon your souls, and may heaven clothe it with power: "COME WITH US, AND WE WILL DO YOU GOOD, FOR THE LORD HATH SPOKEN GOOD CONCERNING ISRAEL."

PUNSHON'S SERMONS.

I.

MEMORIES OF THE WAY.

"And thou shalt remember all the way which the Lord thy God led thee these forty years in the wilderness, to humble thee, and to prove thee, to know what was in thine heart, whether thou wouldst keep his commandments, or no."—DEUT. viii. 2.

A PECULIAR solemnity would be attached to these words in their original utterance, especially in the mind of the person who uttered them, for they were spoken under the shadow of approaching departure. Last words are proverbially impressive, and these were among the last words of the veteran Moses to the people of his charge and love. There had grown in his heart a strong affection for the children of Israel during his forty years' administration of their affairs. He had watched over them with fatherly tenderness, and had guided them through the intricacies of the desert, to the borders of the promised land. Often had he been wearied by their murmurings, often had he been provoked by their unbelief. He had been alternately the object of their mistrust and of their confidence, of their jealousy and of their enthusiasm, and yet their very waywardness only seemed the more warmly to endear them; and, with a love stronger than death, he loved them unto the end. Aware that, by his unadvised speaking at the waters of Meribah, he had barred his own entrance into Canaan, and animated with a passion for the welfare of his people, intenser as the time of their separation drew nearer, he gathered them upon the plains of Moab, and in solemn and weighty words retraced the path they had trod, warned them against their besetting dangers, and exhorted them to fidelity in Jehovah's service. In the midst of this advice, the words of the text occur, summoning them, so to speak, to take a mental pilgrimage over all the track which they had travelled, and to connect it with beneficial uses which might influence their future lives. Such a review of the past is always wise and salutary when it is conducted in a becoming and prayerful spirit, and to such a review of the past, therefore, it is that we invite you to-day. We may not unprofitably accompany the children of Israel in their review of the way which they had trod; we may learn lessons in their company which may effectually benefit ourselves. In order that we may preserve some sort of system in our contemplations, we will notice, in the first instance, the remembrance of the way; secondly, the purpose of God's providence in the journey; and, thirdly, the uses of the memory.

I. In the first place, the REMEMBRANCE OF THE WAY. "Thou shalt *remember* all the way which the Lord thy God hath led thee these forty years in the wilderness." It is a wonderful faculty, this faculty of memory. Its acts seem to be of the nature of miracles wrought continually for the conviction of unbelief. We cannot expound its philosophy; nor tell its dwelling-place, nor name the subtle chords which evoke it from its slumbers. A snatch of music in the street, the sight of a modest flower or of an old tree, a word dropped casually by a passer-by, a face that flits by us in the hurrying crowd, have summoned the gone years to our side, and filled us in a moment with memories of divinest comfort or of deepest sorrow. The power of memory is lasting and is influential. A kindness has been done in secret; but that seed, dropped into the soil of memory, has borne fruitage in the gratitude of years. A harsh word or an inflicted injury, flung upon the memory, has rankled there into lawlessness and into sin. No man can be solitary who has memory. The poorest of us, if he have memory, is richer than he knows, for by it we can reproduce ourselves, be young even when the limbs are failing, and have all the past belonging to us when the hair is silvery and the eyes are dim. How can he be a skeptic or a materialist, for whom memory every moment raises the dead, and refuses to surrender the departed years to the destroyer; communes with the loved ones though the shroud enfolds them; and converses with cherished voices which for long years have never spoken with tongues? I had almost said, but that I know the deep depravity of the human heart, how can he sin who has memory? For though the murderer may stab his victim in secret, far from living witnesses, and may carefully remove from the polluted earth the foul traces of his crime, memory is a witness that he can neither gag nor stifle, and he bears about with him in his own terrible consciousness the blasted immortality of his being. Oh, it is a rare and a divine endowment! Memories of sanctity or sin pervade all the firmament of being. There is but the flitting moment in which to hope or to enjoy, but in the calendar of memory that moment is all time. This, then, is the faculty which the Jewish law-giver calls up into exercise: "Thou shalt remember all the way which the Lord thy God hath led thee these forty years in the wilderness." And in truth there could be no grander history, nor one richer in instruction, than theirs. From the time when they groaned in bondage, and their cry went up unto God, until now, when, after forty years' vicissitudes, they stood upon the threshold of the land of Canaan, each day would have its wonder and its lesson. They had been led by a way which they knew not; they had seen the laws of nature suspended, and the mechanism of the firmament disorganized on their behalf. In Egypt they had quailed beneath the very Omnipotence which had delivered them, and they had crouched trembling at the base of Sinai, while ever and anon loomed through the darkness the flashings forth of the Divinity within. Sustained by perpetual miracle, delivered with an outstretched arm, with the barrenness behind and the plenty before them, they were to "*remember* the way which the Lord had led them in the wilderness."

Brethren, our own, if we will only think of it, has been an instructive history. There is much in the life of each of us, in its rest, and in its change, in its hazard, and in its deliverance, which will repay us if we revisit it to-day. Be it ours to recall the past, to recover the obliterated circumstance, to abide again at each halting-place of our journey, to decipher the various inscriptions which the lapse of time has fretted almost to decay, to *remember*, as the Israelites, the way which the Lord hath led us.

1. There would be in their history, in the first place, *the remembrance of favor, and by consequence of joy.* All through their course they had had very special manifestations of the power and goodness of God. He had brought them out with a high hand from the pride and tyranny of Pharaoh, he had cleared a path for them through the obedient waters, the heavens had rained down sustenance, the rock had quenched their thirst; Jehovah's presence had gone with them through the tangled desert path, by day in guiding cloud, by night in lambent flame; their raiment had not waxed old upon them, neither their foot swelled, for forty years. He had spoiled their enemies in their sight. Sihon, king of the Amorites, and Og,

king of Bashan, had fallen before his power. When the law-giver gathered the tribes in the plains of Moab, he could say: "Not one thing of all that the Lord your God, hath spoken hath ever failed;" and there was not a murmur in the host, and there was not an individual in the congregation that could either gainsay or deny.

Brethren, there could not fail to be great and grateful rejoicing in this remembrance of the loving kindness of the Lord. That loving kindness has compassed us from the first moment of our existence until now, and by his favor he hath made our mountain to stand strong. I would call up before you to-day those scenes in your history upon which you are apt to dwell with joyous and grateful memory. Think of the gracious Providence who cared for your infancy, and who prevented your doings in youth; think of the unexpected deliverances, the unlooked-for surprises of blessing with which you have been visited; pause before the various stones of help which you have erected in the course of your journey; remember the stores of gladness inexhaustible and constantly operating, that have been poured upon you by the bounty of your heavenly Father; the joy of your heart, the joy peculiar to yourselves, the natural and inevitable outflow of childhood's sportiveness and glee, the joy of enlarging knowledge, the joy of some new discovery of the beautiful, of some keener thirst after the true; the joy of travel, the sight of earth's great cities, fair landscapes, and spots renowned in song and story; the joy of home, of parents whose love has cast a spell upon your after-lives, from which you would not be disenchanted if you could—brother, and sister, and wife, and husband, names that mean more to the heart, a thousand-fold, than they can ever mean to the ear; friends that knew you and that understood you, those twin souls who bore with your weaknesses without chiding, and who entered into your dreams with sympathy. The joy of meetings, and of farewells, and of that which came between more sweet than each. The joy of the Church; victory over some besetting temptation; glad seasons of Christian fellowship, which can never be forgotten; sermons that seemed, in their exquisite adaptedness, as if they had been made for you, to counsel in perplexity, to comfort in trouble; sacramental occasions when, in no distempered vision, you "saw heaven opened, and the Son of Man standing upon the right hand of the throne of God." The joy of usefulness, the gladness which thrilled through you when you succored the distressed, or were valiant for the truth, or pitied and reclaimed the erring, or flung the garment of praise over some bewildered spirit of heaviness. The joy that has sprung for you out of sorrow, and has been all the brighter for the contrast; deliverance from danger which threatened to be imminent, recovery from sickness that seemed as though it were about to be mortal; the lightnings that have let the glory through the clouds; the flowers that you have so often plucked from tombs. Call up the mighty sum of gladness now, and as, subdued and grateful in the memory, you think of your past times, many a lip will quiver and many a heart be full, as you *remember* the way which the Lord hath led you in the wilderness.

2. There would, secondly, be in their history *the remembranee of sin, and, by consequence of sin, the remembrance of sorrow.* Nothing is more remarkable as a fact, and more illustrative of the depravity of the human heart, than the frequency with which the children of Israel sinned. Only three days after the wonderful interposition at the Red Sea, their murmurings began. The miracle at Marah, although it appeased their thirst, failed to inspire their confidence, for they tempted God again at the Waters of Strife. Although the manna fell without ceasing, they lusted after the fleshpots of Egypt. Their whole history, indeed, is a record of perpetual sin, a perpetual lapse, now into jealousy, and now into sensualism, now into unbelief, and now, alas, into idolatry. These repeated transgressions, of necessity, introduced them to sorrow, and they suffered, in almost every variety, the strokes of Jehovah's displeasure. They were wasted by successive pestilences; they were devoured by fiery serpents in the wilderness; the earth opened her mouth and swallowed up the rebellious sons of Korah; the Lord went not forth with their hosts to battle; and they fled discomfited and crestfallen before the face of their enemies. Their journey was made protracted and

dangerous. Bereavement visited every tent in turn. One after another the head of each family bowed, and sunk, and fell, until of all those who left Egypt, stalwart and sinewy men, only two, and those of another spirit, remained to enter into the land of promise and of rest; and the very lawgiver who called up the exercise of the memory, and the few old men, upon whose brows the almond tree was flourishing, thinly scattered here and there among the tribes, knew that their heads must bow, their frames dissolve in death, ere the van-standard of the host could be unfurled within the borders of the promised land. There could not fail to be subdued and pensive emotion in this aspect of the remembrance of the way. Our own history has its sorrowful side, too, which it will be well for us to remember to-day. All sorrow, of course, comes originally from sin, but there is some sorrow which we inherit from no personal transgression, but which has been handed down to us, a sad entail of suffering, a disastrous transmission from our earliest fathers. The remembrance of such sorrows stretches far back in the history of every one's life. Perhaps you were cruelly treated in youth, and you can hardly think of it now without shuddering. Perhaps some bitter disappointment made your path ungenial, or some early unkindness came like a frost-blight upon your fresh, young hopes, just when you were beginning to indulge them. Perhaps a long sickness chained you down, and you suffered the illness of hope deferred, and you wondered whether the cheek would ever bloom again in the ruddiness of health, and whether the elastic pulse would ever bound and swell through the veins. Perhaps there are other memories—most likely there are—so dense in their darkness as to cast all the rest into a relief of lesser shadow. The first breaking up of your homes, the stroke that swept you into orphanhood, or that took away the desire of your eyes with a stroke, or that cast you upon a cold world's charities for work and bread. Call up these memories, though the heart bleeds afresh as you think of them. They have their uses; they need not be summoned for the first time in vain. And then the memory of sin—don't hide it, don't be cowardly about it; confront your yesterdays, not in defiance, but in penitence and prayer; your long resistance to the strivings of the Holy Spirit, the veiled impertinence with which you refused to hearken to a father's counsels and were deaf to the entreaties of a mother's prayers. The sins of your youth, which, though you humbly trust are pardoned by the grace of God, plague you still, like the scars of some old wound, with shooting pains in many a change of weather. Your unfaithfulness since the Lord called you, your indulgence since your conversion in things you dared not for your lives have done while you were seeking mercy. How you have cherished some secret idol, or forborne to deliver them that were drawn to death, or dwelt in your ceiled houses, intent only upon you own aggrandizement and pleasure, while the house of God lay waste. Call up these memories, do not disguise them; they will bow you in humility before God.

This is the memory of the way. "Thou shalt remember all the way which the Lord thy God hath led thee." *All the way*—it is necessary that all the way should be remembered—the hill of difficulty as well as the valley of humiliation, the time of prosperity as well as the time of pain. Necessary for our advantage that we may understand our position, learn the lessons of providence and grace; necessary that we may construct a narrative, for every event in our history is connected and mutually interpreted; necessary that we may trace the outworking of Jehovah's plan in the successive achievements of our lives. And if by the memory of joy you are impressed with God's beneficence, kept in cheerful piety, and saved from the foul sin of repining; and if by the memory of sorrow you are molded into a gentler type, taught a softer sympathy, and receive a heavenward impulse, and anticipate a blessed reunion; if by the memory of sin you are reminded of your frailty, and rebuked of your pride, stimulated to repentance and urged to trust in God—then it will be no irksomeness, but a heaven-sent and precious blessing that you have thus "remembered the way that the Lord hath led thee in the wilderness."

II. I come, secondly, to notice the PURPOSES OF DIVINE PROVIDENCE IN THE JOURNEY. These are stated to be three: "to humble thee and to prove thee, to know what was in thine heart, whether thou wouldest keep his commandments or no." The passage tells us that in all God's dealings with the children of Israel, whether he corrected them in judgment or enriched them with bounty, there were purposes at work—purposes of spiritual discipline, intended to induce self-searching and the improvement of their hearts and lives.

1. The first purpose that is spoken of is *to induce humility*—"to humble thee." Every event, alike in their deliverance from Egypt and in their passage through the wilderness, was calculated to show them their own feebleness, and their constant dependence upon a high and upon a superior power. What could human might have effected for them in the way of securing their deliverance from Egypt? Their spirits were broken by long years of slavery; the iron had not only gyved their limbs, it had entered into their soul. They had not the heart, any one of them, to strike for freedom; and if they had even meditated a rising, they were a people of such divided counsels, and so distrustful of each other, that it would have been but a paroxysm of frantic rebellion, which would have rooted the Pharaohs on the empire, and have riveted upon themselves the yoke of a more bitter bondage. When the permission for departure was wrung reluctantly from the plague-stricken king, what could human might have availed for them, when he repented of his momentary graciousness, and pursued after them in hot

haste, and they were on the borders of the Red Sea, with the giant waves barring their progress, and a host of ferocious enemies behind? Everything in their experience taught them their dependence upon God. They were led through a region that no adventurer had ever explored, no foot had ever trod. When they pitched their tents at eventide, they knew not at what hour they should strike them, nor whether they should strike them at all; there might be forced years of encampment in that one spot; there might be forced marches and rapid progress; but they had no control over it: as the pillar went, and wherever the pillar went, they went; and as they sounded forth their matin song of praise, there was not a man in the whole congregation that could tell through what rocky clefts or woody defiles the echoes of the vesper hymn would sound. Their supply was as miraculous as their guidance. No plough had turned up the soil, no river murmured by their side, they had never gazed for forty years upon one solitary blossom of the spring-time, nor had the golden grain ever once in their sight bent gracefully to the sickle of the reaper: they were fed with manna, which they knew not.

> "When faint they were and parched with drought,
> Water at his word gushed out."

Oh! it is the world's grandest illustration of man's absolute feebleness and of God's eternal power. 600,000 fighting men, beside women and children, led by Divine leadership, and fed by Divine bounty, for the space of forty years. Brethren, the dealings of Providence with ourselves are intended to show us our dependence upon God, and to humble us in the dust under his mighty hand. We are very proud, sometimes, and we talk about our endowments, and we boast largely of what we have done, and what we intend to do; but we can do absolutely nothing. The athletic frame—how soon can he bring it down! The well-endowed heritage—how soon can he scatter it! The mental glance, keen and piercing—how soon can he bring upon it the dimness and bewilderment of years! We cannot, any one of us, bring ourselves into being; we cannot, any one of us, sustain ourselves in being for a moment. Alas! who of us can stay the spirit, when the summons has gone forth that it must die? We are free; we cannot help feeling that we are free; and yet we can as little help feeling that our freedom is bounded, that it has a horizon, something that indicates a watchful Providence outside. How often have we aimed at building for ourselves tabernacles of remembrance and of rest, and we have gazed upon the building joyfully as it progressed to completion, and then the breath of the Lord has blown upon it, and it has been scattered, and we have been turned adrift and shelterless; and, lo! dwellings already provided for us of firmer materials and of more excellent beauty, upon which we bestowed no labor nor thought. And so it is with all the matters of human glory. The strong man rejoiceth in his strength, and magnifieth himself in the might of his arms, but the Lord hath made him strong; the wise man glorifieth himself in his intellect, but the clear perception, and the brilliant fancy, and the fluent utterance, these are God's gifts; the rich man rejoiceth in his riches, but the prudence to plan, and the sagacity to foresee, and the industry to gather, these are the bestowments of God.

Ah! why will men sacrifice to their own net, and burn incense to their own drag, when they have absolutely nothing which they have not received; and when every gift cometh from the Father of light, with whom there is no variableness, neither shadow of turning? And in the realm of morals, and in the spiritual life, our feebleness is the same. A conscience void of offence, a good report of those that are without a heavenly purpose or a holy resolve, the inner purification or the comely outgrowth of a beneficent life—we are poor to compass them. We acquire them only by our dependence upon God. Have you learned this lesson, this deep, hard lesson of humility? Forty years' sins you have committed! have they humbled you in the presence of God? Forty years' chastenings have corrected you! have they humbled your pride or fretted you into greater audacity of rebellion? Forty years' mercies have blessed you! have they excited your gratitude or inflated your vanity? Brethren, we must be humbled, if we would be happy. It was in the Valley of Humiliation, you remember, that the lad that had the herb heart's-ease in his bosom kept his serene and his rejoicing home.

2. Then the second purpose of God's providence in the journey is *to prove us.* The idea seems to be, that a skillful chemist employs tests for the purpose of analysis, and to discover the composition of that which he examines, so God uses the occurrences of life as a moral touchstone, to discover the tendencies and inclinations of man. Thus we read God did tempt, test, try, prove Abraham, requiring from him a sacrifice, excessive and apparently cruel, in order that he might know the strength of his servant's faith, and of his filial fear. There were many of those testing circumstances in the history of the children of Israel. They were tested by their mercies, as when, feeling the manna insipid, they lusted after the flesh-pots of Egypt; they were tested by their duties; they were tested by their calamities, as at the Red Sea, and in the conflicts with the hosts of Amalek. They were tested by their companions, as when they formed unholy league with Midianite idolaters, and brought upon themselves that swift destruction which Balak wished for, but which the cowardly Balaam dared not for his life invoke. Brethren, God has his crucible still. In our past lives we shall find circumstances that have tried ourselves, and we shall remember the results of the trial sometimes with devout gratitude, oftener with unfeigned shame. Our afflictions have tried us, and we have thought that we have done well to be angry, and we have arraigned the pro-

ceedings of God at the bar of our limited reason (solemn mockery of judicature!) when, perhaps, the reflection of to-morrow would have approved what the distrust of to-day was so ready to condemn. Our duties have tried us. We have felt the shrinking of the flesh, and the result has been sometimes their reluctant and sometimes their spiritless discharge. Other people have been unjust or unkind to us: we have met with ingratitude or with treachery; our own familiar one, in whom we trusted, has betrayed us; slander has been busy belching out her calumnies against our fair fame; all these things have tested our patience, our endurance, our meekness, our long-suffering, and, like Moses, we have spoken unadvisedly, or, like the disciples, we have had to pray, "Lord, increase our faith," before we could grasp the large and princely idea of forgiveness to seventy times seven. Often companionships have tried us, and we have shown how small has been our self-reliance and how easily we have taken the hue and mold of the society in which we were thrown, and how a pointed finger, or a sarcastic laugh, or a lip scornfully curled, can shame the manhood out of us, and make us very cowards in resisting evil, or in bearing witness for God. Thus have we been, thus has God proved us in the wilderness, and if we are in earnest for heaven, and if we have in any measure profited by the discipline, we shall be thankful for the trial. Placed as we are in a sinful world, exposed to its every-day influences, whether of good or evil, we need a piety which can maintain itself in all circumstances, and under every pressure. The trial will be a matter of choice, preferred by every godly and valiant Christian soldier. He feels as though that were an inglorious heaven that was won without a sacrifice and without a toil; he knows that the promise is not that he shall pass through the wilderness without the sight of an enemy; it is a better promise than that—that we shall never see an enemy that we cannot master, and that by God's grace we cannot completely overcome; and he had rather don his armor for a foeman worthy of his steel, for an enemy that will at once prove his own valor and show the resources of the Captain of his salvation, than he would don it in order to prance in the gorgeous apparellings of some holiday review. Oh! believe me, the piety which the world needs, which the church needs, and which we must have if we would be approved of our Great Master, must not be that sickly sentimentality which lounges on ottomans, and discusses social and moral problems while it is at ease in Sion; it must be the hardy principle pining in inaction, robust from healthy exercise, never so happy as when it is climbing up the slopes of some difficult duties, and has the breeze from the crest of the mountain stirring amid its waving hair; and happy, thrice happy, will it be for you if, as the result of the inspection, you can say, as David did, "Thou hast proved my heart and thou hast visited me in the night; thou hast tried me and shalt find nothing. I am purposed that my heart shall not transgress, concerning the works of men; by the word of thy lips I have kept me from the paths of the destroyer."

3. And then the third purpose of Providence in the journey is "*to know what was in thine heart*—whether thou wouldest keep his commandments or no." The human heart is a microcosm—a little world, containing in itself all the strifes, and all the hopes, and all the fears, and all the ventures of the larger world outside. The human heart! who can unravel its mystery, or decipher its hidden law? The smile may play upon the lip, while beneath there is the broken, burning heart; and, on the other hand, the countenance may have shadow of anxiety, while the sunlight dances gaily on the soul. The human heart! Human knowledge can give us very little acquaintance with it; such knowledge is too wonderful for man; it is high, and he cannot attain unto it; but there is One who knows it, and knows all its tortuous policy, and all its sinister motive, and he is anxious that we should know it, too, and one purpose of his providential dealings with us is, that we may know what is in our heart; and yet of all sciences none is so difficult of attainment as this same science of self-knowledge. Whether it be from the deceitfulness of the object of study, or whether it be from the morbid reluctance, almost amounting to fear, with which men shrink from acquaintance with themselves, there are few that have the bravery to pray, "Lord, make me to know myself." Indeed, it were a hideous picture if it were suddenly unveiled in the presence of us all. When the Lord

would show Ezekiel the abominations of Jerusalem, he led him through successive chambers of imagery, upon the walls of which were portrayed their loathsome and unworthy doings. Ah! if our enormities were to be thus tapestried in our sight, who of us could bear the disclosure? There was deep self-knowledge and deep humility in the word of the old reformer, who, when he saw a criminal led off amid the jeers of the multitude to be hanged at Tyburn, turned around sighing, and said: "There, but for the grace of God, goes old John Bradford." There is a very affecting illustration of what can lurk unsuspected in the human heart, in the 8th chapter of the 2nd book of Kings: "And Elisha came to Damascus; and Ben-hadad, the king of Syria, was sick; and it was told him, saying, The man of God is come hither. And the king said unto Hazael, Take a present in thine hand, and go, meet the man of God, and inquire of the Lord by him, saying, Shall I recover of this disease? So Hazael went to meet him, and took a present with him, even of every good thing of Damascus, forty camels' burden, and came and stood before him, and said, Thy son, Ben-hadad, king of Syria, hath sent me to thee, saying, Shall I recover of this disease? And Elisha said unto him, Go, say unto him, Thou mayest certainly recover. [The disease itself is not fated to destroy thee; there is no decree of that kind]. Howbeit the Lord hath showed me that he shall surely die. And he settled his countenance steadfastly, until he was ashamed; and the man of God wept. And Hazael said,

Why weepeth my lord? And he answered, Because I know the evil that thou wilt do unto the children of Israel; their strongholds wilt thou set on fire, and their young men wilt thou slay with the sword, and wilt dash their children, and rip up their women with child. And Hazael said [shocked at the bare mention of such atrocities], But what, is thy servant a dog, that he should do this great thing?" But, as the old divine quaintly says, "the dog did it after all." Brethren, there lurks this danger in us all; there is no superiority of character in ourselves; there is no firmer power of resistance to evil. In our unaided strength we are no better fortified against the extremes of iniquity than many around us who now wallow in the atrocities of crime. That speculative merchant, whose affairs had become hopelessly embarrassed, and who, in the vain hope of retrieval, plied the too ready pen of the forger, and in that sad moment forfeited the probity of years—how sad must have been his reflections when, to use his own expressive words, he "agonized on," when he thought that he should transmit to his children nothing but the heritage of a blasted name, and that those children would have an up-hill struggle all the way through life, their own blamelessness being a small matter against the terrible opprobrium of their father's misdoings. He who continues in the feast until wine inflames him, imagines that he can tread without danger upon the giddy verge over which multitudes have fallen; but, by little and little, he cherishes the unappeasable thirst for drink until it becomes a morbid physical malady, and, frantic and despairing, he rushes down into the drunkard's grave. That youth who, at the solicitation of some gay companion, ventures, for the first time, into the foul hell of a gaming-house, and who joins in the perilous hazard, would scoff at the prophet who should tell him that, a few years hence, a gambler and a spendthrift, he should live in poverty and die in shame. That young man who, to gain funds, perhaps, for the Sunday excursion, or for the night's debauch, took the money from his master's till with the conscientious intention of replacing it at the time of the quarterly supply, little thought that that deceitful heart of his would land him in a felon's dock, or, upon the deck of the transport ship, waft him to a returnless distance from his country and his home. Brethren, from a thousand causes of disaster and of shame with which our experience can furnish us, and which we read in the history of every-day life, it becomes us, with godly jealousy watching over our own hearts, to guard against the beginnings of evil; and as we think of blighted reputations and of ruined hopes—of many once fair, and innocent, and scrupulous, and promising as we—as we gaze upon the wreck of many a gallant vessel stranded by our side, which we saw steaming out of the harbor with stately pennons—let us remember that in us there are the same tendencies to evil, that it is grace—only grace—which hath made us to differ, and that each instance of calamity and of sin, while it evokes our pity—not our scorn—for those that have so grievously erred, should proclaim in solemn admonition to ourselves, "Let him that thinketh he standeth take heed lest he fall." "To know what is in thine heart, whether thou wouldest keep his commandments or no."

III. If you have thus travelled in the way that you have trodden, there will be MANY USES OF THE MEMORY which we cannot stay to particularize to-day. You will know more of God at the conclusion of your visit than you did at the commencement. You will behold in the way both the goodness and the severity of God—the severity which punishes sin wherever it is to be found, the goodness which itself provides a substitute and finds a Saviour. Where do you not find him, rather? There was the stream gushing forth from the smitten rock—was there not?—and the perishing and thirsty Israelites were happy. "They drank of the rock that followed them, and that rock was Christ." There was the brazen serpent, the symbol of accepted propitiation in the wilderness of sin. "As Moses lifted up the serpent in the wilderness, even so hath the Son of Man been lifted up, that whosoever believeth in him should not perish, but should have everlasting life." Oh, as you gather up those memories—the memory of joy, the memory of sorrow, the memory of sin—as you remember the goodness and the loving kindness of the Lord, his faithfulness to fulfill his promises, his tenderness, which your repeated rebellions have not caused to fail—gather up yourselves in one earnest consecration of flesh and spirit, which I take to be the best consecration of the house which you now dedicate to God—living temples, pillars in the house of God, that shall go out no more forever.

II.

THE BELIEVER'S SUFFICIENCY.

"Not that we are sufficient of ourselves to think anything as of ourselves; but our sufficiency is of God."—2 CORINTHIANS, iii. 5.

THE promise contained in these words is one of the most encouraging and one of the most comprehensive in the Bible. It is the essence of all Christian experience; it is the moral which the Scriptures continually inculcate, and it stands in the heraldry of heaven as the motto on the believer's arms. The all-sufficiency of God has been the support and comfort of the faithful in all ages of the Church. On this rock Abraham built his hope; to this refuge in all times of trial the sweet Singer of Israel fled; by this confidence the great Apostle of the Gentiles was constantly and perseveringly upheld. The all-sufficiency of God gives strength to patience, gives solidity to hope, gives constancy to endurance, gives nerve and vitality to effort. The weakest believer, with this great treasure in possession, is enabled to go steadily forward, sacrificing no duty, resisting all sin; and, amidst every horror and every humiliation, feeling within him the still, clear light of life. To this the most eminent saints are indebted for all they enjoy, for all they are enabled to perform; and though assailed by various foes without, and by various fears within, by this they can return from every conflict, bearing the spoils of victory; and as with the trophies of their triumph they erect the grateful Ebenezer, you may see this inscription written upon them all: "Having obtained help of God, we continue unto this day," feeling most deeply the impotency of the nature they inherit, and penetrated with the sense of the difficulties by which they are surrounded. When faith is in exercise, they point to this as a never-failing source of strength; and in the course of their untried and unswerving pilgrimage, this is their language: "Let the wise man, if he will be so foolish, trust in his wisdom; let the rich man glory in his wealth; let the proud man vaunt his own dignity; let the trifler make the world his defence; *we* dare not trust to such refuges of lies, we dare not build upon foundations that are palpably insecure. We feel our own nothingness; but we feel our own might, because our sufficiency is of God.

From the commencement of the chapter out of which these words are taken, we learn that the same exclusiveness of spirit existed in the days of Paul which exists in certain quarters now, and that the same charge—that of false apostleship—was brought against him that has since been so plentifully flung at eminent ministers of Jesus Christ. It is no small consolation to find that we are thus unchurched in good company. The apostle, however, answers the accusation just as any man would do, who had no particular interest to serve in surrounding a great question with a crowd of arguments anything but luminous—he appeals to the Church amongst whom he had labored, and asks their verdict as to his success as a minister: "Do we begin again to commend ourselves, or need we, as some others, epistles of commendation to you, or letters of commendation from you? Ye are our epistle [your changed hearts, your holy lives, your transformed affections, your heavenly deportment—ye are our epistles] written in our hearts, known and read of all men: forasmuch as ye are manifestly declared to be the epistle of Christ ministered by us, written not with ink [nor anything so fading], but with the Spirit of the living God; not in tables of stone [nor anything so hard], but in fleshy tables of the heart; and such trust have we through Christ to Godward;" then, so anxious is he even in this moment of his triumphant vindication to avoid all appearance of boasting, that he puts in a great disclaimer: "not that we are sufficient of ourselves to think anything of ourselves; all that, whether in us as subjects or by us as the instruments, has been done by the sovereign power of God, who also hath made us able ministers of the New Testament, not of the letter, but of the Spirit; for the letter killeth, but the Spirit giveth life." The Apostle in these verses unfolds the great secret both of ministerial call and of ministerial efficiency. It is God, not man, that makes, not finds, able ministers of the New Testament. The tones of his voice are heard, saying to them, "Son, go work to-day in my vineyard." And it is a remarkable fact, one which we should never forget, that this voice is never heard in a heart where there is no faith; consequently, the prime qualification for a minister of the Christian religion is the heart that has been melted by its love, and a consciousness which has felt it in its power. Without this, all else is unavailing; the attainment of the most profound and extensive knowledge, the grasp of the loftiest and most scholarly intellect, the possession of the most commanding eloquence, the treasures of the most imperial fancy, the research of the most accomplished scholar, all these are useless, worse than useless, if they be not consecrated by the Spirit of the Holy One; only the trappings that decorate the traitor, and make his treason yet the fouler; only the weapons of more imminent danger, and the portents of more terrific and appalling ruin. The most distinguished minister within the compass of the Catholic Church, however eminent he may be, however signally his labors have been blessed, has reason to remember, every moment of his ministerial career, "I am nothing, less than nothing; but my sufficiency is of God." The comfortable and scriptural doctrine contained in the text is not more true of ministers, of whom it was immediately spoken, than of Christians in general, to whom it may be properly applied. The station is different, the strength is the same. Your sufficiency, as well as ours, is of God. To take the words in this extended sense, we may find in them matter of profitable meditation, by considering first the nature of this sufficiency and then the authority which believers have to expect this sufficiency for themselves.

I. First, the sufficiency of God may be considered either as PROPER, or COMMUNICATED. By his essential, or proper sufficiency, we mean that he is self-existent, self-sufficient, independently happy; angels and men may declare that they cannot increase his glory; it is eternal, underived, perfect. He has said that he will never give it to another. There was no necessity in his nature impelling him to create the universe; he could have existed alone, and he did exist alone, long before the everlasting silence was broken by a human footstep, or interrupted by a human voice; and that Divine solitude was the solitude of matchless happiness. The best praises, therefore, the most extensive services of his worshippers, are but reflections of the glory which dwells originally in himself. But it is of the sufficiency of God in relation to his creatures that it is our province especially to speak. And it is in this sense God is good to all, and his tender mercies are over all his works.

1. He is sufficient, in the first place—let us take low ground first—*for the preservation of the universe which his hands have made.* From the sublime account

which the Scriptures give us of creation, we learn that the heavens were made by him, and all the host of them by the breath of his mouth; and as we know that nothing earthly has within it the power to sustain itself, we are further assured that he upholdeth all things by the same word of his power. It is by this ever-breathing word, constantly in exercise, that the sun shines, that the moon walks in brightness, that the stars pursue their courses in the sky; the clouds are marshalled by his Divine decree, and when he uttereth his voice there is a multitude of waters in the heavens. Reason looks at this systematic and continuous regularity, and admires it, and refers it to the operation of second causes, and argues very philosophically about the nature and fitness of things; but piety looks through the complications of the mechanism to the hand that formed it. The universe is to her but one vast transparency, through which she can gaze on God; her pathway and her communion are on the high places of creation, and there, far above all secondary and subordinate agencies, she discovers the hiding of his power. The symmetry of nature is to her more beautiful, because God has produced it. The deep harmonies of the systems come more tunefully upon her ear because the hand of the Lord has awakened them.

"What though no real voice nor sound
Amid the radiant orbs be found?
In faith's quick ear they all rejoice,
And utter forth a noble voice,

> For ever singing as they shine,
> 'The hand that made us is Divine.'"

And what a contemplation does this open to us of the majesty and power of God! Who can understand it? The planets are kept in their orbits, and the seasons continually alternate. Old Ocean dashes himself upon the shore, and every day finds "hitherto" written upon the sand, and the mad surge respects it. The earth yields her increase; vegetable life is evolved; circulation takes place throughout the animal system; man walks and lives, and all these diversified operations are produced at one and the same moment, perpetuated from one moment to another by the simple word of God. Extend your conceptions still further; take hold of the far-reaching discoveries of astronomy. Glance at the numberless suns and systems that are scattered in the broad field of immensity, and remember (for there is no Scripture against it, and probabilities are strongly in favor of the opinion), that they are all inhabited by dependent creatures somewhat like ourselves. Glance at the almost infinite variety of existences with which we are acquainted—whether we walk the earth, or cleave the air, or swim the sea—connect with all these the Scriptural announcement that these are but parts of his ways, and how little a portion is known of them; and then how thought shrinks from the aggregate! how the brain recoils from the contemplation of the sum! and we may well finish the quotation, and say, "The thunder of his power, who can understand?" All our reasonings upon the subject only serve to demonstrate that man by searching cannot find out God. Could you, with the swiftness of a sunbeam, dart yourselves beyond the limits of the known creation, and for ages upon ages continue your pilgrimage in infinite space, you would never—who can grasp that thought? it is too large for us—never be able to reach a place where God is not, never light upon a spot where this glorious Being is not essentially and influentially present. The whole universe is one vast laboratory of benevolent art, over every department of which the Deity presides—a sanctuary, every part of which the Divinity inhabits—a circle, whose circumference is unfathomed, and whose every section is filled with God. But I stop here just for a moment, to remind you of the thrill that comes through the heart of the believer, when, after this exhibition of boundless and colossal power, he can go home, singing—

> "This all-sufficient God is ours,
> Our Father, and our love."

Our sufficiency is of God.

2. Then, secondly, and chiefly, he is sufficient *for the preservation and for the perpetuity of the Gospel plan, in the salvation and ultimate happiness of every individual believer.* Christianity is not to be viewed by us merely as a moral system; that were to place it on a level with the speculations of Confucius, and Socrates, and others. It is something more, it is a course of

Divine operations. We are not to regard it as a mere ethical statement of doctrine made known to us by a bundle of books; we must remember the Divine agency always, by which it is conducted and inspired. We observed before, that no mere man has the power to produce an abiding change upon the hearts of his hearers. Human eloquence is a mighty thing, I know; human reason is a persuasive and powerful thing, I know; under certain favorable conjunctures of circumstances, they have sometimes achieved mighty results. They can shame a Herod, they can make a Felix tremble, they can almost persuade an Agrippa to become a Christian, but they can do no more. I know that immense multitudes have been swayed by the power of a single tongue. The passions have become excited, either to madness or to sympathy, either to deeds of lawless aggression, or to deeds of high emprise; but then there is only a transient mastery obtained. We read of a harp in the classical fables of old, which, when the winds swept it, was said to discourse sweet strains; but then, unhappily, the breeze and the music died away together. So it is with the triumph of the orator: the moment the voice of the speaker ceases the spell is broken, the charm is dissipated; reflection begins to remonstrate against excitement, and the whole affair is forgotten, or comes upon the soul only as the memory of some pleasant song. Nay, truth, celestial truth, can produce no abiding change. Pardon and sanctification are not the necessary consequences of statements of doctrine. Scripture cannot produce them; the truth may appear in all its cogency and in all its power before the mind—it may appear so clear as to extort an acquiescence in what it propounds; but it is uninfluential; it lacks energy, and it lacks a self-appliant power. It may enlighten—that is its province—it can never save. Without the Spirit it is useless; let the Spirit animate it, and it is the power of God. Hearers who sit under the ministrations of the truth without the Spirit may be likened to a man standing upon the brow of a hill which commands the prospect of an extensive landscape. The varied beauties of flood and of field are before him; nature is clad in her richest livery, there is every variety calculated to interest and to inspire; rugged rocks frown as if they would keep sentinel over the sleeping valley; the earth yields her increase, the crystal streamlet leaps merrily along, impressions of the beautiful are everywhere visible, there is just one drawback to the picture, and that one drawback is, that the man who stands upon the summit of the hill is blind. That is precisely the state of the case in reference to truth in the Bible. It is there in all its grandeur, but the man has no eyes to see it. Let the Spirit come and take the scales away and shred off the spiritual ophthalmia, and he sees the landscape stretching before him in all its hues of beauty, and his soul is elevated and he feels the full rapture of the scene. Prevailing truth, therefore, is not of the letter but of the Spirit, for "the letter killeth, but the Spirit giveth life." This Spirit it is that is promised for the carrying out of the Gospel, and it therefore must be successful. I know there is a good deal of difficulty about his mode of procedure: God's word must be fulfilled, that is one thing; man's freedom must be maintained, that is another thing. Man is a moral agent; God has endued him with talents and invested him with an immense delegation of power, and in the distribution of these talents and in the exercise of that power, he has said, in effect, Let him alone; he may do as he lists—just as he lists. He is allowed, for the present, to act as if he had no superior, but for all he is holden finally most strictly responsible. But no coercion is applied, no force is ever in any conceivable instance made use of. One of our most eloquent senators once said, that an Englishman's cottage was his castle. The winds may whistle through every crevice, and the rains penetrate through every cranny, but into that cottage the monarch of England dare not enter against the cotter's will. That is just the state of the case between Christ and the human soul. He has such a respect for the will of that immortal tenant that he has placed within us, that he will never force an entrance. He will do everything else; he will knock at the door—

> "He now stands knocking at the door
> Of every sinner's heart;
> The worst need keep him out no more,
> Nor force him to depart."

But he will not force an entrance. Often, disappointed

and grieved, he turns away from those whom he would fain have enriched and saved, saying, "Ye will not come unto me, that ye may have life." But notwithstanding all this formidable opposition, the Gospel, as the administration of God's truth, backed by the energy of the Holy Spirit, shall finally triumph. We can conceive of no enemies more subtle, more malignant, more powerful than those which it has already encountered and vanquished. Memory cheers us onward and bids hope to smile. God is with the Gospel; that is the great secret. She does not trust in her inherent energy; she does not trust in her exquisite adaptation to man's every necessity and peril; she does not trust in the indefatigable and self-denying labors of her ministers; God is with the Gospel, and under his guidance she shall march triumphantly forward, subjugating every enemy, acquiring a lodgment in every heart, reclaiming the world unto herself, until she has consummated her victory in the ecstasies of a renovated universe, and in that deep and solemn moment when the Son, who gave his life a ransom for all, shall see of the travail of his soul and be abundantly satisfied. O brethren! what a comfortable doctrine is this! If this Gospel is to be conducted from step to step in its progressive march to conquest, do you not see how it guarantees individual salvation and individual defence by the way?

Where art thou in the chapel to-night (would that I could discover thee!) timid and discouraged believer who art afraid of the fatigues of climbing the Hill

Difficulty, and crouchest back abashed and cowering at sight of the lions in front of the Palace Beautiful? Lift up thy head, be not discouraged; thy sufficiency is of God. What frightens thee? Affliction? God is thy help. Persecution? God is thy crown. Perplexity? God is thy counsel. Death? God is thy everlasting life. Only trust in God, and all shall be well. Life shall glide thee into death, and death shall glide thee into heaven. "Who (asks the exulting Apostle, in the 8th of Romans), who shall separate us from the love of Christ? Shall tribulation, or distress, or famine, or nakedness, or peril, or sword?" That is rather a dark catalogue; but mark how the Apostle answers it: "Nay, in all these things we are more than conquerors." It is not a drawn battle; night does not come on to separate the combatants; we have not to send a herald, as they used to do in ancient warfare, to ask permission to bury our dead; we do not come from the field with the dishonored banner trailing in the dust, and the armor hacked, scarred with the wounds we have gotten in the fight. "We are more than conquerors." Oh, the royalty of that language!—"more than conquerors, through him that hath loved us. For I am persuaded that neither death"—he puts that first, because it generally threatens believers most—"neither life," which is really a more solemn and a more perilous thing than death, rightly considered—"neither death, nor life, nor angels"—if any of them should forget themselves so far as to come and preach another

Gospel and try to deceive the very elect—"neither principalities nor powers"—for although the captain of the hosts of darkness may plant all his most formidable battery against us, he cannot shake the palisades of strong salvation, nor snatch away a solitary sheep from the fold of the great Shepherd. "No, nor things present"—though those things present may include famine, nakedness, peril, and sword—"no, nor things to come"—though, in those things to come, there may be an originality of diabolism never dreamed of yet—"and no creature"—nothing but sin, and that is not a creature, that is a foul excrescence, a vile abortion upon the universe of God—keep clear of that—and "no creature shall be able to separate you from the love of God, which is in Christ Jesus our Lord." Oh, the blessedness, the ineffable blessedness of being in the love of God! The blessedness of an approving conscience, the blessedness of increasing knowledge, the blessedness of complete victory, the blessedness of Gospel peace, the blessedness of perfect love! I do not know what that sea of glass means about which we read in the Revelation; I do not pretend to an intimate acquaintance with Apocalyptic disclosures; but I know nothing that can better image the deep, serene, reposing, kingly rapture of the spirit that has finished its course with joy. It is a sea of glass; it hath no billows; not a breath ever, by any possibility, ruffles it. And on this sea of glass, as on a wide and waveless ocean, the believer stands forever, chanting eternally the song of Moses and the Lamb. Oh, lift up your heads and come back to Zion with singing, and let this be the burden of your song:

> "Let doubt, then, and danger my progress oppose,
> They only make heaven more sweet at the close;
> Afflictions may damp me, they cannot destroy,
> For one glimpse of His love turns them all into joy.
> And come joy, or come sorrow, whate'er may befall,
> One hour with my God will make up for it all."

It were very little use our talking in this strain to you, if you were to find out, after all, that it was some aristocratical blessing, some privilege reserved only for the peerage of the faithful, for the favored ones in the family of the King of kings.

II. I come, secondly, to notice THE AUTHORITY WHICH BELIEVERS HAVE TO EXPECT THIS SUFFICIENCY FOR THEMSELVES. And, very briefly, we have a right to expect it, because it is found and promised in the Bible. Every believer, the moment he becomes a believer, becomes an inheritor of the promises. The Bible is not my Bible, nor your Bible—it is our Bible. It is common property; it belongs to the universal Church. We have no sympathy, of course, with those who would monopolize this sacred treasure, and keep this light of the Gospel burning, and that, with a precious dimness, only in the study of the priest, or fettered, as it used to be, like a curiosity, to the altars of the Church. Thank God, these days of darkness are forever gone by. And yet there is a Church, somewhere, professedly Christian, which denies to its members the light and comfort of the Bible, in direct opposition to the command of Him who has said to every one, "Search the Scriptures," thus most absolutely exalting itself against all that is called God. Oh, most foul corruption! Deprive us of the Bible! As well forbid us to gaze on the jewelled sky, or to be fanned by the winged and searching air. Deprive us of the Bible! Call it sin for us to look at the sun, and to bask in the blaze of his enlivening beams. The very same hand which launched yon orb upon his ocean of light, and bade him shine upon the evil and upon the good, has sent this orb into the world, and has sent it on purpose that it may be a lamp to all our feet and a lantern to all our paths. We devoutly thank the good Spirit of the Lord, that he put into the minds of our forefathers to protest against so flagrant and monstrous an impiety; and, thank God, we are *Protest*-ants still. We cannot afford to be thus robbed of our birthright, to be thus cheated out of our inheritance, to be thus basely swindled out of the possession of the Book of God. It is the legacy of the Apostles' labor; the bulwark of the confessors' faith; the purchase of the martyrs' blood. Thank God for the Bible. Let us prove that we love it, by drawing from it all the comfort and blessing, and guidance, and warning, which its heaven-inspired pages are calculated to afford. Well, we have a right, each of us—if we are in Christ—we have a right to expect this sufficiency, because it is promised in the Bible. We gather it from the declarations of Scripture. Listen to them, they are yours: "Thus saith the Lord who created thee, O Jacob, who formed thee, O Israel, Fear not, I have redeemed thee, I have called thee by *thy name.*" What a beautiful thought that is! Just get the meaning and beauty out of it. How many thousands of believers, thousands upon thousands of believers, have there been in the world from the beginning of its history until now—thousands in the patriarchal ages who looked through the glass, and who saw, dimly, the streak of the morning in the distance, and, even with that streak of light, were glad—thousands, in the prophetical times, who discerned it in the brightness of a nearer vision—thousands who basked in its full-orbed lustre, when Christ came into the world—thousands upon thousands, since that time, who have washed their robes and made them white in the blood of the Lamb—thousands, who are now upon the earth, working out their salvation with fear and trembling—thousands upon thousands that shall come into the Church in the time of its millennial glory, when the gates of it shall not be shut day nor night, because the porter shall have no chance of shutting them, the people crowd in so fast. Now, get all that mass of believers, past, present, and future, a company that no man can number; and to each of them God comes in this promise, and says, "I have called thee by thy name, I know all about thee"—that is, I have not a merely vague, indefinite knowledge of thee; as an individual believer I know thy name, I could single thee out of millions, I could tell the world all thy solicitudes, and all thy apprehensions, and all thy hopes, and all thy sorrows—"I have called thee by thy name." Oh, precious promise! Take it to your hearts. "I have called thee by thy name; thou art mine; when thou passest through the waters I will be with thee; and through the rivers"—deeper than the waters—"they shall not overflow thee. When thou walkest through the fire thou shalt not be burned, neither shall the flames kindle upon thee." Listen again: "The Lord God is a sun and a shield"—light and protection; that nearly embraces all our wants—"he will give grace and glory." Is there anything left out? And if there are any of you so perversely clever and so mischievously ingenious in multiplying arguments in favor of your own despair, that you can conceive of some rare and precious blessing that is not wrapped up either in grace or glory—"No good thing will he withhold from them that walk uprightly." "Fear not, for I am with thee; be not dismayed, for I am thy God." "Cast all thy care"—"Nay," the rebel heart says, "there is some little of it I must bear myself; something that has reference to the heart's bitterness, that it alone knoweth; or to the heart's deep, dark sorrow, with which no stranger intermeddles—that I must bear myself." "Cast *all* thy care upon me, for I care for thee." What! distrustful still?

Can you not take God at his word? Hark! he condescends to expostulate with you upon your unbelief: "Why sayest thou, O Jacob, and speakest, O Israel, my way is hid from the Lord"—how often have you said that in the time of your sorrow! you know you have—"my way is hid from the Lord, my judgment is passed over from my God. Hast thou not known, hast thou not heard, that the everlasting God, the Lord, the Creator of the ends of the earth, fainteth not, neither is weary? There is no searching of his understanding. He giveth power to the faint." He does not merely take his swoon away and leave him weakly, he makes him strong. "He giveth power to the faint; and to them that have no might he increaseth strength." Are you still dissatisfied?

The God who knows human nature, knows how much better a teacher example is than precept, and so, sparkling upon the pages of his holy truth, he has left us many bright instances of his interposition on behalf of his saints. Abraham rises early in the morning, goes a three days' journey with the son of his love, intending all the while, with set and resolute purpose, to offer him in sacrifice to the God of heaven. Arrived at the place of their destination, all the ritual preparations are made: the altar is prepared; the willing victim, unresisting, is bound; the sacrificial knife is lifted; no escape, then, surely! But man's extremity is God's opportunity, and the ram is caught in the thicket by its horns, and God's grace is sufficient—none too much—but sufficient still.

The children of Israel are brought to the borders of the Red Sea, hotly pursued by the flower of the Egyptian army; the troops are close upon them in the rear; the Red Sea stretches before them—the inaccessible hills of Baal-Zephon tower on the right hand and on the left. What are they to do? There seems no possible chance of escape. Oh! what are the laws of gravitation when the Lord works for his people! He who made them can alter them at pleasure. The waters erect themselves on either hand, and the bed of the ocean is their triumphal pathway. God's grace is sufficient still. Nehemiah, like a true-hearted patriot as he was, set to work to rebuild the dilapidated walls of Jerusalem. But he began, like some of his successors, in troublous times; Sanballat and Tobiah came to fight against the workmen; they were so hard beset, that they had to work with sword in the one hand and trowel in the other; God's grace was sufficient, and the second Jerusalem rose up in majesty upon the site of the ruins of the first. What! not satisfied yet? Surely that must be an almost invincible unbelief that these instances will not overcome. What is it you say? "Oh, but these are all instances taken from the Old Testament times; the age of miracles is over now—we are not now to expect such interpositions on behalf of God's people." Well, let us try again. Come out of the light of Scripture a little into the light of common life. Tread softly, as you enter that house, for it is a house of mourning; a large family surround the bedside of a dying parent; that parent is a Christian, and knowing in whom he has believed, he is not afraid to die. But he has a large family, and the thought that he shall leave them without a protector, the thought of the forcible disruption of all social ties, presses upon his spirit, and when you look at him, there is a shade of sadness upon his countenance; but you gaze awhile, and you see that sadness chased away by a smile. What has wrought the change? What? Why, a ministering angel whispered to him: "Leave thy fatherless children; I will preserve them alive." He hails the promiser. Faith cries out: "It is he, it is he; my God is present here." He enjoys rapt and high communion with celestial visitants, and thus that chamber of death becomes the gate of heaven. You pass by that house next morning: the half-closed shutter and the drawn blind tell you that he was and is not. You enter—the widow is sitting in sorrow; the first deep pang is scarcely over. The tones of her husband's voice, with which she has so long been familiar, rush, in all the freshness of yesterday, upon her soul, and she is worn with weeping. But she, too, is a Christian, and she flies to the Christian's refuge, and her eye traces those comfortable words: "Thy Maker is thine husband—the Lord of Hosts is his name." It is a dark hour; it has been a dark day; and the darkness has gathered, and settled, and deepened as the day wore on, and now at eventide there is soft and brilliant light, because her sufficiency is of God. You pass by the house again when about a week has elapsed. The last sad rites have been performed; the funeral bell, with its suppressed and heavy summons, sounding like the dividing asunder of soul and body, has tolled; the very clay of her husband has been torn from her embrace. He has died in somewhat straitened circumstances; he was the sole dependence of the family, and, with aching head and throbbing heart, she sits down to calculate about her future subsistence; her heart begins to fail her, but, before she gives way to despair, she consults a friend; he is a wise man, one upon whom the influences of the Holy Spirit have operated long; and he gives her the testimony of a long life of experience: "I have been young, and now am old, yet I have not seen the righteous forsaken, nor his seed begging bread." Dashing away the tears that had blinded her, she struggles and labors on, and feels that though it is her darkest hour, her sufficiency is still of God. That is no uncommon case; I have not drawn largely upon the extravagance of an imaginative fancy to bring it out. I could go into many of our sanctuaries and bid you listen to one, as with a glad heart and free, he sings the converted sinner's anthem: "O Lord, I will praise thee; thou wast angry with me, but thine anger is turned away, and now thou comfortest me." Then I could bid you listen to the experience of another, but faltering and low, for he is just recovering from recent illness: "I was brought low, and he helped me; he saved me even from the gates of death." And then we could point you to a third, and say: "This poor man cried, and the Lord heard him, and saved him out of all his troubles." And where are the damnatory clauses that forbid you to partake of these blessings? What statute of limitations is there that bars you from the enjoyment of this great and gracious heritage? Brethren, are you in Christ? Then all that belongs to the covenant is yours. Yours is the present heritage, yours is the future recompense of reward.

"Our sufficiency is of God." Is it so? Then you will be sustained in trial; you won't succumb to its power; it won't over-master you; you will regard it as sent of God, intended to work lessons and changes of some providential discipline within you. You will be grateful for it; you will know that when it comes, although it looks harsh and repulsive outside, you have entertained angels unawares, you will find after it has gone away. Oh! we learn many lessons when the head is low, that we do not learn in the heyday of prosperity and blessing. Just as it is in the natural world: you know when the sun is set, the stars come out in their placid beauty, and

> "Darkness shows us worlds of light
> We never saw by day;"

and we should never have known they were there if the darkness had not come. So in the night of God's providential dispensations, the stars of the great promises come shining out, broad and bright upon the soul; and we rejoice in their light and go on our way rejoicing.

Or, changing the figure, in the glad summer-time, when the leaves are on the trees, we go out, such of us as can get into the country—we go out into the thick woods and walk under the trees in shadow, and their branches interlace above us, and the leaves are green and glossy, and so thick above that we cannot see the sky through; and then we forget that there is another world, and our hearts are revelling in all pleasure and all blessedness of this. But when the blasts of winter come and scatter the leaves down, then the light of heaven comes in between, and we remember that here we have no continuing city, and are urged to seek one that is to come. Oh! take hold of God's sufficiency then, and go bravely to the meeting of trial, and you will find that trial,

> "God's alchemist old,
> Purges off the dross and mold
> And leaves us rich with gems and gold."

Is your sufficiency of God? Then it will animate you to duty. Listen to this confession of weakness: "Unto me, who am less than the least of all saints, is this grace given." Less than the least! What a pressure of weakness there must have been upon that soul! Listen to this exulting consciousness of power: "I can do all things through Christ that strengtheneth me." They are the antipodes of sentiment—are they not? Weakness the most helpless and feeble—power the most exultant and proud; and yet that confession of weakness, and that exulting consciousness of power, were the utterance of the same lips, and the expression of the experience of the same individual. What made the difference? In the one case he relied upon his own resources; in the other, he took hold of the sufficiency of God. Take hold of the sufficiency of God, and nothing will be able to resist you; you will go forward strong in the Lord, and in the power of his might, overcoming sin and overcoming evil in its every form, and planting for yourself and for your Master an heritage of blessing in this world and in that which is to come.

"Our sufficiency is of God." Is there a poor straggling sinner that is rejoicing to think that the minister has forgotten him, and that while he has been endeavoring to bring out all the heart of the text—privilege and promise exceeding great and precious, for the benefit of believers—no word of warning can be extracted out of it for those that are yet ungodly? Wait a little. What is the lesson you are to learn from the subject? Just this: that there is a sufficiency in God to punish. All his attributes must be equally perfect. He must be just, as well as the free and generous justifier of him that believeth in Jesus. Oh, I beseech you, tempt not against yourselves that wrath which needs only to be kindled in order to burn unto the lowest hell. "Kiss the Son, lest he be angry, and ye perish from the way." Perish out of the way—just as men fling away any obstacle or hindrance that interrupts their progress, so shall God fling the wicked out of his way. "Kiss the Son, lest he be angry, and ye perish from the way, when his wrath is kindled but a little. But a little—oh, it will need but a little kindling to doom you to the perdition of hell. Brethren, you need not perish: there is a sufficiency, thank God! there is a sufficiency in Christ to save. Our sufficiency is of God. And with this promise that I fling forth into the midst of you, and pray that God would bind it as a spell of sweet enchantment on your souls, I close my words to-night: "Wherefore he is able to save unto the uttermost"—to the uttermost of human guilt—to the uttermost of human life—to the uttermost of human time. May God save your souls, for the Redeemer's sake!

III.

THE MISSION OF THE PULPIT.

"Therefore seeing we have this ministry, as we have received mercy, we faint not; but have renounced the hidden things of dishonesty, not walking in craftiness, nor handling the word of God deceitfully; but by manifestation of the truth commending ourselves to every man's conscience in the sight of God."—2 Cor. iv. 1, 2.

This is the Apostle's recorded judgment as to the mission of the ministry which he had received of the Lord Jesus, and the duties of which he discharged with such singular fidelity and zeal. In the preceding chapter, he magnifies its superiority alike of glory and of substantial usefulness over the dispensation of the law, and then in a few weighty words separates himself entirely from all false teachers, and establishes himself, upon the ground of holy character and exalted office, as Heaven's high remembrancer among the nations—a true witness for God amidst a dark and alien world. He takes care, at the very outset, to assure those to whom he speaks, that he is of the same nature, and originally of the same sinfulness, as themselves: "Therefore seeing that we have received this ministry, as we have received *mercy*, we faint not." We are not—as if he had said—a distinct order of beings: there is no natural superiority of character which might make the minister proud, or which might make the hearer distant, and callous, and unsympathizing. We once were sinners; we have yet the memory of bondage; we have received mercy, and are anxious to tell to others the tidings that have led to our redemption. As we have received mercy we faint not, but have renounced the hidden things of dishonesty, the secret immoralities of pagan priests; not walking in craftiness, not retaining our hold upon the consciences of men by deceivableness of unrighteousness, and by juggling, lying wonders; not handling the Word of God deceitfully, not preaching an adulterated truth or a flexible Gospel; not pliant to the prejudices, or silent to the vices of those who hear us; "but, by manifestation of the truth, commending ourselves to every man's conscience in the sight of God."

All this, affirmed by the Apostle of the ministry of olden time, may be affirmed of the ministry of reconciliation now. That ministry, wickedly maligned on the one hand, imperfectly fulfilled on the other hand, has yet its mission to the world. The unrepealed command still stands upon the statute-book: "Go ye into all the world, and preach the Gospel unto every creature." And it is a prayer often earnestly and passionately uttered by those on whom its obligations have fallen, that, repudiating artifice and idleness, they may, by manifestation of the truth, commend themselves to every man's conscience in the sight of God. I purpose,

God helping me, briefly to notice from these words—in the first place, the business of the ministry; secondly, the instrumentality which it employs; and thirdly, the thought that hallows it.

I. The ministry—this is my first position—has a business with the world. It is the Divinely-appointed agency for the communication of God's will to man. As a Divine institution it advanced its claims in the beginning, and in no solitary instance have they been relinquished since. This Divine authorization and enactment are still in force. The Bible says, when Christ ascended up on high, "he led captivity captive, and received gifts for men; and he gave some apostles, and some prophets, and some evangelists, and some pastors and teachers, for the perfecting of the saints, for the work of the ministry, for the edifying of the body of Christ." There might be something special, perhaps, in this original commission, but the principle of its Divine origin is evidently presented as the principle of the ministry itself; for St. Paul, who was not then called, who speaks of himself afterward as one born out of due time, earnestly and anxiously vindicates the Heavenly origin of his apostleship: "I certify you, brethren, that the Gospel which was preached of me is not of men; for I neither received it of men, neither was I taught it but by the revelation of Jesus Christ." This it is which is the elevation of the Christian ministry, which exalts it far above human resources and human authority. It travels on in its own majestic strength—Heaven-inspired and heaven-sustained. Moreover, the same passage which tells us of the institution of the ministry announces its duration, and tells of the period when it shall be no longer needed—till we all come, in the unity of the faith and of the knowledge of the Son of God, unto a perfect man—unto the measure of the stature of the fullness of Christ.

This period, thus divinely appointed for the cessation of the ministry, has obviously not yet arrived. The world sees but little yet of millennial glory; there is yet an alienated heart in its debased and rebel tribes; there is nothing in the pursuits which it follows, nor in the natural impulses which move it, to incite to holy aim or to induce spiritual living. It has no self-suggestive memory of God. It has passions as blind and powerful, and a will as perverse as ever. Death is in the midst of it, and, though the corpse may be sometimes embalmed with spices, or tricked out with flowers, or carried 'neath obsequious plumes to burial, the chill is at its heart, the breath of the plague is in the tainted air, and there is need, strong and solemn need, for the anointed witness who may stand between the living and the dead, that the plague may be stayed. There are some, I know, who tell us that the mission of the pulpit is fulfilled. They acknowledge that, in the earlier ages, in the times of comparative darkness, when men spelt out the truth in syllables, it did a noble work; but the world has outgrown it, they tell us; men need neither its light nor its warning; the all-powerful Press shall direct them, the educational institute shall assist them in their upward progress, they shall move onward and upward under the guidance of the common mind. And, while this is the cry of infidelity and indifferentism, there are some among ourselves who have partially yielded to the clamor. They have deplored (as who must not?) the apparent ineffectiveness of existing agencies, the feebleness of the efforts for evangelical aggression, and, in their eagerness to conciliate prejudice and disarm opposition, they have compromised somewhat the high tone of Christian teaching, and have studiously avoided the very terminology of the Bible, so that the great truths of God's will and man's duty, of Christ's atonement and the sinner's pardon, of the Spirit's work and the believer's growth—those old gospels whose sound is always music and whose sight is always joy, are hardly to be recognized, as they are hidden beneath profound thought, or veiled within affected phrase. But the Divine institution of the ministry is not to be thus superseded. It has to do with eternity, and the matters of eternity are paramount. It deals and would grapple with the inner man; it has to do with the deepest emotions of the nature, with those instincts of internal truths which underlie all systems, from which a man can never utterly divorce himself, and which God himself has graven on the soul. So far as they work in harmony with its high purpose, it will hail the helpings of all other teaching; but God hath given it the monarchy, and it dare not abdicate its throne. The opposition that you sometimes meet with of worldliness and infidelity to the pulpit, if you analyze it, you find that though it may have derived from the oppressions of priestcraft in bygone ages somewhat of plausibility and force, it is but one phase of the method in which the human heart discovers its rooted and apparently unconquerable enmity to God. Hence it is one of the worst symptoms of the disease which the ministry has been calculated and instituted to remove. The teaching of the political agitator, of the philanthropic idealist, of the benevolent instructor—why are they so popular? The teaching of the religious minister—why is it so repulsive to the world? Mainly from this one fact, that the one reproves, and the other exalts human nature—the one ignores, the other insists upon the doctrine of the Fall. You will find, in all the schemes for the uplifting of man not grounded on the Bible, the exaltation of his nature as it is, lofty ideas of perfectibility, assertions that it needs neither revelation nor heavenly influence to guide it in the way of truth. Thus the Gospel is presented only as one among many systems which all men may accept or reject at pleasure. Its restraints are deemed impertinence, its reproofs unnatural bondage. The talk of such teaching is frequently of rights, seldom of duties. They are complimented on their manliness who ought to be humbled for their sin, and, by insidious panderings to their pride, they are exhorted to atheism, self-reliance, or habitual disregard of God. Both kinds of teaching, the worldly and the religious alike, aim at the uplifting of the nature. But then they look at it from different standpoints, and, of course, they apply to it different treatment. The one is an endeavor to exalt the nature without God; the other would take hold of his strength and work to the praise of his glory. The one regards humanity as it once was before sin had warped it, able to tower and triumph in its own unaided strength—the other sees it decrepit or ailing, the whole head sick and the whole heart faint; and yet, by the balm of Gilead, to be restored to pristine vigor. The one, deeming that no confusion has come upon its language, nor shame upon its many builders, would have it pile up its Babel towers until they smite the skies—the other sees the towers in ruins, splintered shaft and crumbling arch bearing witness that they were once beautiful exceedingly, and that by the grace and skill of the heavenly Architect, they may grow up again into a holy temple in the Lord.

It is absolutely necessary, in this age of manifold activities and of spiritual pride, that there should be this ever-speaking witness of man's feebleness and of God's strength. And, however much the opposition against the ministry may tell, and it does tell, and it ought to tell, against the vapid and frivolous, against the idle and insincere, it is a powerful motive for the institution of the ministry itself; just as the blast that scatters the acorns, roots the oak the more firmly in the soil. So long as men are born to die, so long as the recording angel registers human guilt, so long as human responsibility and retribution are unheeded truths, so long as there is one solitary sinner tempted by the black adversary, so long will the ministry have a business with the world; and it is the earnest prayer of those who have undertaken it that they may in some humble measure, in all fidelity and with dauntless courage, with genial sympathy, with pure affection, be witnesses for God, like that glorious angel whom the evangelist saw with the light upon his wings, having the everlasting Gospel to preach unto every nation and people and tongue.

II. I observe, secondly, THE BUSINESS OF THE MINISTRY IS MAINLY WITH THE CONSCIENCE OF MEN. Every man has a conscience; that is, a natural sense of the difference between good and evil—a principle which does not concern itself so much with the true and false in human ethics, or with the gainful and damaging in human fortunes, as with the right and wrong in human conduct. Call it what you will, analyze it as you may—a faculty, an emotion, a law—it is the most important principle in our nature, because by it we are brought into sensible connection with, and sensible recognition of, the moral government of God. It has been defined sometimes as a tribunal within a man for his own daily and impartial trial; and in its various aspects it answers right well to all the parts of a judicial tribunal. It is the bar at which the sinner pleads; it prefers the accusation of transgression; it records the crime; it bears witness to guilt or innocence; and as a judge it acquits or condemns. Thus taking cognizance of moral actions, it is the faculty which relates us to the other world; and by it God, retribution, eternity, are made abiding realities to the soul. As by the physical senses we are brought into connection with the physical world, and the blue heavens over it, and the green earth around us, are recognized in their relation to ourselves; so by this moral sense of conscience we see ourselves, in the light of immortality, responsible creatures, and gain ideas of duty and of God. How mighty is the influence which this power has wielded, and yet continues to wield in the world! There are many that have tried to be rid of it, but there is a manhood at its heart which murder cannot kill. There are many that have rebelled against its authority, but they have acknowledged its might notwithstanding, and it has rendered them disturbed and uneasy in their sin. There are multitudes more that have fretted against its wholesome warnings; and often when—because it has warned them of danger or threatened them with penalty—they have tried to stifle and entomb it, it has risen up suddenly into a braver resurrection, and pealed forth its remonstrances in bolder port and louder tone. But for its restraint, many of the world's reputable ones would have become criminal. But for its restraint, many of the world's criminals would have become more audaciously bad. It has spoken, and the felon, fleeing when no man pursued him, has been chased by a falling leaf. It has spoken, and the burglar has paled behind his mask, startled at his own footfall. It has spoken, and the coward assassin has been arrested in his purpose, and has paused irresolute ere he has struck the blow. Its vindictive and severe upbraiding after the sin has been committed has often lashed the sinner into agony, and secured an interval of comparative morality by preventing sin for a season. It has been the one witness for God amid the traitor faculties—single but undismayed, solitary but true. When the understanding and the memory, and the will and the affections, had all consented to the enticements of evil, conscience has stood firm, and the man could never sin with comfort until he had drugged it into desperate repose. It has been the one dissentient power among the faculties, like a moody guest among a company of frantic revellers, whom they could neither conciliate nor expel. When God's judgments have been abroad in the world, and men would fain have resolved them into ordinary occurrences or natural phenomena, conscience has refused to be satisfied with such delusive interpretations, and, without a prophet's inspiration, has itself deciphered the handwriting as it blazed upon the wall. It has forced the criminal oftentimes to deliver himself up to justice, preferring the public shame of the trial and the gallows-tree to the deeper hell of a conscience aroused and angry. Yes, and it has constrained from the dying sinner a testimony to the God he has insulted, given when the shadows of perdition were already darkening upon the branded brow.

Oh, brethren, that must be a mighty power which has wrought and which is working thus! And it has wrought and is working in you; and, as such, we acknowledge it. We can despise no man who has a conscience. Although with meanness and with sin he may largely overlay it, we recognize the majestic and insulted guest, and are silent and respectful as in the presence of a fallen king. We see the family-likeness, although intemperance has bloated the features and has dulled the sparkle of the eye. There is a spirit in man, and the inspiration of the Almighty giveth him understanding. Now it is with this faculty in man that the minister has mainly to do. His work, his business, is to bring out the world's conscience in its answer to the truths of Divine revelation. Recognizing in it something which can respond to its own duty, the ministering witness without will constantly appeal to the answering witness within. Regarding all other faculties, however separately noticeable, as avenues only to the conscience, he will aim constantly at the ears of the inner man. To come short of this is to come short of duty. To fail in this is to fail in a work which our Master has given us to do. We should form but a very unworthy estimate of our own high calling if we were to aim at the subjugation of any subordinate faculty, and, that accomplished, sit down as if our work were done. The minister may appeal to the intellect—of course he may. All thanks to him if he clear away difficulties from the path of the bewildered. All thanks to him if he present truth in its symmetry of system, and in all the grand and rounded harmony of its beautiful design. But he must press through the outworks to the citadel, through the intellect to the conscience, that the understanding, no longer darkened, may apprehend the truth, and that the apprehended truth may make the conscience free. The imagination may be charmed by the truth, which is itself beauty; but only that it may hold the mirror up to conscience, to see its own portrait there photographed directly from on high, and which, with such marvellous fidelity, gives all the scars upon the countenance, and every spot and wrinkle upon the brow. The passions may be roused by the truth, which is the highest power—not that people may swoon away under terrific apprehensions of wrath, or only or mainly that people may escape hell and enter heaven, but that the conscience may resolve on a holy life, that there may result the comely outgrowth of a transformed and spiritual character, and that through the impending fear of perdition and the promised water of life, a man may issue into the wealthy place of confidence in God, assimilation to his image, that attachment to right which would cleave fast to it, even were its cause hopeless and its friends dead, and that perfect love which casteth out all possible fear.

It is not the intellect, then, but the conscience—not the imagination, but the conscience—not the passions, but the conscience—to which the minister is to commend himself in the sight of God. If he speaks to the intellect, the philosopher can rival him. If he speaks to the imagination, his brightest efforts pale before the dazzling images of the poet's brain. If he speaks to the passions, the political demagogue can do it better. But, in his power over the conscience, he has a power that no man shares. An autocrat undisputed, a czar of many lands, he can wield the sceptre over the master-faculty of man. Oh! very solemn is the responsibility which thus rests upon the religious teacher. To have the master-faculty of man within his grasp; to witness of truths that are unpopular and repulsive; to reprove of sin, and of righteousness, and of judgment; to do this with his own heart frail and erring, with the moral conflict battling in his own spirit the while. "Who is sufficient for these things?" breaks often from the manliest heart in its seasons of depression and unrest. But there is a comfort broad and strong, and I feel that comfort now supporting me. While pained by my own unworthiness, and by the trifling of multitudes over whom ministers weep and yearn—pained by the short-sighted and self-complacent indifference of the church and the world—pained by the thousand difficulties which Satan always puts in the way of the reception of the truth as it is in Jesus; I say there is a comfort of which I cannot be deprived: that all the while there is a mysterious something moving in you—in you all—barbing the faithful appeal, pointing the solemn warning, striking the alarum in the sinner's soul. There! listen to that! That belongs to thee. That heart so callous and ungrateful—it is thine. That sin that the minister reproves—thou hast committed it. That doom so full of agony and horror—thou art speeding to it. How wilt thou escape the damnation of hell? Many a time and oft, when the minister without has gone sheafless to his home, and in tears has offered his complaint, "Who hath believed our report?" the minister within, by God's good grace, has been a successful harvest-man, and gathered sheaves into the garner; and often when, to the eye of the human minister, there has been no ripple on the waves, deep in the depths of the soul have swelled the billows of the troubled sea; and in the keenest acknowledgment of the truth he was endeavoring to impress, men's consciences have borne him witness, their thoughts meanwhile accusing, or else excusing one another.

Again, the great instrumentality which God has empowered us to use is the truth. You will have no difficulty in understanding what the Apostle means by the truth, because he calls it "the word of grace," and "our Gospel." The revelation of God in Christ, the life and teaching and wondrous death of Jesus, was the truth, alone adapted to the supply of every need, and the rescue from every peril. The Apostle was no ordinary man. Well-read in the literature of the times, observant of the tendencies and the inclinations of man, he would be ready to acknowledge truth everywhere.

He knew that there had been truth in the world before. He would see it in Pagan systems, gleaming faintly through encumbered darkness. Fragments of it had fallen from philosophers in former times, and had been treasured up as wisdom. It had a somewhat healthy circulation through the household impulses and ordinary concerns of men. But it was all truth for the intellect, truth for social life, truth for the manward, not the God-ward relations of the soul. The truth which told of God, which hallowed all morality by the sanctions of Divine law, which provided for the necessities of the entire man, was seen but dimly in uncertain traditions. Conscience was a slave. If it essayed to speak, it was overdone by clamor, or hushed by interest into silence. The higher rose the culture, the deeper sank the character. The whole world seemed like one vast valley, fertile and gay with flowers, but no motion in the dumb air, not any song of bird or sound of rill; the gross darkness of the inner sepulchre was not so deadly still, until there came down a breath from heaven that brought life upon its wings, and breathed that life into the unconscious heaps of slain. Thus, when Christ came with his Gospel of purity and freedom, all other truth seemed to borrow from it a clearer light and a richer adaptation. The ordinary instincts of right and wrong were sharpened into a keener discernment, and invested with a more spiritual sensibility. The Gospel founded a grander morality; the Gospel established a more chivalrous honor; the Gospel shed out a more genial benevolence. All the old systems had looked at man as a half-man; only on one side of his nature; that part of him that lay down to the earth. The Gospel took the whole round of his faculties, both as lying toward earth and as rising toward heaven. Love to man—the ordinary, commonplace philanthropy of every day, the philanthropy that wings the feet of the good Samaritan, and that sends all the almsgivers upon errands of mercy—love to man was not known in its fullness, until the Gospel came. "Thou shalt love thy neighbor" was a command of old, but then the Jews first contracted the neighborhood, and then they contracted the affection. The Jew's neighbor was not the Samaritan, but one within his own exclusive pale and sphere. But when love to God came, like a queenly mother leading out her daughter by the hand, then men wondered at the rare and radiant beauty that had escaped their notice so long; and when they loved God first, then it was that from that master-love the streams of love to man flowed forth in ceaseless and in generous profusion. And the Gospel is just the same now. It is the great inspiration of ordinary kindnesses, and of the every-day and rippling happiness of life. It is *the* truth for man; *the* truth for man's every exigency, and for his very peril—blessing the body and saving the soul. By the truth, then, which we are to commend to every man's conscience, we understand the truth as it is in Jesus—the truth which convinces of sin and humbles under a sense of it; the truth which reveals atonement and flashes pardon from it; the truth which leads the pardoned spirit upward to holiness and heaven. Now, we are to bring that conscience and that truth into connection with each other; that is the great business for which we are gathered here. In order that there may be the bringing of the one into connection with the other, there must be variety in all truth, suited to the various states in which the conscience of the hearers may be found.

Now, for the sake of argument, we may take it that there are three stages in which nearly the whole of the consciences of humanity are ranged: those whose consciences are slumbering, torpid, inert, lifeless; those whose consciences are quick, apprehensive, alarmed; and those whose consciences have passed through those former stages, and are now peaceful, happy, and at rest.

1. First, *there are some consciences that have no apprehension of God—no spiritual sensibility at all.* It is a very sad thought that this has been, and continues to be, the condition of the vast majority of mankind. Think of the vast domain of paganism, where the truth of God is lost for lack of knowledge, with its monstrous idols, fertile of cruelty, and its characters exemplifying every variety of evil. You may look through universal history; you can see the track of passion in the light of the flames which it has kindled; you can see the works of imagination throned in bodiless thought, or sculptured in breathing marble; you can see the many inventions of intellect on every hand, but for conscience placed on

its rightful seat, and exerting its legitimate authority, you look almost in vain. Even in Christian England there are multitudes of whom it may be said that God is not in all their thoughts, to whom conscience is a dull and drowsy monitor, who live on from day to day in the disregard of plainest duties, and in habitual, hardening sin. Are there not some here? It may be you go to your place of worship, but to little purpose; you are rarely missed from your accustomed seat, but you have trifled with conscience until it rarely troubles you, and when it does, you pooh-pooh it as the incoherences of a drunkard, or the ravings of some frantic madman. Brethren, I do feel it a solemn duty to manifest God's arousing truth to you. I appeal to the moral sense within you. You are attentive to the truth; the Word is suffered to play around your understanding; I want it to go deeper. I accuse you fearlessly of heinous and flagrant transgression, because you have not humbled yourselves before Heaven; and God, in whose hands your breath is, and whose are all your ways, you have not glorified. I charge you with living to yourselves, or that, going about to establish your own righteousness, you have not submitted yourself to the righteousness of God. I arraign you as being guilty of base ingratitude, inasmuch as when Christ was offered, the just for the unjust, that he might bring you to God, you refused to hearken. And you have trodden under foot the blood of the covenant, and counted it an unholy thing. I accuse some of you, moreover, of trying to secure impunity by your vile treatment of God's inward witness. You have deposed conscience from its throne; you have tried to bribe it to be a participator with you in your crimes; you have overborne it by interest, or business, or clamor, or pleasure; you have limited its scrutiny to the external actions, and not allowed it to sit in judgment over the thoughts and intentions of the inner man. When it has startled you, you have lulled it to sleep, and you have done it on purpose that you might the more easily and the more comfortably sin. Brethren, I am not your enemy because I have told you the truth. That very conscience which you have insulted bears me witness that it is the truth which I now minister before you. I warn you of your danger. Oh! I would not fear to shake you roughly if I could only bring you to a knowledge of yourselves. It is a sad and disastrous thought that there are some consciences here so fatally asleep that they may never be roused except by the peal of the judgment trumpet or by the flashing of the penal fires.

2. Then *there are some whose consciences are aroused*, and who are going about, it may be, in bitterness of soul. You have seemed, perhaps, hard and impenetrable, but there has been a terrible war in your soul; your conscience has been at work; it is at work now. Oh! I have a power over you from this fact—that I have got an ally in your own bosom testifying to the truth of the things I speak before you. You may fret against that power, but you cannot rob me of it. You

cannot get the barb out; all your endeavors to extract it only widen and deepen the wound. My brother, oh! let me manifest Christ's redeeming truth to thee. Christ has died; all thy wants may be supplied through his wondrous death. Is thy heart callous and ungrateful? He has exalted the law and made it honorable. Hast thou dishonored justice? He has satisfied its claims. Hast thou violated law? He has lifted up the majesty of its equity. Is there in thy spirit unrest and storm? Come to him; thy conscience is like the Gali lean lake—it shall hear him, and there shall be a great calm. Doth the curse brood over thee, and calamity appal thy soul? Flee to his outstretched arms, and as thou sobbest on his bosom hear his whispered comfort: "There is, therefore, now no condemnation unto them that are in Christ Jesus, who walk not after the flesh, but after the Spirit." See the clouds disappear, the tempest hath passed by, the storms rage no longer; lift up thy head, serene, peaceful, smiling, happy. Let us hear thy experience: "In whom I *have* redemption through his blood, even the forgiveness of sin, according to the riches of his grace."

3. But some of you have got still further, and are *happy in the sense of the Redeemer's love.* You are in the fairest possible position for the true soul-growth day by day. You rejoice in Christ Jesus now. You have victory over the carnal mind now. All antagonistic powers are made subject now. Conscience has resumed its authority, and is sensitive at the approach of ill, and

eager for the completed will of God. I rejoice to manifest God's discipling, training, growing, comforting, nourishing truth to you. Self is not the master-principle within you now; you are not paralyzed by craven fear. There is a good land and fair before you. Rise to the dignity of your heritage. What a future awaits you! to be day by day more like God, to have day by day bright visions of the throne, day by day increased power over sin, increased progress toward heaven, increased fellowship with the Divine; and then when the tabernacle falls down there opens another scene—angelic welcomes, the King in his beauty, and a house not made with hands eternal in the heavens.

III. "By manifestation of the truth commending ourselves to every man's conscience in the sight of God." In the sight of God. Ah! that is the thought that hallows it. All our endeavors for the enlightenment of the ignorant are under the felt inspection of Almighty God. His eye marks the effort; his voice, "I know thy works," is constantly in-spoken to the soul. It is necessary that we should feel this in order to fit us for our duty. If we do not feel this we shall have no courage. Depend upon it, the heroism which the pulpit needs, which it never needed in this world's history so much as it needs to-day—the heroism which the pulpit needs, which the ministry must have, will not be wrought in the soul unless this thought be there. There is so much to enslave a man—the consciousness of his own unworthiness and weakness, in his best and holiest moments; the love of approbation which, from a natural instinct, swells often into a sore temptation; the reluctance to give offence lest the ministry should be blamed, the anxiety as to what men think of him and say of him—oh! how often have these things checked the stern reproof or faithful warning, made a preacher the slave instead of the monarch of his congregation, and, instead of the stern, strong, fearless utterance of the prophet, made him stammer forth his lispings with the hesitancy of a blushing child. Depend upon it, it is no light matter; it requires no common boldness to stand single-handed before the pride of birth, and the pride of rank, and the pride of office, and the pride of intellect, and the pride of money, to rebuke their transgressions, to strip off their false confidence, and tear away their refuges of lies. But if a man have it burned into his heart that he is speaking in the sight of God, he will do it—yes, he will. God-fear will banish man-fear. He will feel that for the time the pulpit is his empire and the temple is his throne, and, like another Baptist, he will thunder out his denunciations against rich and poor together, with his honest eyes straight flashing into theirs, "Except *ye* repent, *ye* shall all likewise perish."

"In the sight of God." Give him that thought, and he will be tender as well as brave; he will look upon his congregation as immortal, and will see in each one before him (oh, that thought is overwhelming!) an offspring of the Divine, an heir of the Everlasting; and in this aspect of it he will tremble before the majesty of man; he will be awe-struck as he thinks of trying to influence them for eternity. There will be no harshness in his tones, there will be no severity in his countenance. If the violated law must speak out its thunders, it will be through brimming eyes and faltering tongue. He will remember his own recent deliverance. Like Joseph, he will scatter blessings round him with a large and liberal hand; but there will be no ostentation, there will be no vanity; for he will remember that he is but the almoner of another's bounty, and that his own soul has only just been brought out of prison. He will be like one shipwrecked mariner who has but just got upon a rock, and is stretching out a helping hand to another who yet struggles in the waters; but he that is on the rock knows that the yawning ocean rages and is angry, near. Oh! let us realize that we are in sight of God, and we shall have larger sympathies for man, we shall have more of the spirit of Him who came eating and drinking, who was a friend of publicans and sinners. There will be no fierce rebukes, no proud exclusivism, no pharisaical arrogance then. The sleeper will not be harshly chided; the remonstrance of affection will yearn over him, "My brother, my brother!" and the tear will gather in the eye as the invitation is given, or the regret is breathed, "Ye will not come unto me that ye may have life;" "Come, all ye that are weary and heavy laden, and I will give you rest."

"In the sight of God." That will help us to persevere. We shall be constant as well as brave and tender, if we realize continually that we are in the sight of God. Though difficulties multiply, this will prevent us from becoming weary and faint in our minds; we shall remember him who endured the contradiction of sinners against himself; and, through perverseness or obstinacy, whether men will bear or whether men will forbear, we shall labor on for the cause of Christ and for the good of souls. We shall not be satisfied with good report, with extensive popularity, with decorous congregations, with attention settled, and seriousness upon every countenance. We shall want souls. We shall press right away through to the great end of restoring the supremacy of conscience, and bringing the disordered world back again to its allegiance to God. This is our life-work, and we are doing it day by day—unfaithfully, imperfectly, but we are doing it. Moral truth upon the mind of man is something like a flat stone in a churchyard, through which there is a thoroughfare, and hundreds of pattering feet go over it day after day. Familiarity with it has weakened the impression, and time has effaced the lettering. But God has sent us with a friendly chisel to bring it out again into sharpest, clearest, crispest, distinctest outline before the spirits of men. This is our life-work; and we are laboring on amid the driving sleet and pelting rain; jostled now and then by the rude and heedless passenger; fitfully looked at by those who flit away to the farm and the merchandise; regarded with a sort of contemptuous admiration by those who admire our industry, while they pity our enthusiasm. Patient, earnest workers, we must labor on, and we intend to do it. God helping, the ministry of reconciliation will continue to be proclaimed, within reach of every man in this land, Sabbath after Sabbath, universally, unto those who will come, without money and without price. And everywhere we shall have our reward. I, for my part, cannot labor in vain. What think you would sustain me under the pressure of the multiplied excitement and multiplied sorrow and labor, but the thought that I cannot labor in vain? The words I have just spoken have been launched into your ears, and have lodged in your conscience, and I cannot recall them. Simple, well-known Bible truths have gone into your conscience, and I cannot recall them. But they shall come up some day. You and I may never meet again until we stand at the judgment-seat of God. They shall come up *then—then*—and, verily, I shall have my reward. I shall have it when some fair-haired child steps out to spell out the syllables upon the flat stone, and goes away with a new purpose formed in his heart. I shall have it when some weather-beaten man, bronzed with the hues of climates and shades of years, takes the solemn warning, numbers his days, and applies his heart unto wisdom. I shall have it in the welcome given to my ascending spirit by some whom I first taught, it may be unworthily, to swell the hosanna of praise, or to join with holy sincerity in all the litanies of prayer. I shall have it in the smile that wraps up all heaven in itself, and in those tones of kindness which flood the soul with ineffable music—"Well done, thou good and faithful servant; enter thou into the joy of thy Lord." I leave with you and the Spirit—I dare not trust you alone—the Word of his grace, praying that He who alone can apply it, may give it life and power.

IV.

SOLICITUDE FOR THE ARK OF GOD.

"And when he came, lo, Eli sat upon a seat by the wayside watching; for his heart trembled for the ark of God."—1 SAM. iv. 13.

WHAT news from the battle-field?—for the Philistines are out against Israel, and the Israelitish armies are marshalled, and have gone forth unto the fight. A few days ago a reverse befell them, but they have sent for a fancied talisman, and they are marching now with the ark of God in their midst, deeming that its presence in their camp will assure victory to their side. There is expectation in the streets of Shiloh, doubt and hope alternating in the spirits of its townsmen; for though the ark is a tower of strength, yet their defeat has disheartened them, and dark rumors, moreover, of the Lord's kindled anger, and of sad prophecies alleged to have been spoken, are rife among the people; so that many a glance is strained wistfully toward the plains of Aphek, whence the couriers may bring tidings of the war. There are quivering lips in the city, and cheeks blanched with sudden fear; for the tidings have come, and they are tidings of disaster and of shame: the glory of Israel hath fallen upon its high places; the shield of the mighty hath been vilely cast away; thirty thousand of the people have fallen with a great slaughter; and the sacred symbol of their faith itself has been carried off in triumph by the worshippers of Ashtaroth and Dagon. Loud is the wail of the widows, and terrible the anguish of the remnant that are left, oppressed by the national dishonor. But yonder, near the gate, there is one feeble old man, with silvered hair and sightless eyes, before whom, as each mourner passes, he subdues his sorrow into silence, as in the presence of grief that is mightier than his own. It is Eli, the high priest of God; he hears the tumult, but is yet unconscious of its cause. But now the messenger comes in hastily to unfold his burden of lamentation and of weeping. "And the man said unto Eli, I am he that came out of the army, and I fled to-day out of the army. And he said, What is there done, my son?" Oh, terrible are the tidings that are now to come upon the heart of that old man, like successive claps of thunder. "And the messenger answered and said, Israel is fled before the Philistines"—here the patriot mourns—"and there hath been also a great slaughter among the people"—here the spirit of the judge is stricken—"and thy two sons also, Hophni and Phineas, are dead"—here the father's heart bleeds. Strong must have been the struggle of the spirit under the pressure of this cumulative agony, but it bears nobly up. Ah, but there is a heavier woe behind: "And the ark of God is taken.

And it came to pass when he made mention of the ark of God"—not till then, never till then—"that he fell from off the seat backward by the side of the gate, and his neck brake, and he died." The grand old man: he may have been feeble in restraint and criminal in indulgence, but there is majesty about this his closing scene which redeems his errors and shrines him with the good and true. The patriot could survive the dishonor of his country; the judge, though weeping sore, could be submissive under the slaughter of the people; the father, his heart rent the while with remorseful memories, could have upborne under the double bereavement: but the saint swooned away his life when deeper affliction was narrated of the disaster that had happened to the ark of God. "And it came to pass that when he made mention of the ark of God that he fell from off the seat backward by the side of the gate, and his neck brake, and he died."

Brethren, this is just the character, the type of character, that we covet for the churches of to-day—men of broad souls, large-hearted and kindly in their human sympathy, bating not a jot in all earthly activities and philanthropy, but reserving their highest solicitudes for the cause and service of the Lord Jesus Christ. "An impossible combination," scoffers are ready to observe, "and unlovely even if it were possible. The narrow fanaticism will contract the human affection; the man will be so absorbed in the possibilities of the shall-be as to forget the interests of the now; he will live in a world of the ideal, and the life that now is, and that presses upon us so incessantly on every side, will degenerate into a brief history of dwarfed charities and aimless being." Nay, surely not so, my brother. That love must ever be the kindliest, even on its human side, which has the furthest and the most open vision. That cannot be either a small or a scanty affection which takes eternity within its scope and range. The Christian, the more he realizes his Christianity, and embodies it, becomes of necessity pervaded by an affection, bounded only by the limits of humanity.

"Pure love to God its members find—
Pure love to every son of man."

And this love, which the thought of eternity thus makes indestructible, is raised by the same thought above the imperfections which attach themselves to individual character, so that it sees the broad stamp of humanity everywhere, and discovers, even in the outcast and trembling sinner, an heir of the Everlasting, an offspring of the Divine.

And this, the perfection of character, is the character which we covet for you. You will find very many instances in Scripture in which, in words full, full to overflowing, of the warmest human affection, regard for the spiritual is discovered, not in ostentatious obtrusion, but in developments of incidental beauty, to be the reigning passion of the soul. Who can for a moment doubt the strong human affection of the beloved disciple, who, loving at first, drank in a deeper lovingness as he lay upon the Master's bosom, and to whom, as the fittest for such a mission, was committed the charge of that meek sufferer with a sword in her heart—the sad and saintly mother of our Lord? Listen to his salutation to Gaius the well-beloved: "I wish above all things"—this is my chiefest and most fervent desire—"I wish above all things that thou mayest prosper and be in health, even as thy soul prospereth." This is the principal thing after all. Remember David and all his afflictions. See the persecuted monarch fleeing from his infuriated and bitter enemies, hunted like a hart upon the mountains, lodged, with small estate and diminished train, in some fortress of Engedi or in some cave of Adullam! Of what dreams he in his solitude? What are the memories that charge his waking hours? Does he sigh for the palace and the purple, for the sceptre and the crown? No—Hark! His royal harp, long silent, trembles again into melody! "How amiable are thy tabernacles, O Lord of Hosts! My soul longeth, yea, even fainteth, for the courts of the Lord: my heart and my flesh crieth out for the living God." See him again when he is crossing the brook Kedron, when the hearts of his people have been stolen from him by his vile and flattering son; when he has lost his crown and is in danger of losing his life; what is his chiefest anxiety in that time of adversity, and in that crisis of peril? "And the king said unto Zadok, carry back the ark of God into the city. If I shall find favor in the eyes of the Lord he will bring me again, and show me both it and his habitation." As if he had said, "The ark of God—all that is tender and all that is sacred are in my history associated with the ark of God —carry back the ark of God into the city. I am hunted like a hart upon my own mountains; I have no longer a sceptre of authority; I am going upon a precarious expedition; I know not what may become of me. Carry back the ark. Don't let it share our fortune; don't let it be exposed to insult and pillage, and the chances of war. Carry back the ark carefully. Whatever becomes of me, carry back the ark of God into the city; though I wander in exile, lie down in sorrow, and am at last buried in the stranger's grave." But what need of multiplying examples? It was his religious home, the metropolis of faith, the place which God's presence had hallowed, which was referred to when the happy Israelite, rejoicing in recovered freedom, and remembering long years of bondage, struck his harp and sang, "By the rivers of Babylon there we sat down; yea, we wept when we remembered Zion." And this, I repeat it, brethren, the perfection of character, is the character we covet for you. As Christians you are bound to cultivate it. It is the highest affection in heaven: "The Lord loveth the gates of Zion more than all the dwellings of Jacob." It is the highest affection of the incarnate Son: "The zeal of thine house hath eaten me up." It is the highest affection of the Apostle, the highest style of man: "Neither count

I my life dear unto myself, so that I might finish my course with joy, and the ministry which I have received of the Lord Jesus, to testify the Gospel of the grace of God."

Oh, that God would raise up amongst us Elis in our spiritual Israel, who, with reverent and earnest solicitude, would have their hearts tremble for the ark of God. His heart trembled for the ark of God, and wherefore? Because the ark of God was in peril. In peril from its enemies—in greater peril from its friends. And, brethren, the cause and kingdom of Christ, pure religion and undefiled before God and the Father, the faith for which we are valiantly and constantly to contend, is in this hazard to-day. It also is in peril: in peril from its enemies; in greater, deeper, deadlier peril from its friends.

These are the points which I will endeavor, briefly, God helping me, to illustrate on the present occasion.

I. In the first place, THE ARK OF GOD IS IN PERIL FROM ITS ENEMIES. There never was a period, perhaps, when the ark of God was carried out into a hotter battle, or was surrounded by fiercer elements of antagonism. There is, for instance, *idolatry*, holding six hundred millions of our race in thrall. Idolatry, which has succeeded in banishing from their perceptions all thought of the true God—which holds all that vast world of mind under the tyranny of the vilest passions, and under the dark and sad eclipse both of intellectual and spiritual knowledge.

There is, again, *imposture*, reigning in Mohammedan realms over one hundred and forty millions of souls; imposture, accommodated with the most exquisite ingenuity to the prejudices of the population among which it was to spread, complimenting Moses to cajole the Jew, speaking respectfully of Jesus to seduce the nominal Christian, offering a voluptuous heaven to the licentious Pagan, and gathering in the indifferent by the wholesale conversion of the sword—imposture thus founded and perpetuated over some of the fairest provinces of the globe in foul and ferocious despotism until now.

There is, again, *superstition*, the corruption of Christianity by Greek and papal admixtures, blinding the world with the utter falsehood of half truths, dazzling the senses and emasculating the understanding, trafficking in sin as in merchandise, and selling escape from its penalties cheap. Imposture, under whose strange system atheist and libertine, infidel and Jew, may join hands together and with equal rights wear the sacred garments, and, in robes upon which the cross is broidered, may gather together to make war against the Lamb.

There is, again, *skepticism*, that cold and soulless thing, that mystery of iniquity, which doth already work, chilling the ardor of the church and hardening the unbelief of the world—skepticism, bribing intellect to sustain it with sophistry, and genius to foster its errors, and poetry to embalm them in song—skepticism, that travels through the universe in search of truth and beauty, that it may enfeeble the one by its misgivings, and blight the comeliness of the other by its wintry breath.

All these, enemies of Christianity from the beginning, and retaining their ancient hate against it, now are the Philistines of its spiritual field. They are not content, as in former times, with holding their own; they have a resolute purpose of aggression. They have habit, and numbers, and prejudice on their side; they have warriors and a priesthood, zealous and valiant in their service. They have no chivalry about them to restrain them from any style of warfare. They smart under multiplied defeats, and they know that in the heart of every man in the world there are interests and sympathies in their favor. There is reason, then, is there not, for that cry, "Men of Israel, help!" there is reason, strong and solemn reason, why the Elis of our Israel should sit by the wayside, watching, for their hearts tremble for the ark of God. It is not necessary to enlarge upon this point. I do not want to preach specially to-night in reference to these extraneous matters—matters, I mean, extraneous to the Church of Christ, which hinder the progress of the work of God in the world. I want to come nearer home in discussing our second point:

II. Just as it was in the days of Israel, so it is now—THE ARK OF GOD IS IN STRONGER, DEEPER, DEADLIER PERIL FROM ITS FRIENDS. Vainly might the Philistines have fought, vainly might the foe have striven, if there had not been in the heart of the camp the springs of deep and destructive evils, if the chosen children of Israel had not been traitors and unworthy of themselves. And there are, if you will only examine into the subject, strange analogies subsisting between the causes which prevented the victory of Israel of old, and the causes which operate with such fearful disaster against the progress of the truth of God to-day.

1. In the first place, there was in the camp of Israel of old the presence of *superstition*, a blind reliance upon external forms. The Israelites, though their lives were loose and their devotions therefore iniquity, felt safe in the prospect of the battle, because they had the presence of the ark. At other times they cared nothing about it, were indifferent altogether as to its welfare; but in the hour of danger, they rallied round it as an amulet of strength, and in place of contrition before God, and in place of humblings on account of sin, they vaunted that the Lord was in the midst of them, and conveyed what they deemed to be the symbol of his presence with arrogant and obtrusive gladness to the camp. And it is to be feared, brethren, that there is much of this vain and formal confidence clogging our piety now. Are there not hanging upon our skirts, ostensibly one with us in fellowship and spirit, many of whom we stand in doubt before God, and over whose defective consistency we mourn? Nay, are we not all conscious, each for himself—let the spirit of searching come in—are we not

all conscious of compromise, if not, indeed, of betrayal? Our church, our organization, our influence, the decorum of our services, the activity of our agencies, an attractive ministry, a respectable gathering, a well-furnished sanctuary, a well-replenished treasury—have not these stolen our hearts away from the Divine, the spiritual, the heavenly? Our spirit—bounds it after the Divine Spirit as it once did? Our ear—listens it as intently for his whispers? Our eye—has it as keen an insight for his coming? Or is the very symbol of his dwelling, which, in the olden time, transformed the wilderness from the sepulchre into the home, become an occasion of sin, if not an object of idolatry? Oh, for some brave old Hezekiah to come amongst us and write Nehushtan upon the mutilated brass, and break it into pieces before God! Do not mistake us; we are no iconoclasts, to dissolve all organizations, and mutilate the whole and perfect symmetry of truth, and with distempered zeal to tear away the inscriptions on her holy and beautiful house. We rejoice in precious ordinances, and crowded sanctuaries, and in those grand institutions of benevolence which redeem our age from lethargy. But when the trust of the individual or of the church is placed in these things, God's Holy Spirit is dishonored, and the life of our religion becomes of dwarfed growth and sickly habit, from the very care with which we screen it from the breath of heaven. Brethren, are there not in the Divine Word many intimations of the tendency which we now deplore, to let the very highest and holiest customs degenerate into the indifference of formalism? That the brazen serpent lifted up in the wilderness received in after ages idolatrous homage, I have already reminded you. And such was the danger of idolatry to the children of Israel, that God would not trust any one of them to be present at the funeral of their great law-giver. No human eye must witness his obsequies, but, in solitary possession of his God-prepared sepulchre, the lordly lion stalked, and the bald old eagle flew. The combined power of healing and of speech constrained the worship of the men of Lystra for the Apostles Barnabas and Paul. Maltese superstition, which had branded him as a murderer whom the viper stung, in sudden reaction deified him when he declined to die. And in the time of the Saviour, the temple had become a house of merchandise; anise and cummin were of more account than righteousness and truth, and enlarged phylacteries and public prayers, and a countenance preternaturally sad, were the low and degenerate substitutes for a renewed heart and a holy life. And, brethren, it becomes us solemnly to be on our guard in this matter, for the same tendency exists still. The formal and the careless will creep into our worship, and, if we are not watchful, will eat out the heart of our religion. If, as individuals, our trust is in our attendance on religious ordinances, or our participation of sacramental emblems and our fellowship in church communion, or the comeliness of our external moralities, and if, in the strength of these, unfurnished with the higher gifts of the Divine Spirit, we go out to dare the dangers and fight the battles of our daily life; and if, as a church, as a confederacy of Christian people, we talk about our numbers, and our agency, and our influence, what are we doing but perpetrating—perpetrating, too, with still greater aggravation and enormity—the error and the sin of the people of Israel of old? We carry the ark into the battle, but we leave the God of the ark behind us; and there is strong and solemn need that the Elis of our Israel should sit by the wayside, watching, for their hearts tremble for the ark of God.

2. I observe, secondly, that there was *inconsistency* in the camp of Israel. The times were times of apostasy and of idolatry; the priests, who should have been the leaders of the people, committed abominable iniquity; there were sensuality and oppression in the service of the holy shrine, so that men abhorred the offering of the Lord, and, by consequence, the whole land became infected with the contagion of this evil example. There was still an affectation of reverence for the sanctuary, and of attachment to the ark; but the Lord of the sanctuary and the God of the ark were not the true objects of worship and of love. And is it not so largely now? Are there not amongst those who habitually gather themselves for worship, numbers, not, perhaps, consciously insincere, but strangely defective? and numbers more—spots in our feasts of charity—who come among us like so many whited sepulchres, all symmetry without, but all rottenness within: Achans, whose

rapacious covetousness can hardly hold itself from the prey: Reubens, whose unstable souls are luring themselves to their own destruction: Judases, with fawning lip, and grasping hand, but hiding in the coward heart the guilty purpose of betrayal? Are there not such amongst us? Yes, there are those who intrude themselves into our assemblies, eluding all human scrutiny, wearing the garb of sanctity, and remaining in their imposture, perhaps, until some overwhelming pressure crushes them, and brings scandal upon the cause that they have dishonored. And in public life are we not accustomed to hear a noisy zeal for the holy name of God on the part of men who rarely use it except in imprecation and in blasphemy—ostentatious helpings-on of the ark by those in whose esteem it figures only as an imposing thing for public procession, or as a relic of sanctity to be unveiled to the curious in some hour of rejoicing and of display? Brethren, this inconsistency imperils alike our own salvation and the progress of the cause of God. The Church must be consistent, every individual in the Church must be sincere and thorough in his piety, before the work is done. It may be, or it may not be, that there is the hypocrite here to-night—the systematic and habitual impostor—who has assumed the garb of godliness that he may the better sin; if there be, in God's name let him forsake his hope, for it will perish, and let him at once, before the hail sweeps his refuges of lies away, seek mercy of that Saviour whom he has insulted and betrayed. And what is our condition? Grey hairs have come upon us, signs of feebleness, tokens of lassitude and age, and we have not known it. Oh! a more sincere and decisive godliness is wanted from us all, if we would either pass untarnished through the terrible temptations of the world, or be found worthy to bear the vessels of the Lord. Brethren, we must resolve that whatever of insincerity may have attached to our profession shall at once be forsaken, and that we will from this time forward, God helping us, renew our baptismal vows, and be valiant for the truth upon the earth. If in our pursuit of pleasure there has been the indulgence of frivolity, and perhaps of licentiousness—if in our high-reaching ambition for renown there have been oppression and time-serving, and the concealment of principle, and practices that are corrupt and unworthy—if in our labor for competence there has been compliance with unhallowed custom, or complicity with wrong—if we have followed the maxims of trade, rather than the maxims of truth—if there has been over-reaching and cupidity in our commercial life, we have sinned, and our profession of religion only makes our sin more truly scandalous, and more completely sin. And it behooves us all now, from this very hour, to put away the sin from us with loathing, and fall humbled and penitent before God. We must have holiness—inner and vital heart-holiness—if we would cleave unto the Lord with full purpose of heart.

Brethren, when I see out in the broad world the

palpable inconsistencies of professors of religion—a man devout in the sanctuary and detestable at home, saintly on the Sabbath and sordid all the week, ostentatious in the enterprises of benevolence, but grinding his own workmen and tyrannical to the poor—when I see a man, whose citizenship is ostensibly in heaven, distance the keenest worldling around him in the race of fashion, or in the strife for gold—when I see a man, whose religion teaches the divinest charity, censorious in his spirit, and narrow in his soul—when I see a man, to whom God has given a fortune in stewardship, grudging to dispense to him that is in want; when I see a man, whose Divine Saviour rebuked his own disciples for intolerance, professing to follow his footsteps, and yet harshly excluding thousands from his fold; or when in the world of opinion I see religion represented as vindicating the most monstrous atrocities, as preaching eternal reprobation, as advocating an accursed system of slavery, as upholding an aggressive war—what have I to think but, as it was in the days of ancient Israel, the ark of God is carried out by the uncircumcised to battle, and there is need—strong, solemn, and passionate need—that the Elis of our Israel should sit upon the wayside, watching, for their hearts tremble for the ark of God.

3. And then there was, in the third place—and it is the last particular that I shall mention—there was in the camp of ancient Israel *indifference.* I do not mean to say that there was not a sort of patriotism—a natural

and common wish for victory—a desire to free themselves from the Philistine thrall. But patriotism, to be real and to be hallowed, must have all-heartedness; and this was lacking. They had no confidence in their leaders; there was among them the element of disunion. The laxity of their lives had of necessity enfeebled somewhat their moral principles, so that the high and chivalrous inspirations of the true lover of his country were emotions that were above them and beyond them. Hence, they went out into the battle-field, but they went with paralyzed arms; conscience made cowards of them, and, recreant and panic-stricken, they fled at the first attack of the foe. And, brethren, can there be any question that a lack of whole-hearted earnestness is one of the chief sources of peril to the ark of God to-day? Oh, if Laodicea is to be the type of the Church, it is no wonder that the world sneers and perishes! If religion, clad in silken sheen, has become a patronized and fashionable thing—a something that men cleave to as they cleave to the other items of a respectable life—something that they wear as a sort of armorial bearing for which they pay small duty either to God or man—it is no wonder that the world should be heedless of the message, and should subside into the drowsy monotony in which the messengers dream away their lives. Brethren, the poisonous trees do little harm in the vineyard; they are uprooted as soon as they are seen. It is the barren trees, that cumber the ground and mock the husbandman, that are the curses of the vineyard of the Lord. Cases of flagrant apostasy but little hinder the progress of the work; their inconsistency is so palpable and manifest. They are the true hinderers, under the shadow of whose luxury, and idleness, and frivolity, the Church sits at ease in Zion, while they are eating out its inner life as the vampire sucks out the life-blood of the victim that it is all the while fanning with its wings. Oh, brethren, we need all of us a baptism for a deeper and diviner earnestness, that we may bear our testimony for God. We are a witnessing Church; this is our character and our mission. But, alas! our witness has sometimes been feeble and has sometimes been false. We have been altogether too secular and too selfish. We have not been prophets —not we; but stammering, hesitating, blushing children, ashamed of the message that our Father has bidden us deliver. We have sought morality rather than holiness, serenity rather than sacrifice, smooth things to conciliate the world rather than strong things to conquer the world. We have been content to grasp all the world's wealth and honor that we could, and then, in the great wreck, some on boards and some on broken pieces of the ship, to get ourselves safe to land, rather than, freighted with heavenly treasure, to cast anchor in the fair haven with colors flying, and amid the glad welcome of the multitudes on shore. Oh, there is room, brethren, indeed there is, for the taunt of the infidel: "Ye Christians are as infidel as I am; ye do not believe in your own system; if you did, like a fire in your bones, it would burn you into action, if by any means you might save some." Oh! everything around us is rebuking this lethargic and this professional piety. Everything is in earnest—suns in their constant shining, and rivers in their ceaseless flow; the breeze that stops not day nor night to bear health upon its wings, the spring tripping up the winter, the seed-time hastening on the harvest—all are activity, faltering not, any one of them, in the sure and steady purpose of their being. Error is in earnest; Pagans are self-devoted; Mohammedanism has her resolute and valiant sons; Popery compasses sea and land to make one proselyte; infidels walk warily and constantly, scattering the seeds of unbelief. Society is in earnest; the sons of enterprise do not slumber; the warriors—how they hail the clarion call, and rush eagerly into the battle; the students—how they consume the oil of the lamp and the oil of life together; Mammon's votaries—are they the laggards in the streets? Oh, everything around us seems to be lashed into intensest energy, while we—ingrates that we are, God forgive us!—with the noblest work in the universe to do, and the most royal facilities to do it with; with the obligations of duty, and gratitude, and brotherhood, and fellowship; with the vows of discipleship upon us; with death at our doors and in our homes; and with the sad, wailing sound, as if it came from places where men were and are not: "No man hath cared for my soul" —we are heedless and exclusive, selfish and self-aggrandizing, and, worst of all, as self-satisfied with our grudged obedience, and our scanty effort, and our heartless prayer, as if no sinners were in peril and as if no Christ had died. And is it really so? Has that mightiest motive lost its power? Is Mammon really more potent than Messiah? Has the crucifix a holier inspiration than the cross? Is it true that war can move men's passions, and science stimulate their souls, and trade intensify their energies, and ambition flame their blood? and is Christianity nothing but a worn-out spell—a dim memorial of ancient power—an extinguished volcano, with no fire slumbering in its mighty heart? Is it true? Thy cross, O Jesus, has it lost its magnetism? does it no longer draw all men unto thee? Thy love, O Saviour, bôundless, unfathomable, all-embracing, doth it constrain no longer the souls for whom thy blood was shed? It is yours to answer these questions; do it as in the sight of God. But, oh! when we see the terrible indifference around us—when we see the awful contrast between the intensity of our beliefs and the smallness of our doings for Christ—what wonder is it that the Elis of our Israel, who, with all their faults, feel their heart-strings quiver in solicitude for the interests of Zion, should sit by the wayside, watching, because their hearts tremble for the ark of God?

May God the Holy Ghost come down, and write these truths upon the hearts of all, for his name's sake!

V.

THE INCARNATION OF CHRIST.

"Forasmuch then as the children are partakers of flesh and blood, he also himself likewise took part of the same."—HEB. ii. 14.

SOME eighteen hundred years ago, in the land of Judah, and in the city of Jerusalem, a strange restlessness had come upon the public mind. If a stranger just about that time had visited the Holy City, and had made himself acquainted with the inner life of its inhabitants, he would have found them all engrossed with one absorbing theme. It had superseded, as matter of interest, commerce, and conquest, and the intrigues of faction, and the subjects of ordinary politics. It had become the unconfessed hope of matrons and the deep study of earnest men. So prevalently had it spread, that it became identified with every thinking of the Hebrew mind, and with every beating of the Hebrew heart. This topic was the advent of a Deliverer who had been promised of God unto their fathers. Their holy books contained circumstantial directions, both as to the signs of his coming, and as to the period about which he might be expected to appear, and these various prophecies converged to their fulfillment. There were rumors, moreover, of certain meteoric appearances, which in Eastern countries were deemed the luminous heralds of the birth of a great king; and the heart of many a patriot Jew would throb more quickly, as in his vain dream of material empire he saw the Messiah, already, in vision, triumphing over his enemies, and his followers flushed with the spoil. In the midst of this national expectancy, events of strong significance were occurring in a quarter from which the eyes of the world would have turned heedlessly or in scorn. The national census was decreed to be taken throughout the Jewish provinces of the Roman empire in the time of Augustus Cæsar. In obedience to the imperial enactment, each man, with his household, went up for enrollment to his own—that is, his ancestral city. The unwonted influx of strangers had crowded the little inn in the little city of Bethlehem, one of the least among the thousands of Judah; so that the out-buildings were laid under tribute to furnish shelter to later comers. In the stable of that mean hostelry a young child was born. There was nothing about him to distinguish him from the ordinary offspring of Jewish mothers, and yet, at the moment of his birth, a new song from angel harps and voices rang through the plains of Bethlehem and ravished the watchful shepherds with celestial harmonies. Small space had passed ere wondering peasants beheld a star of unusual brightness hovering over that obscure dwelling; and by and by the inn was thrown into confusion by the arrival of a company of foreigners from afar off—swarthy and richly apparelled, who made their way to the stable with costly gifts and spices, which they presented to the new-born babe, and bowed the knee before him in homage, as to a royal child. Rapidly flew the glad tidings of great joy—passed from lip to lip, until the whole city was full of them—scorned by haughty Pharisees with scoffs and doubting—hailed with devout gladness by the faithful few who waited for the consolation of Israel—agitating all classes of the people—startling the vassal monarch on his throne—"Unto you is born this day in the city of David a Saviour, who is Christ the Lord."

Brethren, it is ours in this day to rejoice in the blessing which on that day descended on mankind. Blindness, indeed, hath happened unto Israel, so that they see not the glorious vision. And there are many among ourselves to turn away their eyes from the sight. But the advent of the Saviour has been the chiefest joy of the multitudes who once struggled like ourselves on earth, and who now triumph through his grace in heaven; and multitudes more, rejoicing in his true humanity, and happy in their brotherhood with Immanuel, cease not to thank God for the unspeakable gift, that, "forasmuch as the children are partakers of flesh and blood, he also himself likewise took part of the same."

The great fact, of course, which the Apostle wishes

to impress upon us, is our Saviour's assumption of humanity. And there are certain salient characteristics of that incarnation, upon which, in order that we may have it presented in all its aspects of blessing before our minds, we may not unprofitably dwell.

I. We observe, in the first place, then, that THE SAVIOUR'S ASSUMPTION OF HUMANITY WAS AN ACT OF INFINITE CONDESCENSION. It is obviously impossible that the language in which the Apostle here refers to Christ could be used legitimately of any being possessed essentially of the nature of flesh and blood. The language before us, applied to any mere man, even the holiest, even the most heroic, would be impertinent and without meaning. There is obviously implied the fact of his preëxistence, and of his preëxistence in a nature other and higher than that which he assumed. In a subsequent verse the implication is further made, that this preëxistence was in a nature other and higher than the angelic. For in his descent from the highest to recover and save, he took not hold on angels—they perished without redemption and without hope; but he took hold on the seed of Abraham. In the former chapter the Apostle rather largely illustrates his superiority to the angel: "When he bringeth in the first-begotten into the world, he saith, Let all the angels of God worship him." Just as when a crown prince goes a travel into some foreign realm, all the choicest of the nobility are selected to wait upon his bidding and follow in his train, so when He bringeth his first-begotten

.nto the world—a foreign realm to him—he says, "Let all the angels of God"—all the principalities and powers in heavenly places—worship, bow down to, wait upon, minister to him. Again, "of the angels he saith, Who maketh his angels spirits, and his ministers a flame of fire. But unto the Son he saith, Thy throne, O God, is forever and ever; a sceptre of righteousness is the sceptre of thy kingdom." From the scope and tenor of these passages—indeed, from the scope and tenor of the Apostle's entire argument, we are swift to conclude, and we are bold to affirm, the proper and unoriginated Godhead of the Saviour; that it was God made man for man to die. Yes, brethren, that stoop of illimitable graciousness was from the highest to the lowest. And in mysterious union with the child-heart of that unconscious babe the veiled Divinity slumbered. That weary and hungry traveller along the journey of life—it was Jehovah's fellow! That meek sufferer whose head is bowed to drink the cup of bitterness to the dregs—it was the true God, and eternal life! Strange marriage between the finite and the infinite; incomprehensible union between the divine and human!

There are scoffers in the world, I know, who dismiss the mystery of the incarnation, and deride it as the figment of fancy, or as the vision of fanaticism. They are of two kinds mostly: some who try everything by the standard of their own ideas, and who exalt their own reason—at best of no great tallness, and which prejudice has dwarfed into yet pigmier stature—into abso lute dictatorship over the realm of mind; and others more degraded, who seek a license for their desperate wickedness amidst the skepticisms of a still more desperate infidelity, who dismiss the narrative of the incarnation because it is a mystery, something that is not patent to the senses, which they aver to be the only means of knowledge. All the while they live in a mysterious world where there are thousands of secrets which their hearts cannot unravel. In the ordinary resources of life, in the daily benefits which Providence pours forth ungrudgingly, they take their churlish share of blessings whose wherefore they understand not. They are themselves a mystery, perhaps, greater than aught. They cannot, any one of them, understand that subtile organism which they call man, nor how that strange essence or principle, which they call life, floods them every moment with rapture; and yet, with marvellous inconsistency, credulous on matters where no mystery might be expected to abide, they are skeptical in matters where mystery exists of necessity, and where the absence of it would be a suspicious sign: "For canst thou by searching find out God; canst thou find out the Almighty unto perfection?"

Brethren, the incarnation of Christ is a mystery—an inexplicable and solemn mystery. But were there no mystery, on the other hand, think you, in the event of Christ being a mere man? How stands the case? There is an individual obscurely born; reared in village humbleness; looked on by his kindred according to the flesh with coldness, if not with dislike; with no aristocratic connections, with no noble patronage; telling to all to whom he ministered, with a strange candor, that he required absolute service; that he had no preferments in his gift; that he had no bribes to win the allegiance of the sordid; that it was more than likely, if they followed him, that they would have to forsake all else, to part at once with all that was lucrative and all that was endearing; to be secluded from ecclesiastical privilege; to be traduced by slander; to be hunted by persecution; nay, to hold life cheap, for whosoever killed them, in the blind zeal of his partisanship, thought he had done God service. Now, look at that individual. In spite of all these disadvantages, by the mere force of his teaching and of his life, he gathers a multitude of followers; charms the fisher from the lake; charms the soldier from the standard; charms—strangest of all—the publican from the loved seat of custom; and not only these, who might, perhaps, be imagined to risk little by the venture, but charms the physician from his practice, the scholarly student from the feet of his master, the ruler from his pride and luxury, the honorable counsellor from the deliberations of the Sanhedrim. The chief authorities combine against him; but his doctrine spreads. His name is attainted as a traitor; but he is held dearer than ever. His death gratifies his bloodthirsty and relentless foes; but his disciples rally, and his cause lives on. His tomb is jealously guarded and hermetically sealed, but it is somehow found empty notwithstanding. He shows himself alive by many infallible proofs. He soars, after forty days, from the crest of a mountain, and he has established an empire in the minds of thousands upon thousands, which promises to be extensive as the world, and to be permanent as time. And you ask us to believe that all this could be accomplished by the unaided resources of a mere man like ourselves! Were not that a mystery than all other mysteries greater and surpassing far? Then, look at that individual in the days of his flesh. He exerts, on the testimony of numerous and unexceptionable witnesses, miraculous power. He has power over the elements, for the winds are still at his bidding, and the lawless sea obeys him. He has power over inorganic matter and over vegetable life, for he blasts the fig-tree by a syllable, and five loaves and two fishes swell up, as he speaks, into a royal repast for full five thousand men. He has power over the ferocious passions, for he strikes down the advancing soldiery, and at his glance the foul demoniac is still. He has power over sickness, for the numbed limbs of the paralytic quicken, as he speaks, into strengthened manhood, and the leprosy scales off from its victim, and leaves him comely as a child. He has power over death, for at his word the maiden rises from her shroud; and the young man stops at the gate of the city to greet his mercy on his way to burial; and weeping sisters clasp their ransomed brother, a four days' dweller in the tomb. And you ask us to believe that all this can have been accomplished by the unaided resources of a mere man like ourselves! Were not that a mystery than all other mysteries greater and surpassing far? "Ah," but say some, "he was a good man, we acknowledge; a great teacher, a model man, a representative man, the highest man, God specially honored him. He may almost be said, indeed, to have had an inferior and derived Divinity. It is no wonder, therefore, that he should thus perform miracles, and that he should thus have founded a dominion." Nay, pardon me, but this only deepens the mystery, for this model man, whose frown was dismissal from his presence, of whose inimitable morals Rousseau, the infidel, said, that if the life and death of Socrates were those of an angel, the life and death of Jesus were those of a God—this model man claimed all his life to be Divine, made the impression of his pretensions upon the minds of the Jews so strong that they stoned him for blasphemy, received Divine honors without once rebuking the offerers, "thought it not robbery to be equal with God," and distinctly predicted that he should come again in the clouds of heaven. Oh, Jesus of Nazareth cannot possibly be simply a good and benevolent man. There is no escape from this alternative—no middle position in which he can abide—he is either an impostor or God. Now, unbeliever, you who dismiss the mystery of the incarnation, and treat it with solemn scorn or with derisive laughter, solve this mystery of your own. You pass through life in your pride and in your skepticism, scouting this mystery of Godhead, and yet shut up to the far greater mystery—either a good man who has spoken falsehood, or an impostor who has cheated the world. But we, with reverent trust, and from the lowest depth from which gratitude can spring, can say, "Great is the mystery of godliness, God manifest in the flesh."

II. I observe, secondly, THE SAVIOUR'S ASSUMPTION OF HUMANITY WAS NOT ONLY CONDESCENDING, BUT VOLUNTARY. This, indeed, follows inevitably from the foregone conclusion of his Divinity. Being Divine, he could be under no restraint of overwhelming necessity. To accommodate the theological language to human infirmity, we are apt to speak of God sometimes as if influenced by external things. But really it is not so; every Divine act is spontaneous and self-originating. Jesus Christ, therefore, could be under the bond of no possible obligation. Law was himself in spoken precept. Justice was himself engraven on the universe. Mercy was himself, the radiation of his own loving-kindness upon his people. Every decision of wisdom, every administration of physical government, every act of omnipotence, was his own; not in independent action, but in the harmonious union of the Divine nature. It is manifest, so far as his Divine nature was concerned, that his assumption of humanity must have been disinterested and voluntary; the strong upwelling of his tenderness for the hapless creatures he had made. There is something in the spontaneity of his offering which redeems it from the suspicion of injustice, and which vindicates the Father from the accusations of those who charge him with vindictiveness and cruelty. It would seem, indeed, as if the Saviour had foreseen, in the days of his flesh, that there would rise audacious rebels, who would thus cast a slur upon his Father's kindness, for he defends him by anticipation: "Therefore doth my Father love me, because I lay down my life, that I might take it again. No man taketh it from me, but I lay it down of myself. I have power to lay it down, and I have power to take it again."

But as to the human nature which vicariously suffered, you remember that at the time there was the proposition of incarnation, there was also the proposition of equivalent recompense. The promise of the joy was coeval with the prospect of suffering. Hence the Apostle: "Who for the joy that was set before him endured the cross, despising the shame." A world ransomed from the destroyer, a mediatorial kingdom erected upon the ruins of earth's spoiled thrones, a name that is above every name, honored in heaven by prostrate obedience and undying song, honored on earth by every confessing lip and every bending knee—this was the joy set before him; and for the sake of all this he endured patiently the cross, despised, looked down with holy contempt upon, mysterious and inconceivable shame. Besides, there can be no availableness in exacted suffering. There is something in the voluntariness of the incarnation which at once exalts our reverence and augments our affection for our Surety and Friend. We judge of the excellency of virtue by the willinghood with which it is practised. We cannot enter into a proper comparison, because we are all under the bond of one common obligation; but we all know that the virtue shines the most brightly which is practised amidst hazard and suffering, rather than that which is accorded where duty is inviting, and where obedience is profitable. Viewed in this light, what a wealth of disinterested generosity there is in the incarnation of Christ. The voice was heard from the midst of the throne: "Here I am; send me. Lo I come. In the volume of the book it is written of me, to do thy will, O my God." In another passage: "I delight to do thy will." Now, just think of what the will of God in this instance comprehended. The veiling the essential glory, the tabernacling in human flesh, the homeless wandering, the pangs of desertion and treachery, the abhorred contact with evil, the baptism of fire, beside the crown of sorrow, the dread hiding of the Father's countenance in portentous eclipse. And into this more than Egyptian darkness Jesus delighted to enter, for the sake of fallen man. When he assumed the form of a servant, and, actually incarnate, entered upon the work of redemption, it was with no reluctant step, in no hireling spirit. It was his meat and his drink; as necessary and pleasing to him as his daily sustenance, to do the will of his Father which was in heaven. Steadily pursuing one purpose, he was heedless of all that hindered; he felt irrepressible longings for its accomplishment; and his soul was like a prisoned bird that dashes itself for freedom against the grating of the cage: "I have a baptism to be baptized with; how am I straitened till it be accomplished." Steadily pursuant of that purpose, he was heedless of all that hindered. Now passing through a threatening mob, now turning from an offered crown, now resisting wisely the temptations of the enemy, now casting behind him the more dangerous, because more affectionate remonstrances of his disciples, and now repelling the suggestive aid of twelve legions of angels from heaven. Oh, as sinners like ourselves, at far off, reverent distance, watch him in his redemptive course—as, one wave after another wave, the proud waters go over his soul, and he dashes off the spray, and holds on his course, unfaltering and steady, to the end—with what depth of gratitude should we render him the homage of our hearts, and with what earnestness and self-accusation should we take to ourselves the burden of every melancholy sigh!

> "For all his wounds to sinners cry—
> I suffered this for you."

III. I observe, thirdly, THE SAVIOUR'S ASSUMPTION OF HUMANITY WAS NOT ONLY CONDESCENDING AND VOLUNTARY, BUT IT WAS COMPLETE. It was no mock assumption of humanity. The whole nature was taken on.

He had a human body with all its infirmities; he had a human soul with its completeness of faculty and its capability of endurance, with its every capacity, with its every affection. There were three reasons which seemed to render this entire assumption of human nature necessary. It was necessary, first, because the man had sinned, and upon the man, therefore must come the brand of Jehovah's displeasure. It was necessary, secondly, that the world might have the best and utmost manifestation of God, and that humanity, too gross and bewildered to comprehend ideas that were purely spiritual, might see in the Incarnate Son the highest embodied possibility of being. It was necessary, thirdly, that the felt need of the people in all ages of the world's history might be supplied—the need of perfect pureness allied to perfect sympathy—of the strength which was omnipotent to deliver, married to the tenderness that was brave and deep to feel. The complete humanity of Jesus has been attested by abundant authentications. In every legitimate sense of the word he was a man with man. He did not take our sinful nature upon him; that is only an inseparable accident of humanity; it came in after the creation, and it should go out before the end. Therefore, in every legitimate sense of the word, he was man with man. He was born helpless as other children are. His early years were spent in the house o his reputed father, working at his handicraft for bread. He grew in wisdom and in stature as other children grow; not at once, but by the slow ripening of years developed into the maturity of man. When he entered on his public ministry and went out among his fellows, he sustained, as they did, the relationships of mutual dependence and help. He was no self-elected reformer. He was no turbulent inflamer of unholy passions. Faulty as was the government under which he lived, he was a loyal subject, paid the tribute money without murmuring, and submitted himself to every ordinance of man. He was no dark ascetic; he was a brother of the multitudes, mingling in all the grief and cheerfulness of life. If men invited him to their houses, he went and sat down with them at their boards. If they asked him to their marriage festivals, he graced them with his presence, and turned the water into wine; and mingled his tears with theirs when the light of their homes was quenched, and when some loved one was suddenly withdrawn. His care for them who trusted him ceased not with his own danger, for, having loved his own, he loved them to the end. His filial affection was conspicuous throughout every part of his life, and shone radiant as a star through the darkness of his agony. He was the man Christ Jesus. How is it that you identify him with our nature? What are the peculiar characteristics by which you understand that such a one is partaker of humanity? Does human nature hunger? He hungered in the plain where the delusive fig-tree grew. Does human nature thirst? He felt the pang sharply upon the cross. Is human nature wearied under the pressure of travelling and of toil? He sat thus upon the well. Does human nature weep unbidden tears? Pity wrung them from him as he gazed upon the fated and lost Jerusalem; and sorrow wrung them from him at the grave where Lazarus lay. Does human nature shrink and fear in the prospect of impending trial, cowering beneath the apprehended peril, and pray that dread pangs may be spared it? In the days of his flesh, when he poured out his supplications with strong crying and tears, "he was heard, in that he feared." He was the man Christ. Come, ye seekers after the sublime, behold this man—marred enough by sorrow, but not at all by sin; decorated with every grace, yet disfigured by no blemish of mortality; raying out warmth and life into the hearts and homes of men; with not an act that you can trace up to selfishness, and not a word that you can brand as insincere; with his whole life of kindness, and his death an expiation—behold the Divine Man! Talk of the dignity of human nature—it is there, and you can find it nowhere in the universe beside. "The boast of heraldry, the pomp of power," the skill to make canvas speak or marble breathe, or to play upon men's hearts as upon a harp of many tunes, the mad ambition that would climb to fame by slopes where the trampled lie, and where the red rain drops from many a heart's blood—what are their claims to his? Hush, ye candidates for greatness, and let him speak alone. Erase meaner names from thy tablets, thou applauding world, and chronicle this name instead. Shrine it in your living hearts, those of you who trust in his atonement, and who come by his mediation unto God; grave it there, deeper than all other names—the man Christ Jesus.

IV. I observe, fourthly, THE INCARNATION OF THE SAVIOUR WAS NOT ONLY CONDESCENDING, AND VOLUNTARY, AND COMPLETE, BUT IT WAS ALSO, AND CHIEFLY, ATONING.—The great purpose for which he came into the world could not be properly accomplished but through death. It was through death that he was to destroy him that had the power of death, that is, the devil. Intimations of this had come previously into the world, in the visions of seers, from the lips of prophets, in the adumbrations and typical shadowings of some great Offerer, who, in the end of the world, should appear to put away sin by the sacrifice of himself. All other purposes, however separably noticeable, become subordinate and subsidiary to this. Hence Christ did not become partaker of flesh and blood that he might give to the world a spotless example. Although holiness, illustrious and unspotted, does beam out from every action of his life, he was not incarnate in order that he might impress upon the world the teachings of pure morality; although such were the spirituality of his lessons, and the power with which he taught them, that "never man spake like this man." He did not assume our nature merely that he might work his healing wonders, showing, before the bleared vision of the world, omnipotence in beneficent action. All these things, however separably noticeable, were not vast enough or grand enough to have brought the Saviour from heaven. Miracles, precepts, kindnesses, all these were collateral blessings—flowers that sprung up, as at the tread of the fabled goddess, wherever he appeared. Large and full in his sight, through all the years of his incarnate life, more distinctly, more vividly, in the last years of his ministry, loomed the shadow of the figure of the cross: "That is the end of my toil; that is the consummation of my purpose. I am straitened till I get to that; I have not fulfilled my mission and expressed all the Divine energy that I am to pour out upon the world until I reach that. There is the goal of all my endeavors; there I see my true office before me—the surety of insolvent humanity, the friend of a forsaken race, the refuge and succor of endangered man." If you will think for a while, you will see how all the other characteristics of the incarnation converged here, and were each of them necessary in order to give this, the master-purpose, its efficacy and its power. It was necessary that a being of holy estate should condescend, Divinity sustaining humanity under the pressure of agony, and imparting to humanity a plenitude of atoning meritoriousness. It was necessary that the offering should be voluntary, because there could be no availableness in exacted suffering; and the offering must be profoundly willing before it could be infinitely worthy. It was necessary that the whole nature should be taken on, because the man had sinned and the man must die; and as humanity, in its federal representative, the first Adam, had been drawn to death, so humanity, in its federal representative, the second Adam, might have the free gift coming upon all men unto justification of life.

Now, you see how far we have got in our search for an accepted propitiation. We have got a willing victim. We have got a willing victim in the nature that had sinned; we have got a willing victim in the nature that had sinned with no obligation of his own, and all whose merit, therefore, could be to spare for the redemption of the sinner. Justice herself required only another exaction, and that is, that this willing victim should be free from taint, whether of hereditary or actual crime. Now, the miraculous conception freed from the hereditary taint of human nature; and, thus freed from hereditary defilement, he was born, not of blood, not in the ordinary method of human generation, nor of the will of the flesh, nor of the will of man, but of God. And he moved about in the midst of his fellows in an atmosphere of impurity, yet escaping its contagion. Like the queenly moon shining down upon the haunts of beggars, and dens of thieves, yet preserving its chastity and its brilliance unimpaired, he moved among the scum and offscouring of human society, and could say, "Which of you convicteth me of sin?" He was holy, harmless, undefiled, separate from sinners; evoking from heaven its attesting thunders; charming the wondering earth with spotlessness which it had never seen before; and (crown of triumph!) wringing from baffled demons the reluctant acknowledgment, "We know thee who thou art, the Holy One of God." Here, then, is the perfected offering—a willing victim; a willing victim in the nature that had sinned, and free from taint, free from obligation, man's eternal Saviour, God's incarnate Son. Follow him in the shadow of his passion. Close upon the agony of Gethsemane came his arrest by the treachery of one whom he had honored. Patiently he bears the ribaldry and insult in the dishonored judgment-hall of Pilate. Wearily he treads the pathway to Calvary, bearing his own cross. Now, the cross is reared. The multitude are gathered about the hill of shame. The nails are fastened into the quivering flesh; and in agony and torture ebbs his pure life away. The last ministering angel leaves him, for he must tread the wine-press alone. Darkness gathers suddenly round; and—oh, mystery of mystery!—the Father hides his face from the Beloved. Darkness deepens in the sky and in the mind—how long, the affrighted gazers know not. A cry bursts through the gloom, sharp, shrill, piercing. All is silent—it is finished! The night, that had climbed up strangely to the throne of noon, as suddenly dispersed. The multitude, that eager and wondering had gathered round the hill of shame, separated to their several homes, talking about the tragedy they had witnessed. The moon rose on high as calmly as if the sun had not set on a scene of blood. But, oh! what a change those few hours had wrought in the fortunes of the world. Christ had died, the just for the unjust, that he might bring us to God. Go, tell it to that despairing sinner—that man, I mean, who has the cord about his neck, and the pistol at his throat, who is just about to escape from the terrible harrowings of an alarmed conscience, by the dreadful alternative of self-murder. Go to him; be quick; tell him he need not die, for Christ has died, has died to bear his sins away. Proclaim salvation from the Lord for wretched dying men. Sound it out from the summit of that hill-side of Calvary, and let the sister hills echo it, until round the earth has spread the rapturous hosanna—Salvation! Go with it to the wretched, and miserable, and poor, and blind, and naked; it is just the thing they need—Salvation! Ring it out through every avenue of this vast metropolis of a world, till it rouse the slumbering dust, and awake the coffined dead—Salvation! Take it to your own hearts—be sure of that; and, in the fullness of your own experience, let us hear your song: "There is, therefore, now no condemnation to them that are in Christ Jesus, who walk not after the flesh, but after the Spirit."

How is it with you, brethren? How is it with you to-night? Have you any personal interest in the incarnation of the Saviour? Has the realizing change by which you are enabled to understand the purposes of the Saviour's advent come upon your heart? Have the purposes of his advent been fulfilled in your experience? He came "to destroy him that had the power of death," that is, the devil—to counter-work him on his own ground; is he slain in you—vanquished and overcome in you? He came "to deliver them who through fear of death were all their lifetime subject to bondage;" are you freed from the tyranny? Have you entered into the liberty wherewith Christ has promised to make you free? He has accomplished his purpose. Many a one has gone blithely to the stake in the name of Jesus; many a one has marched steadily with eyes open to meet the last enemy, trusting in Jesus. No, not much fear of death about Stephen, when in the gloom of that fierce council he looked up and saw heaven opened, and the Son of Man standing at the right hand of the throne of God, and all that were in the council, looking steadfastly on him, saw his face as it had been the face of an angel. Not much fear of death in Paul. That is more patent to your experience, perhaps; for he was a blasphemer once, we know—a persecutor once, an injurious man once; but he obtained mercy, and he is presented in what I take to be one of the sublimest passages of Scripture: "I am in a strait betwixt two"—frail, erring, sinful, mortal man poised, so to speak, in balance between both worlds, having the choice of either, and not knowing which to take—"I am in a strait betwixt two, having a desire to depart and to be with Christ, which is far better; but to remain in the flesh is more needful for you." Not much fear of death there. He came "to deliver them who, through fear of death, were all their life-time subject to bondage." How is it with you? Does the Spirit take of the things of Christ and show them to you? Does he witness to you of your own personal adoption into the family of God? If you hesitate to say that, can you say, as the old woman in Scotland said, when questioned upon the fact of her adoption: "I can say this: either I am changed or the world is changed." Can you say that? Has the cautery begun its work? Is the proud flesh getting eaten out by the live coal from the altar? Are you ceasing to do evil and learning to do well—bringing forth fruits meet for repentance? Do you hate sin with ever-increasing hatred, and press forward to the cultivation of the things that are of good report and lovely? Alas! it will be sad for you if the incarnation of Christ should be to you a mystery forever, if there be no light coming upon his purposes, no experience of the fulfillment of them in your own hearts. Oh, seek first the kingdom of God and his righteousness. Hallow this dedicatory service by the dedication of your own hearts to God. Let there be this sacrifice, a living sacrifice, holy and acceptable, which is your reasonable service.

VI.

ZEAL IN THE CAUSE OF CHRIST.

"For whether we be beside ourselves, it is to God: or whether we be sober, it is for your cause. For the love of Christ constraineth us; because we thus judge, that if one died for all, then were all dead; and that he died for all, that they who live should not henceforth live unto themselves, but unto him who died for them, and rose again."—2 COR. v. 13–15.

IT is always an advantage for the advocate of any particular cause to know the tactics of his adversary. He will be the better prepared for the onset, and repel the attack the more easily. Forewarned of danger, he will intrench himself in a position from which it will be impossible to dislodge him. The Apostle Paul possessed this advantage in a very eminent degree. In the earlier years of his apostleship, the Jew and the Greek were the antagonists with whom he had to contend. Having been himself a member of the straitest sect of the Jews, he knew full well the antipathy with which they regarded anything which set itself by its simplicity in contrast with their magnificent ritual; and he knew also the haughty scorn with which they turned away from what they deemed the unworthy accessories of the

Nazarene. And, well read as he was in classic literature, and acquainted with all the habits and tendencies of the Grecian mind, he could readily understand how the restraints of the Gospel would be deemed impertinent by the voluptuous Corinthian, and how the philosophic Athenian would brand its teachers mad. And yet, rejoicing in the experimental acquaintance with the Gospel, he says, for his standing-point of advantage: "We preach Christ crucified, to the Jews a stumbling-block and to the Greeks foolishness, but to them that are called, the power of God and the wisdom of God." And in the words of the text, addressing some of those very Corinthians upon whom the Gospel had exerted its power, he seems to accept the stigma and vindicate the glorious madness: "For whether we be beside ourselves, it is to God: or whether we be sober it is for your cause. For the love of Christ constraineth us; because we thus judge, that if one died for all, then were all dead: and that he died for all, that they who live should not henceforth live unto themselves, but unto him who died for them, and rose again." The great purpose of the Apostle in these words is to impress upon us the fact that the cause of Christ in the world, sanctioned by the weight of so many obligations, fraught with the destinies of so many millions, should be furthered by every legitimate means; that for it, if necessary, should be employed the soberest wisdom; and for it, if necessary, the most impassioned zeal. He vindicates the use of zeal in the cause of Christ by the three following considerations: First, from the condition of the world; secondly, from the obligations of the Church; and, thirdly, from the master-motive of the Saviour's constraining love. To illustrate and enforce this apostolic argument, as not inappropriate to the object which has called us together, will be our business for a few brief moments to-night.

I. The Apostle argues and enforces the use of zeal in the cause of Christ, in the first place, from THE CONDITION OF THE WORLD. The Apostle speaks of the world as in a state of spiritual death. He argues the universality of this spiritual death from the universality of the atonement of Christ. "For the love of Christ constraineth us, because we thus judge, that if one died for all, then were all dead"—dead in sin, with every vice luxuriant and every virtue languishing; dead in law, judicially in the grasp of the avenger; nay, "condemned already," and hastening to the second death. We need not remind you that this is by no means the world's estimate of its own condition. It is short-sighted, and, therefore, self-complacent. There is a veil over its eye; there is a delusion at its heart. In that delusion it fancies itself enthroned and stately, like some poor lunatic, an imaginary monarch under the inflictions of its keeper. The discovery of its true position comes only when the mind is enlightened from on high. "We thus judge," not because there is in us any intuitional sagacity, or any prophetical foresight, by which our judgment is made more accurate than the judgment of others; but the Holy Spirit has come down, has wrought upon us—has shown us the plague of our own hearts—and from the death within we can the better argue the death which exists around. And that this is the actual condition of the world, Scripture and experience combine to testify. The Bible, with comprehensive impartiality, concludes all "under sin;" represents mankind as a seed of evil-doers—"children that are corrupters;"—sheep that have wandered away from the Shepherd and Bishop of their souls. In the adjudication of Scripture there is no exemption from this common character of evil, and from this common exposure to danger. The man of merciful charities, and the woman of abandoned life—the proudest peer, and the vilest serf in his barony—the moralist observer of the decalogue, and the man-slayer, red with blood, all are comprehended in the broad and large denunciation: "Ye were by nature children of wrath, even as others." And out in the broad world, wherever the observant eye travels, you have abundant confirmation of the testimony of Scripture. You have it in your own history. The transgressions and sins which constitute this moral death abound in our age no less than in any former age of mankind. There are thousands around you who revel in undisguised corruption. There are thousands more externally reputable who have only a name to live. You have this confirmation in the nations of the Continent—some safely bound by the superstition of ages; others subsiding into a reactionary skepticism. You have this confirmation further away in the countries which own Mohammedan rule, and cherish the Mohammedan's dream—where you have unbridled lust, and a tiger's thirst for blood. You have this confirmation in the far-off regions of heathenism proper, where the nature, bad in itself, is made a thousand-fold worse by its religion—where the man is the prey of every error, and the heart the slave of every cruelty—where men live in destruction, and where men die in despair. Travel where you will, visit the most distant regions, and search under the shadow of the highest civilization—penetrate into the depths of those primeval forests, into whose original darkness you might have imagined the curse would hardly penetrate, and the result is uniformly the same. Death is everywhere. You see it, indeed, in all its varieties; now in the rare and fading beauty which it wears just after the spirit has fled from the clay, when its repose seems the worn-out casket, which the soul has broken, and thrown away; now, when there is shed over it a hue of the sublime, and it is carried amid tears to burial; and now, when corruption has begun its work, and its ill odor affects the neighborhood, and spreads the pestilence—you see it in all its varieties, but uniformly death is there. We gather from our melancholy pilgrimage no vestige of spiritual life. Mourners go about the streets, and there are mourners over many tombs.

Although, as we have observed just now, a thorough and realizing estimate of the world's condition comes only when the judgment is enlightened from on high, the wise men of the world, the minds that have in all ages towered above their fellows, have felt an unsatisfactoriness for which they could hardly account; they have had a vague and morbid consciousness that all was not right somehow, either with themselves or with their race; they have met with disturbing forces, signs of irregularity, tokens of misery and of sin that have ruffled, somewhat, the philosophic evenness of their minds. Each in his own way, and from his own standpoint, has guessed at the solution of the problem, and has been ready with a suggested remedy. The peoples are imbruted; educate them. The nations are barbarous; civilize them. Men grovel in sensual pleasure; cultivate the æsthetic faculty; open up to them galleries of pictures; bring them under the humanizing influences of art. Men groan in bondage; emancipate them, and bid them be free! Such are some of the tumultuous cries that have arisen from earnest but blind philanthropists, who have ignored the spiritual part of man's nature, and forgotten altogether the Godward relations of his soul. All these, as might have been expected, valuable enough as auxiliaries, worth something to promote the growth and comfort of a man when life has been once imparted, fail, absolutely fail to quicken the unconscious dead. In all cases the bed has been shorter than that a man could lie on it, and the covering narrower than that he could wrap himself in it. The inbred death lay too deep for such superficial alchemy; corpses cannot by any possibility animate corpses; and the compassionate bystander from other worlds, sickened with the many inventions, might be constrained to cry, "Amid all this tumult of the human, O for something Divine!" And the Divine is given—Christ has died for all men. There is hope for the world's life. This is a death whereby we live; this is a remedy commensurate with existing need, and intended entirely to terminate and extinguish that need.

That squalid savage, whose creed is a perpetual terror, and whose life is a perpetual war—Christ hath died for him. That fettered and despairing slave, into whose soul the iron has entered, valued by his base oppressor about on a par with the cattle he tends, or with the soil he digs—Christ hath died for him. That dark blasphemer, who lives in familiar crime, whose tongue is set on fire of hell, whose expatriation would be hailed by the neighborhood around him as a boon of chiefest value—Christ has died for him. That dark recluse, whom an awakened conscience harasses, and who, in the vain hope of achieving merit by suffering, wastes himself with vigilant penance well-nigh to the grave—Christ has died for him. Oh, tell these tidings to the world, and it will live. Prophesy of this name in the motionless valley, and the Divine Spirit who always waits to do honor to Jesus, will send the *afflatus* from the four winds of heaven, and they shall leap into life to his praise.

Now take these two points. Think, in the first place, of the condition of the world—a condition so disastrous, that nothing but death can illustrate it—a condition which prostrates every faculty, which smites the body with unnumbered cruelties, which dwarfs the mind with prejudices or distorts it into unholy passion, which banishes the soul and mind within a man in hopeless estrangement from happiness and God; and then think of the death of Christ, providing for the furthest need, overtaking the utmost exile, pouring its abundant life upon the sepulchred nations, diffusing light, liberty, hope, comfort, heaven: and I appeal to your enlightened judgment whether you are not bound, those of you who believe in Jesus, to labor for the world's conversion with intensest energy and zeal. Oh, if temporal miseries elicit sympathy, and prompt to help; if the anxieties of a neighborhood gather around a drowning child, or are fastened upon the rafters of a burning house, where, solitary and imploring, stands a single man, already charred by the flame, how much of sympathy, of effort, of liberality, of zeal, of prayer, are due to a world lying in the wicked one, and panting after the second death! You will agree with me, that there is more than license for the poet's words:

> "On such a theme,
> 'Tis impious to be calm!"

And you will rejoice—will you not?—to take your stand, to-night by the Apostle's side, and to cry, when men deem your zeal impertinence and your efforts fanaticism, "If we be beside ourselves, it is to God: and if we be sober, it is for your cause."

II. The Apostle argues the necessity for zeal in the cause of Christ, secondly, from THE OBLIGATIONS OF THE CHURCH, in that he died for all, that they should live—should not henceforth live unto themselves, but for him who died for them and rose again. The Apostle's argument is this—none of us has life in himself; if we live at all, we live by imparted life; we live because life has been drafted into our spirits from on high. Then it is not our own; it belongs to Him who has purchased it for us with his own blood, and we are bound to employ it in his service, and for his glory. This also is the conclusion of an enlightened judgment. We judge this as well as the other, and this is in accordance with the whole tenor of Scripture. Time would fail us to mention a tithe of the passages in which devotion—the devotion of the heart and of the service of God, are made matter of constant and of prominent demand. I will just mention one passage that may serve as an illustration of all: "I beseech you therefore, brethren, by the mercies of God, that ye give your bodies as a living sacrifice." Have you ever gauged the depth of consecration that slumbers in the heart of those words—"a living sacrifice;" to be absolutely and increasingly devoted to God, as if the knife were at the throat, and the life-blood streamed forth in votive offering? Nay, better than that; because the life-blood could stream out but once, but the living sacrifice may be a perpetual holocaust, repeated daily for a lifetime—a living sacrifice, holy and acceptable unto God, which is your reasonable service. From the doctrine of this passage, and of numberless others kindred to it, it would appear that the regenerate heart is not at liberty to live for itself, nor to aim supremely at its own gratification; it must live for him who has "died for it, and who has risen again." You cannot fail, I think, to perceive that compliance with this exhortation is utterly antagonistic to the ordinary procedure of mankind.

In an age of organization against idolatry, there is one proud, rampant idolatry which retains its ascendency amongst us. Selfishness is the most patronized idolatry in the world. It is the great image whose brightness is exceeding terrible, and before which all men bow; it is a throne, and an empire, and the likeness of a kingly crown; it equips armies and mans armaments to gratify its lust of power. Fastnesses have been explored and caverns ransacked to appease its thirst for gold. It presides over the councils of kings and over the diplomacy of cabinets; for it the merchantman grindeth down his manhood, for it the treader-under-foot of nations marcheth in his might and in his shame; its votaries are of all handicrafts—of the learned professions, and of every walk in life. It hath sometimes climbed on to the judgment-seat, and perverted justice there. The cowled monk hath hidden it beneath his robe, and it hath become for him an engine of oppression, and it hath occasionally robed itself in holy vestments, and entered the priest's office for a morsel of bread. No grace nor virtue of humanity is free from its contamination. It has breathed, and patriotism has degenerated into partisanship; it has breathed, and friendship has been simulated for policy; it has breathed, and charity has been blemished by ostentation; it has breathed, and religion has been counterfeited for gold; its sway is a despotism—its territory wherever man hath trodden, and it is the undisputed anarch of the world. Now it is against this principle in human nature, throned within us all, doggedly contesting every inch of ground, that Christianity goes forth to combat. The Gospel absolutely refuses to allow self to be the governing power, and assaults it in all its strongholds with precepts of sublime morality. To the selfishness of avarice it goes up boldly, even while the miser clutches his gold, and says: "Give to him that asketh of thee, and from him that would borrow of thee turn not thou away." To the selfishness of anger it addresses itself, even when the red spot is yet on the brow of the angry: "Let not the sun go down upon thy wrath;" "Bless them that curse you, pray for them that despitefully use you and persecute you." To the selfishness of pride, even in its haughtiness and arrogance, it says: "In honor preferring one another, be clothed with humility, let each esteem another better than himself." To the selfishness of indifference to the concerns of others, "Look not on thine own things, but likewise upon the things of others;" and to the selfishness of souls and criminal neglect of the great salvation, it speaks in tones of pathos which that must be a callous heart that can withstand, "Ye know the graces of our Lord Jesus Christ, who, though he was rich, yet for our sins he became poor, that we, through his poverty, might be made rich." Oh, how small, alongside of august and heavenly precepts like these, are the sublimest maxims of any merely ethical morality!

It is said that, once, during the performance of a comedy in the Roman theatre, one of the actors gave utterance to the sentiment, "I am a man; nothing, therefore, that is human, can be foreign to me," and the audience were so struck by the disinterestedness, or so charmed by the novelty, that they greeted it with thunders of applause. How much greater wealth of kindly wisdom and prompting to unselfish action lies hidden in the Gospel of Christ, shrined there as every-day utterances passed by the most of us very slightingly by! Oh! let there be anything like the genial practice of this divine morality, and the world would soon lose its aspect of desolation and of blood; oppression and over-reaching, and fraud and cruelty, would be frowned out of the societies of men, and this earth would be once more an ample and a peopled paradise. By selfishness, as we have thus endeavored to describe it, we mean that grasping, monopolizing spirit which gets all and gives nothing; heedful enough of its own fortunes, careless of the concerns and interests of others.

This is the principle in our nature which Christianity opposes, and with which it ceaselessly wages war. But there is a sort of selfishness which, for the sake of distinction, we may call self-love, which is instinctive, and therefore innocent—that merciful provision by which we are prompted to the care of our own lives and to the avoidance of everything that would disquiet or abridge them. This principle in our nature Christianity encourages; to this principle Christianity addresses itself; and hence it has connected, married in indissoluble union, man's chiefest duty and man's highest pleasure. Godliness is profitable unto all things, having the promise of the life that now is. What has the dark, morbid, unhappy sensualist to do with it? Godliness hath the promise of the life "that now is," as well as "that which is to come." In keeping thy commandments there is a present reward. "Take my yoke upon you and learn of me, for I am meek and lowly in heart, and ye shall find rest unto your souls; for my yoke is easy and my burden is light." "In thy presence there is fullness of joy; at thy right hand there are pleasures for evermore." Just as it is in man's physical organization, and its adaptation to the material world around him, when body and mind are alike in health, we can neither eat, nor drink, nor talk, nor walk, nor sleep, nor sing, nor perform any of the commonest actions of life, without a sensation of pleasure; so it is in the spiritual life: there is pleasure in its every motion. There is pleasure even in the sting of penitence; it is

> "A godly grief and pleasing smart,
> That melting of a broken heart."

There is pleasure in the performance of duty; there is pleasure in the enjoyment of privilege; there is pleasure in the overcoming of temptations, a grand thrill of happiness to see trampled under foot a vanquished lust or slain desire; there is pleasure in the exercise of benevolence; there is pleasure in the importunity of prayer. Hence it is that the Apostle seeks to rivet the sense of personal obligation by the remembrance of personal benefit. "We thus judge, that he died for all, that they which live should not henceforth live unto themselves, but unto him who"—owns them? No. Claims them? No. Will judge them? No; but—"to him who died for them and rose again." Gratitude is to be the best prompter to our devotion. Those who live to Christ, those who live by Christ, will not tamely see his altars forsaken, his Sabbaths desecrated, his name blasphemed, the blood of the covenant wherewith he was sanctified accounted an unholy thing. Brethren, are you of that happy family? Have you obtained life from the dead through his name? Then you are bound to spend it for his honor, and, watching with godly jealousy for every possible opportunity of doing good, to spend and be spent for them who have not yet your Master known. I call on you to answer this invocation; it belongs to you. There is no neutrality, believe me, in this war—and if there be some of you that would like to be dastardly and half-hearted trimmers, you will find by and by that you have got the hottest place in the battle, exposed to the cross-fire from the artillery of both parties. I call on you decisively to-night to answer this invocation. Call up before your minds the benefits you have individually received; think of the blessings which the death of Christ has procured for you—the removal of the blighting curse which shadowed all your life, the present sense of pardon, mastery over self and over sin, light in the day of your activity, and songs in the night of your travail; the teaching Spirit to lead you into still loftier knowledge, and the sanctifying spirit to impress upon you the image of the heavenly; that Divine fellowship which lightens the present, and that majestic hope which makes the future brighter far. Think of the benefits which the resurrection of Christ has conferred upon you; light in the shadowed valley, the last enemy destroyed, support amid the swellings of Jordan, a guide upon the hither side of the flood, angelic welcomes, the King in his beauty, and "a house not made with hands, eternal in the heavens." And then, as the sum of favor is presented, and gratitude arises and the fire burns, and the heart is full, and the frame quivers with the intensity of its emotions, just remember that there is a world lying in the wicked one, that there are multitudes, thousands upon thousands, in your own city, at your own doors, for whom the Saviour died, who never heard his name; that there are multitudes for whom he has abolished death who have never felt his resurrection's power. Let your tears flow; better, far better a tear for God's sake and the world's sake than the hard-heartedness and darkness of sin. Lift up your voice in the midst of them; lift it up, be not afraid. Say unto the cities of Judah, "Behold your God." Men will call you mad, but you can give them the Apostle's answer, "If we be beside ourselves, it is to God; if we be sober, it is for your cause."

III. The Apostle argues the necessity of zeal in the cause of Christ, in the third place, from the master motive of THE SAVIOUR'S CONSTRAINING LOVE. "The love of Christ constraineth us"—forces us along, carries us away as with the impetuosity of a torrent, or rather as when cool heavens and favoring air speed the vessel steadily to the haven. Love is at once man's most powerful motive and his highest inspiration, both in the life that now is and that which is to come. From love to Christ spring the most devoted obedience, the most untiring efforts in his service. There are other springs of action, I know, by which men are influenced to a profession of religion. Interest can occasionally affect godliness from sordid aims, and behave itself decorously amid the respectabilities of the temple-going and alms-giving religion; but it will give its arm to any man that goes down to the house of Rimmon; and if there is a decree that at the sound of all kinds of music they are to fall down before another image which has been erected in the plains of Dura, they will be the most obsequious benders of the knee. Men sometimes practise obedience under the influence of fear. A sudden visitation, a prevailing epidemic, an alarming appeal, will strike into momentary concern; but when the indignation is overpast, and the craven soul has recovered from its paroxysms of terror, there will often be a relapse into more than the former atrocities of evil. Convictions of duty may and sometimes will induce a man, like an honest Pharisee of the olden time, to observe rigidly the enactments of the law; but there will be no heart in his obedience, and no holy passion in his soul; but let the love of God be shed abroad in his heart by the Holy Ghost given unto him, let there be a perception of love in God, let there be sight of the Crucified as well as of the cross, and there will be disinterested, and cheerful, and hearty obedience. Zeal for God will become at once a passion and a principle, intensifying every purpose into ardor, and filling the whole soul with the vehemence of absorbing desire. This is the emotion from whose natural and inevitable outflow the Apostle vindicates impassioned zeal.

Opinions are divided as to whether the constraining love spoken of in the text, refers to Christ's love to us or to our love to him, which the sense of his love has enkindled in the soul. I do not think we can go far wrong if we take both meanings, inasmuch as no principle of exposition is violated, and as we need the pressure of a combination of motive, that we may be zealously affected always in this good thing. Ye, then, if there are any of you here who need rousing to energy in the service of Christ, think of his love to you; how rich its manifestations, and how unfeigned; how all other love of which it is possible for you to conceive shrinks in the comparison! There have been developments in the histories of years of self-sacrificing affection, which has clung to the loved object amid hazard and suffering, and which has been ready even to offer up life in its behalf. Orestes and Pylades, Damon and Pythias, David and Jonathan, what lovely episodes their histories give us amid a history of selfishness and sin! Men have canonized them, partly because such instances are rare, and partly because they are like a dim hope of redemption looming from the ruins of the fall. We have it on inspired authority, indeed, "Greater love hath no man than this"—this is the highest point which *man* can compass, this is the culminating point of that affection which man can by possibility attain, the apex of his loftiest pyramid goes no higher than this—"greater love hath no man than this, that a man lay down his life for his friend; but God commendeth his love toward us, in that while we were yet sinners Christ died for us." A brother has sometimes made notable efforts to retrieve a brother's fortunes, or to blanch his sullied honor; but there is a Friend that sticketh closer than a brother. A father has bared his breast to shield his offspring from danger, and a mother would gladly die for the offspring of her womb; but a father's affection may fail in its strength, and yet more rarely a mother's in its tenderness.

"I saw an aged woman, bowed
'Mid weariness and care;
Time wrote in sorrow on her brow,
And 'mid her frosted hair.

"What was it that like sunbeam clear
O'er her wan features ran,
As, pressing toward her deafened ear,
I named her absent son?

"What was it? Ask a mother's breast,
Through which a fountain flows,
Perennial, fathomless, and blest,
By winter never froze.

"What was it? Ask the King of kings,
Who hath decreed above,
What change should mark all earthly things
Except a mother's love!"

And "can a woman forget her sucking child, that she should not have compassion on the son of her womb? Yea, they may forget, yet will I not forget thee." O Jesus of Nazareth, who can declare thee? "Herein is love, not that we loved God, but that he loved us, and sent his Son to be a propitiation for our sins." Think of that love—love which desertion could not abate—love which ingratitude could not abate—which treachery could not abate—love which death could not destroy—love which, for creatures hateful and hating one another, stooped to incarnation, and suffered want, and embraced death, and shrank not even from the loathsomeness and from the humiliation of burial; and then, with brimming eye, and heart that is full, and wonder "Why such love to me?" you will indeed be ungrateful if you are not stirred by it to an energy of consecration and endeavor, which may well seem intemperate zeal to the cool reckoners with worldly wisdom. Then take the other side of the argument; take it as referring to your love to Christ, which the sense of his love has enkindled in the soul. The deepest affection in the believing heart will always be the love of Jesus. The love of home, the love of friends, the love of letters, the love of rest, the love of travel, and all else, are contracted by the side of this master-passion. "A little deeper," said one of the veterans of the first Napoleon's old guard, when they were probing in his bosom for a bullet that had mortally wounded him, and he thought they were getting somewhere in the region of the heart —"a little deeper and you will find the Emperor." Engraven on the Christian's heart deeper than all other love of home or friends, with an ineffaceable impression that nothing can erase, you find the loved name of Jesus. Oh! let this affection impel us, and who shall measure our diligence or repress our zeal? Love is not bound by rule; there is no law that can bind it; it is never below the precept, it is always up to the precept, but it always has a margin of its own. It does not calculate, with mathematical exactitude, with how little of obedience it can escape penalty and secure recompense; like its Master it gives in princely style; it is exuberant in its manifestations; there is always enough and to spare. And if meaner motive can prompt to heroic action—if from pure love of science astronomers can cross ocean familiarly, and dare encounter dangers, just that they may watch in distant climes the transit of a planet across the disc of the sun—and if botanists can travel into inhospitable climes and sojourn among inhospitable men, only to gather specimens of their gorgeous flora—and if, with no motive but love of country, and no recompense save bootless tears and an undying name, a Willoughby could sacrifice himself to blow up a magazine, and a Sarkeld could fire the Cashmere Gate at Delhi, surely we, with obligations incomparably higher, with the vows of profession on our lips, with death busy in the midst of us, and souls going down from our doors into a joyless and blasted immortality, ought to present our life-blood, if need be, for the cause of Christ, and for the good of souls. Let the scoffers spurn at us as they will; we are far superior to such poor contumely. Heaven applauds our enthusiasm, and we can vindicate it in the Apostle's words: "If we be beside ourselves, it is to God; and if we be sober, it is for your cause."

VII.

THE CHRISTIAN'S INHERITANCE.

"Whom have I in heaven but thee? and there is none upon earth that I desire beside thee. My flesh and my heart faileth: but God is the strength of my heart, and my portion forever."—PSALM lxxiii. 25, 26.

"MY flesh and my heart faileth." Who does not understand that? It is the common lot—the uniform and continual experience of the race. "The voice said, Cry. And he said, What shall I cry? All flesh is grass, and all the goodliness thereof is as the flower of the field; the grass withereth, the flower fadeth, because the spirit of the Lord bloweth upon it; surely the people is grass." This announcement of mortality, coming thus solemnly in a voice from heaven, finds its echo in the experience of mortals themselves; for however they may attempt to disguise it—with whatever study, perseverance, and hypocrisy they may conceal their feelings—it is an undeniable and startling truth that the living know that they must die. Death, my brethren, is a theme of mighty import. Eloquence has been exhausted upon the wide-spread magnitude of its desolation; there is not a place where human beings congregate which does not tell them that they are mortal. Is it a family?

Death enters and makes household memories painful, and turns home into the dwelling of the stranger. Is it a market-place? It is a busy, stirring throng which fills it as ever, but they are new faces that meet the eye, new voices which fall upon the ear. Is it a congregation? Our fathers, where are they? The prophets, do they live forever? Is it a world? Every thirty years its mighty heart is changed in continual supercession; one generation comes upon the heels of another, and the bones of our fathers form the dust on which we tread. And yet, strange to say, there is an almost universal listlessness upon the subject, and the saying of the poet seems well-nigh to be verified, that

> "All men think all men mortal but themselves."

Look at the man of the world—does not he seem as if he thought he should live forever—as if he thought only on the paltry, perishable matters with which he happens to be surrounded? Circumstances may indeed now and then occur in his history which may compel a transient recognition of eternity: his eye may perhaps rest upon the Bible, or a funeral procession may cross his path as he walks the streets of the city, or a passing bell, with its slow and solemn tolling, may break suddenly upon his ear, and the thought comes on his mind for a moment that there may possibly be such a thing as death. But it was but for a moment; it was a stray thought of eternity—one whose advances are at once forbidden as an unwelcome intruder; he was ruffled for awhile—taken aback for an instant—but time passed away, and he has become as still, and as slumbering, and as senseless as before. Brethren, we might rebuke that insensibility from the records of ancient history. It is recorded of Alexander, the conqueror of one world, that he wept because there was no other world to conquer. Alas! men now-a-days have sadly degenerated; they have no such ambition, they mourn over no such cause of grief. However, there is, brethren, whether men reck of it or not, there is another world to conquer. The battle is not with the confused noise of war, or garments rolled in blood; the enemies are not flesh and blood, but principalities and powers, and the rulers of the darkness of this world, and spiritual wickedness in high places. The prize is not an earthly crown, but a kingdom of whose brilliancy the Macedonian never knew. Yet many never enter this battle-field, and many who do, after a few brief and ineffectual struggles, grow tired, and ingloriously lay down their arms. Brethren, we are anxious that you should not be thus cowardly in the day of battle; we would have you quit yourselves like men and be strong; and we know of nothing that is better calculated to arouse your fortitude and bring into play that high and fearless heroism which we are exhorted by the Apostle to add to our faith, than the consolation of the words of the text, bringing before us, as they do, the Christian's personal inheritance, and hope, and future prospects: "Whom have I in heaven but thee? and there is none upon earth that I desire beside thee. My flesh and my heart faileth: but God is the strength of my heart, and my portion forever."

We need not spend time in endeavoring to prove to you, that it is one characteristic of the wicked that "God is not in all his thoughts." He may not go so far as openly to deny either his being or intelligence, but could you search his heart you would discover it to be a matter of the supremest indifference. A faint whisper of the Divine existence never obtrudes itself into his schemes, whether of aggrandizement or pleasure; and he is content, so far as he is concerned, to enjoy the uncared-for inheritance of this world. Nay, oftentimes his presumption is more galling and flagrant still: aspiring to be his own deity, he pays homage to himself, and with Eastern devotion does he worship at the shrine of his idol.

How, then, was this stray spirit to be won back to God? This was the question which engaged the Divine attention, and the answer to which became to the angelic host a matter of mystery and wonder. The law was undoubtedly powerless; it had been broken, its requirements flagrantly violated, and wherever man went it proscribed him a fugitive and a rebel. Moreover, it is the tendency of the law rather to irritate than to heal—rather to beget unfriendliness than tenderness toward the law-giver in the breast of the criminal. Hence you may bring God before the sinner's mind in his character of a God of judgment; you may manifest to the sinner the frowns of his angry countenance; you may collect all the arguments of terror which language can gather, and you may arm these arguments of terror with additional energy by descanting on the thunder of his power; you may set before him the horrible spectacle of his own impending death, and the unknown horrors of that eternity which is on the other side; you may disquiet him with all these appliances (and it is quite right he should be disquieted); you may induce a partial reformation of life and character (and it is necessary that he should reform); you may set him trembling at the power of the lawgiver (and a thousand times rather let him tremble than sleep); but where, in the midst of all this, is there obedience to the first and great commandment? Is the love of God shed abroad in his heart? Has it dawned upon the darkness of his mind? has its gentle influence acted like a salutary and composing charm over his alarmed breast? No; all your appliances have failed, there has been no conviction implanted except the conviction of fear. The thunders of executive justice and the power of judicial vengeance have failed to impress his heart; there it is, like a fortress, firm, impregnable, granite-like on its adamantine rock; and that which was intended to draw the soul into closer communion to God, has only driven him to a more hopeless distance from God. How, then, was this stray spirit to be won back to God? Oh, brethren, "what the law could not do, in that it was weak through the flesh, God sending his own Son in the likeness of sinful flesh"—mark the words; not in the *reality* of sinful, but in the *likeness* of sinful, though in reality of human —"in the likeness of sinful flesh, and for sin, condemned sin in the flesh." By the mysterious incarnation of the Mighty One all difficulties were removed. The dignity of the throne remained unsullied, while the milder beams of mercy were made to fall upon it; and God could at once be just, and yet the free and generous justifier of them that believe in Jesus. The all-comprising offering of the Saviour's blood made at once an atonement, an at-one-ment between God and man. The moment the man exercises faith in Christ the reconciliation is complete. The Lord is his defence; the holy one of Israel his refuge; and he who a while ago was an alien, unredeemed and desolate—a worthy companion of the beast in his lair, a fit follower on the serpent's trail—is now clothed, in his right mind, careering along in the enterprise of godliness, a fellow-citizen of saints and of the household of God. And this brings us immediately to speak of our present meditation, God as the recompense of the believing soul. "Whom have I in heaven but thee? and there is none upon earth that I desire beside thee."

We find three thoughts, my dear brethren, which tend forcibly to impress this matter upon our minds.

I. In the first place, GOD IS THE CHRISTIAN'S INHERITANCE AS THE LIGHT OF HIS INTELLECT. There is nothing for which man is more accountable than for his possession of mind—for his improvement and abuse of those powers with which the mind is gifted. It is a beneficent gift from a beneficent Being, but, then, by partaking of the nature of the immortal, it entails upon him the responsibilities of an immortal also. Few are the subjects which it cannot penetrate; difficulties but urge it to a course of loftier efforts, and, like the avalanche of snow, it gains additional momentum from the obstacles that threaten to impede it. Our position is this: Mind never finds its level, never finds its rest, until it is fixed upon the things above; active, inquiring, speculative, impassioned; like the eagle towering from his eyrie on the cliff, its course is right upward to the sun, and in the beams of uncreated light alone it finds its home, and its kindred, and its joy. The great purpose of man in the present world is to pass from a passive to an active state of being. And it is, in fact, this transition, effected by the agency of the Holy Spirit, which is that regeneration of which Scripture speaks. By nature, man is under the dominion of habit; the Spirit brings him under the dominion of principle. By nature, a man exercises himself in all his doing without reference to God; in grace, the Spirit dwells in the heart as the sanctifier and the guide. By nature, a man, under temporary impulses of master-passions, may put forth energies which awe a world, but they are of the earth, earthy; but the Spirit, so to speak, implants heavenly ideas in his mind, and he gets power and capacity to think of God. By nature, the man cleaves to the dust, is conversant only with what is contemptible and low, and at last sinks into perdition; in grace he draws himself up to his full stature, asserts his native royalty, and, as a heaven-born and heaven-tending subject, claims kindred with the King of the other world. In fine, by nature the man walks in darkness, the shadows of the night are around him, and he knoweth not whither he goeth; in grace, the morning has broken delightfully on the steps of the traveller, and he is revived and invigorated by the light of day.

Brethren, there is one point here which, if you are all like-minded with myself, you will hail with no common satisfaction. I am loth to part with those I love; I am loth to regard them as strangers, because they change their residence, and are just gone to live on the other side of the stream. I won't pay death the compliment of telling him he has divided the Church. He cannot do that. There is only one army of the living God:

> "Part of the host have crossed the flood,
> And part are crossing now;"

but it is one army; there is but one body growing up into Christ—its living head. The head and the upper members in heaven, the lower members on earth; but it is but one system and one body; and at no very distant period the whole body shall be drawn into the upper sanctuary, and stand out to the gaze of the admiring universe in the full stature of the perfect man. I hail with joy, therefore, anything that has a tendency to bring me even in thought near to the loved and gone before. I welcome as the visit of a ministering angel the voice of kindness which brings me tidings from the realms where my friends are reposing.

The thought, then, that gives me such satisfaction, is this, that now, even now, clogged as we are by the frailty and weakness of the body, we and those departed ones who have died in the faith are walking in the same light. We are told that the Lord is the light of his people in heaven; we know that the Lord is the light of his people on earth. We are told that the glory of the Lord is the sole illumination of the heavenly Jerusalem; we know that the glory of the Lord illuminates the earthly Zion; the lamp of light above, the spirit of light beneath—the same light, for they are both God. There is a beauty in this conception—don't you see it?—because it gives us the notion of alliance; it repudiates the idea of this earth of ours as cast off from God's fatherhood, a shrouded and forgotten thing. It takes hold of it in its degradation, and fastens round it one end of the chain, the other end of which is bound to the throne of the Everlasting himself. And, oh! is it not a beautiful thought, ay, while here to-night in the sanctuary we are opening our Bibles, and imploring the Spirit of God to shine down upon the truth, faith looks through the clouds—and they are very thin ones—and sees a host of bright spirits above, engaged in the same employment, desiring to look into the same things. We are one with them after all. The light may fall, the light does fall, with a more gushing flood-tide upon their eyes, but it is the same light. There they are, with the Great Teacher in the midst of them, poring everlastingly upon the tale of pleading love. Such students and such a teacher, who would not join; and, as the light of the intellect, adopt at once and forever the words of the text: "Whom have I in heaven but thee? and there is none upon the earth that I desire beside thee."

II. And then again, God is the Christian's inheritance, not only as the light of his intellect, but as the refuge of his conscience. Whenever human nature reflects on God, it must reflect on him as an object of distrust and dread. We think of him as a being of unimagined power, of enormous power; we are ignorant, moreover, how he stands affected toward us—and the fancy of ignorance will always be found to be the fancy of fear. The uncertainty in which the manner of his existence is shrouded, the vast extent of his creation, the wise and sage policy of his government, the retirement in which he dwells, the clouds and darkness that are round about his footstool, the inscrutable majesty which surrounds his throne—all these things have a tendency to inspire us with alarm, so that we may say with Job, "When I consider, I am afraid of him." The case might have been different in the primeval paradise, when the Lord walked in the garden in the cool of day; but ever since he has withdrawn himself from mortal society, mortals view him with dismay; and the Athenians only spoke the language of unassisted reason, when they reared their altar "to the unknown God."

And if we appeal to nature, to the external world, to remove this distrustfulness of God, we shall find ourselves but little benefited. This, you know, is one of the very tritest prescriptions of the Theophilosophers and Latitudinarians of the present day. "Go to nature," they say; "look at the external world; see everything around you; look there, and see written with pleasing characters that one great lesson of the universe, that God is love." Well, I will go to the external world, if such is to be the theme. I look around me, and I discover many things upon which the eye can gaze, to which the ear can listen, upon which the heart can dwell, which rejoices me when I think that the God that made them all is surely a God of love. There are the smiling landscapes, and beautiful enamelled earth, and soft music of the summer's breeze, and the loud laugh of the bounding stream, and the innocence of domestic enjoyments and ennobling principles, and the peace and love and animation which cluster around the hearth-stone of many a cottage home. Oh, it is a delightful thought that the God who made all these things, is surely a God of love! Ah, but then there are the sweeping floods, and the resistless tempests, and the mighty thunder, and the jealousies and heart-burnings of domestic society, and the wholesale slaughters of aggressive war, and the wrath of the devouring pestilence, and, to crown all, death, grim and ghastly death, crushing the generations as the moth is crushed. What am I to believe, but that the God of the universe is a mighty judge? Nature can tell me nothing then. She just tosses my poor mind about in the most distressing alternations, first of confidence, and then of dread. And yet often when the mild voice of Christianity—rather of natural religion—assures me that God is love, I am not disposed to believe it. But then there is a reason for this. This is not, like the other, conjured up out of the land of shadows, the mere result of man's intellect or of speculation and theories; it has its base and origin in the secrecies of his own nature. The fact is, in every mind there is a law of right and wrong, and along with it a consciousness that that law has been habitually violated. There is a restless apprehension of the law and the Law-giver, a dread foreboding of guilt and judgment; and a man cannot believe that God is love, while his conscience tells him that that God is to be viewed as an enemy. The comforting voice of reason and of religion may testify to the benevolence of God in heaven; but so long as there is a secret misgiving within—so long as there is the yet unsettled controversy between his Maker and himself, all ideas of confidence are banished from his mind, and, like Adam of old, in the very slyness of his crime, he would hide himself from his Maker among the trees of his garden.

And here it is that Christianity comes to our assistance, just as she always does when we most need her, and one feels the force of those deep and thrilling words—"Behold the Lamb of God, that taketh away the sins of the world." This told of a Saviour, and a Saviour who has borne his cross and carried his sorrow, the man looks about him for the unwonted spectacle, puts off his fainting for awhile, gazes at the illustrious victim, and "Who is it?" he cries: "who is that mighty one that has come down to the rescue? Who is it that has agonized in the garden, that has bled under the scourge, and died upon the cross? Who is it?" Why, who should it be but the very Being whom he has so basely and so ungratefully insulted? and with the grace of love and the tenderness of the man Christ Jesus, there is blended the majesty of the King of kings. Oh, he cannot doubt after that; that is an argument likely to overturn all his skepticism. He looks at the cross, and sees that God is righteous; but he looks at the Crucified, and he sees that God is love; and, with clasped hands and streaming eyes and grateful heart, he sings, "Whom have I in heaven but thee? and there is none upon earth that I desire beside thee."

III. And then, again, GOD IS THE CHRISTIAN'S INHERITANCE, ALSO AS THE REST OF HIS SOUL. The restlessness of human ambition has become proverbial. It is grasping as the leech, insatiable as the grave. The moment one scheme has succeeded, it pants for the enjoyment of another. The moment it has scaled one eminence of fancied bliss, its cry is "up," ay, from the summit of the Alps. "O that I had the wings of the dove, and then would I fly away and be at rest." This restless craving for something better than earth, although it is the companion of our fallen nature, very plainly tells us an important truth—that the earth and its concerns can never satisfy an immortal spirit. It pants for something higher, something more refined, something more intellectual, something more like God. That which alone can satisfy, can fill the immortal mind, must be something in which it can feel secure, and something with which it can be satisfied; for to be secure is to be safe, and to be satisfied is to be happy.

1. Take the first thought, then—that of *security*. We are in a dangerous world; at every step of our track we feel the necessity of celestial guardianship, and that tutelary and sustaining influences should be shed upon us from on high. Well, let us once get it into our hearts—not into our heads simply by an intellectual conviction, but into our hearts as a happy alliance—let us get it into our hearts that the Lord is our defence and the Holy One of Israel our refuge, and what can make us afraid? Omnipotence pledged in our behalf! Why, the very idea should make heroes of us all! He may, he most likely will have to pass through the furnace; the hand of affliction may be laid upon him; the wind may sweep swiftly over the desert, rocking to and fro the canvas tents of his earthly shelter; but you can hear him crying in the pauses of the storm—"It is the Lord; let him do what seemeth to him good." He

may have to suffer the bitterness of bereavement; death may deprive him of the beloved of his soul; there may be the breaking up of the domestic homestead; the fresh laceration of the already bleeding spirits, and the tearing asunder of hearts that have grown together; but, in the midst of this unparalleled suffering, you can hear his unmoved faith, saying—"The Lord gave, and *the Lord* hath taken away"—not the Chaldæan, nor the Sabean, nor the whirlwind, nor the flood—"THE LORD hath taken away. Blessed be the name of the Lord." A fiercer flood may roll upon him, a heavier wave may threaten to overwhelm him, the fires of vengeance may be poured on his head, but even in death's grasp his failing voice is heard—"Though he slay me, yet will I trust in him. Whom have I in heaven but thee? and there is none upon earth that I desire beside thee."

2. And then take the next thought, that of *happiness.* The question of man's chief good has been in all ages speculated upon and determined. All the theorizers on the subject have been convinced of this—that it could consist in nothing inferior. And so far they are right. That which alone can fill the immortal mind, must have some analogy to the constitution of that mind; and it must therefore be steadfast, proof against the fitfulness of ever-changing circumstances; not here to-day and vanished when we need it to-morrow; not present in the summer time when the breezes blow, and failing in the winter time when the blast of the hurricane comes down; but steadfast, always the same and always avail-

able. And it must be progressive, keeping pace with the soul, lasting as long as the soul, keeping abreast with it in its triumphal march to holiness and God. Well, there are many candidates in the field. Just bring them to the test-stone for awhile. Pleasure is a candidate, and she brings before the soul a very glowing description of herself and her ways. She tells him that the voice of the siren shall make music in his ears, and that the loud laugh of festivity shall be heard in his dwelling, that the voice of song and dance and carnival shall yield him succession of delight. But he asks, "Is she steadfast?" And he hears that she never enters the chambers of sorrow, has no comfort for the dark slumber and hopeless winter of age. A bird of passage, she flaps her giddy wings in the sunshine, but at the first approach of the stormy season speeds her flight into more favored climes. Then honor is a candidate, and she tells him of a wreath of laurels, of the swellings of the heart as it listens to its own praise, and of the untold happiness of being the conversation of the world. But he asks, "Is she steadfast?" And they tell him that chaplets of distinction often fade in a night; they tell him that the most fickle thing in the fickle universe is popular applause—how the same lips that shouted "Hosanna to the Son of David!" shouted shortly afterward, "Crucify him! crucify him!" and how the mob-idol of to-day has often been the mob-victim of to-morrow. Then wealth is a candidate; and she tells him of the pleasure of hoarding, of the joys of possession, of the pomp, and power, and flattery, and obsequiousness which money can procure. But he asks, "Is she steadfast?" He hears that she brings with her her own discontent; that the cares of keeping are worse than the cares of getting; that often in times of panic, like the scared eagle, wealth takes to itself wings and flies away; and even if a man enjoy it all his life long, though failure and panic may not come to strip the lord of his property, death shall come and strip the property of its lord.

Well, then, after all these, the joys of earth, have been tried and severally found wanting, God brings his claims before the mind, offering to be the soul's refuge and everlasting home. True itself, it does not shrink from the test. God's aids are steadfast, they avail in the winter as well as in the summer; in the dark season of adversity as well as when the sun shineth on the path; when frost depresses the spirit as well as when sunshine fills it with laughter; when friends troop up and when friends forsake equally; when fortune smiles and when the world turns the cold shoulder. Are they always the same? Are they not? Oh! if the decorums of the sanctuary would permit it to-night, are there not many of you who could rise up in your deep baptism of sorrow and sing in the words of the poet?—

"When our sorrows most increase,
Then his richest joys are given;
Jesus comes in our distress,
And agony is heaven."

Are they progressive? Will they last as long as the soul? Will they keep young as it does, and keep pace with it as it travels along toward holiness and God? Oh, yes! for before all the immense and varied landscape of blessings upon which the eye can rest, existed the fullness of Deity; beyond it, stretching forth, a broad, fathomless infinity—

> " An ocean of love and of power,
> Which neither knows measure nor end."

3. Passing over several topics that might be worthy of our meditation, just let us glance for a moment at the *support offered to the Christian in the hour and article of death.* Come with me, then, will you? it will do you good. Come with me to the Christian's death-bed; and if there is a cold-hearted and skeptical infidel of your acquaintance, bring him with you, that he may learn at once the worthlessness of human pride and the glory of the God of love. Stretched upon a couch lies the poor sufferer—

> " Whose weak, attenuated frame
> Shows naught of being but a name."

Is this the man—is this the being who but a little while ago towered in all the strength of his pride? Is this clenched hand that which clasped yours in friendship but a little while ago? Ah, how true it is that he cometh forth as a flower and is cut down! But what is it fills that closing eye with such unwonted brightness? What is it that kindles that pallid cheek into such angelic animation? Ah! there is a mightier than you, and a mightier than death; there is God in that death-chamber. There is an awe and a solemnity which tells of the presence of God. Listen! listen to the unfaltering firmness with which that voice sings: "My flesh and my heart faileth; but God is the strength of my heart and my portion forever." Is that enthusiasm? Are these the accents of frenzy? Does madness talk so calmly? Has the prospect of dissolution no chilling influence? Can a fictitious excitement support the soul at such an hour? Ah! that is a stout-hearted hypocrisy that can brave the agony of dying. But here is triumph in death. Stoicism boasts of her examples; patriotism has a long list of worthies, for whom the world has woven garlands of undying bloom. But here is a man, a poor, frail, erring, insignificant man, going with his eyes open, with the full consciousness of his position, down the dark valley, to meet, to grapple with, and to master his last enemy. There is a spectacle of the morally sublime that I challenge the wide universe to equal. And this sublime spectacle is not of the wisdom of men; it is just the power of God. But while we have been talking about him, the man has died; the last convulsion is past; the last breath is drawn; the last pulse has completed its feeble throb—

"Oh change, oh wondrous change!
  There lies the soulless clod:
The sun eternal breaks; the new immortal wakes—
  Wakes with his God."

There is high festivity in the realms of the blest at the accession of another member to the rejoicing family. And the harpers harping with their harps rest in their music awhile, and the angels, who pry forever into the mysteries of God, take holiday from their researches for awhile, and all heaven is gathered to witness the coronation of the rejoicing believer as the crown is placed on his head by the Master for whom he has done and suffered so much. Ah! what strange act is that? He takes the crown and casts it again at the feet of the giver, and he says, assigning his reason—listen, we shall hear, for the music is still just now—what is it? "Ah, Lord, the harp, and the robe, and the crown, and the palm, what are all these to me? These are only the appendages of the recompense. Thou art my reward; thou art my portion; whom have I in heaven itself but thee?" And then the harpers harping with their harps break out again, they can hold in no longer, and heaven is filled as with an irrepressible gush of melody, "Not unto us, not unto us, but unto thy name be all the glory." And that is the end. Who does not say, "Let me die the death of the righteous, and let my last end be like his?" Ah, but there are many people that pray that prayer, who would like to die the death of the righteous, but who do not like to live the life of the righteous. But they go together; believe me they go together. If you would die the death of the righteous, you must live the life of the righteous, even a life of faith in the Son of God, "who hath loved you and given himself for you." There are some in this assembly to-night, who are not living the life of the righteous; you have not given yourselves unto Christ and his people, and there is no hope of that death for you.

There is another death which I dare not trust myself to describe—scenes of agony over which I draw the veil—the very thought of which freezes the vitals and curdles the blood! Oh! come to Jesus; do not tempt upon yourselves any such doom as that. Get Christ for you all. "I live," as says the rejoicing Apostle; "yet not I, but Christ liveth in me"—so shall everything lead you up to God. It could not lead you to undervalue the life you now live; it would not make you love less this beautiful world; everything around you will only have mystic meanings which will be interpreted only by Christ; you will be led thus from nature up to nature's God. Then, as you pass through scenes of beauty and blessedness, your full heart, taking refuge in the language of poesy, will sing—

"Lord of earth, thy forming hand
Well this beauteous frame hath planned:
Woods that wave, and hills that tower,
Ocean rolling in its power;
All that strikes the gaze unsought,
All that charms the lonely thought.
Yet, amid this scene so fair,
Oh! if thou wert absent there,
What were all those joys to me;
Whom have I on earth but thee?"

Then, travelling through the path of your pilgrimage, God, your own God, will bless you, and will wipe away all tears from your faces, and will uplift you in the endurance and prepare you for the duties of life; and your pilgrimage will go on calmly; mellow eventide will come upon you, yet at eventide there shall be light. The last stroke will be struck, the last enemy encountered, the last change realized, and amid the ranks of the ransomed you pass to pay your first homage to the throne, and even then, taking refuge again in the language of poesy, will your thoughts be the same—

"Lord of heaven, beyond our sight
Rolls a world of purer light;
Where, in love's unclouded reign,
Parted hands are clasped again;
Martyr's there and seraphs high,
Blest and glorious company!
While immortal music rings
From unnumbered seraph strings.
Oh, that scene is passing fair!
Yet if thou wert absent there,
What were all those joys to me?
Whom have I in heaven but thee?"

May God bring us all to sing that song forever, for his name's sake.

VIII.

THE HEAVENLY CONQUEROR.

"And I saw, and behold a white horse; and he that sat on him had bow; and a crown was given unto him; and he went forth conquering and to conquer"—Rev. vi., 2.

How animating is the sound of war! How easily can it awaken the ardors of the unrenewed and unsanctified heart of man! There is no profession in which he can gain more renown and applause than in the profession of arms. It is the birthplace of what men call glory. Custom has baptized it honorable; it carries with it a pomp and a circumstance of which other professions are destitute; it has nerved the arm of the patriot, it has fired the genius of the painter, it has strung and swept the poet's lyre; nations have bowed before its shrine, and even religion has prostituted herself to bless and consecrate its banners. Yet it must not be forgotten that for the most part human conquerors are just murderers upon a grand scale—mighty butchers of human kind. Their victories are won amid extermination and havoc; their track is traced in ruin; there is human life upon their laurels; and if they wish to acquire a name, they have got one; let them glory as they can in its possession—the voice of blood proclaims it from the ground, and it is vaunted from earth to heaven by the wailings of orphaned hearts, and by the deep execrations of despair. The sacred writings, however, tell us of one conqueror whose victories were peacefully achieved, whose battles were bloodlessly won; or if his onward march was discolored by blood, it was *his own.* It is the Lord Jesus Christ who is thus evidently set before us; he who "died the just for the unjust, that he might bring us to God." In the fulfillment of the various duties connected with the mediatorial office which he had undertaken, he is frequently represented as going out to battle against his adversaries, as routing them by the word of his mouth, and returning in exultation and triumph. Instances of this you will easily and at once remember. Thus, in the forty-fifth Psalm: "Gird thy sword upon thy thigh, O most mighty, with thy glory and thy majesty. And in thy majesty ride prosperously because of truth and meekness and righteousness; and thy right hand shall teach thee terrible things." Again, in the eleventh chapter of Luke: "When a strong man armed keepeth his palace, his goods are in peace: but when a stronger than he shall come upon him and overcome him, he taketh from him all his armor wherein he trusted, and divideth his spoils." And yet, again, according to the mysterious apocalypses of the Book of Revelation, "Then shall all make war with the Lamb, and the Lamb shall overcome them." It matters not how numerous or how powerful his enemies may be—alike over the powers of darkness with their legioned hosts of foes—alike over the corruption of the human heart with all its ramifications of depravity—alike over the false systems into which the corruption has retreated, as into so many garrisoned and fortified towns, "a crown is given unto him, and he goeth forth conquering and to conquer." It is not my intention to enter into all the details of this interesting and absorbing strife. I should just like to concentrate your attention upon one phase of the conflict—the battle of the old serpent the devil, the great origin of evil, under whose generalship the others are mustered, and to whose commands they submittingly bow. Behold, then, the combat beyond all others important—*the combat between Christ and Satan for the human soul*, and, as you trace the progress of the fight, remember with encouragement, and say that "He goeth forth conquering and to conquer." It will be necessary, in order that we have the whole matter before us, that we introduced the *cause* of strife, the *battle*, and the *victory*.

I. As to the cause of strife. You know that when the all-comprising benevolence of God found heaven too small for the completion of his vast designs, this earth arose in order and in beauty from his forming hands. After by his Spirit he had garnished the heavens, and scattered upon the fair face of nature the labor of his hand and the impress of his feet, as the fairest evidence of Divine workmanship, the last and most excellent of his works below, he made man in his own image, after his own likeness. The soul, then, was the property of him by whom it was created, who imparted to it its high and noble faculties, by whom, notwithstanding its defilement, it is still sustained, and from whom proceed the retributions which shall fix its doom forever. Man was created in possession of that moral purity, that absolute freedom from sin, which constituted of itself assimilation to his Maker's image. And so long as he retained that image, so long was he the Divine property, and the Divine portion alone. But the moment he sinned, the moment of the perversion of his nature, of the estrangement of his faculties, of the alienation of his heart, he came under a different tenure, and became a vassal of a different lord.

Satan himself, once an inhabitant of the high realms of glory, but hurled from that giddy height for disobedience and pride, was mysteriously permitted to tempt our first parents in the garden, with the full knowledge, on their part, that, standing as they did in their representative, and public character, if they fell the consequences of that one transgression were entailed upon all their posterity. With the circumstances of the original temptation you are of course familiar, and the issue of it you have in that one verse in the book of Genesis: "Because thou hast done this, thou art cursed above all cattle, and above every beast of the field; upon thy belly shalt thou go, and dust shalt thou eat all the days of thy life." This tells us of the contravention—the direct contravention—of a known law: a law which God, as the supreme Creator, had a perfect right to institute; a law which man, as a dependent creature, was under binding obligations to obey. It was instituted avowedly as a test of obedience; and this is all we would answer to the labored sarcasms of foolish infidelity. Any wayfaring man, though a fool, can curl his lip and declaim against the insignificance of the act from which such mighty issues sprang; but he forgets that the moment the temptation was yieled to, there was in human nature a very incarnation of the devil. Under that demoniacal possession the man was prepared for any infraction, from the eating of the forbidden fruit to the subversion of an almighty throne; and he who, under such circumstances, would violate a known command, however trifling, would not, if the circumstances had been equal, have shrunk away from the endeavor to scale the battlements of heaven, and pluck the crown of divinity from the very brow of the Eternal. Hence it was, by yielding to the suggestions of the tempter, and to his infamous temptation, that the portals of the palace were flung wide open for the strong man armed to enter; and hither, alas! he came with all his sad and fearful train, enthroning himself upon the heart, setting up his image, as Bunyan hath it, in the market-place of the town of Man-soul; fortifying every avenue, filling every chamber, corrupting every faculty, enervating every inhabitant, and announcing every moment the symbols of his own resolve to grasp and hold it forever. Here then is in brief the cause of this celestial strife. The soul, a colony of heaven, had been taken usurped possession of, by the powers of hell, and the effort to restore it to allegiance was the main cause of this celestial war.

Still further to impress you with the weighty causes of the strife, let us remind you for a moment of the character of the government thus by daring usurpation acquired. The dominion which Satan exercises over the human soul is *despotic* in its character. He is not a monarch, he is an autocrat; he admits no compromise, he brooks no rival, he pours his uncleanness upon every part, and reigns supremely over every power and every faculty of man. True, the man is not always conscious of his slavery; that is one of the cunningest secrets of his power, that he persuades his vassals that they are free, and their offended language to any one who questions the fact is, "We be Abraham's children that were never in bondage to any man." He brands them as is own, and then, content to wear his badge, they may choose their own trappings. He has no uniform. Some of his soldiers are in rags and others in purple, and his very choicest veterans have stolen the livery of heaven. There is not one within the compass of the whole human family who is not subject to his authority, naturally led captive by the devil at his will. And then, this government of Satan over the human soul is not only despotic but *degrading*. Slavery in any form is essentially connected with degradation, and in the case before us the connection must be regarded as the most palpable and emphatic of all. The essence and exaltation of moral dignity are assimilations to the image of God. Whatever recedes from that image must of necessity debase and degrade. Now the course of man's life, as it has been, ever since the fall, a course of constant and increasing recession from God, presents a spectacle of moral degradation which is grievous to behold: the whole nature has fallen; the understanding has become darkened, and is conversant only with what is contemptible and low; the affections, which once soared sublimely upward, now cleave to worldly objects, objects that perish in the using; the passions have become loyal servants of the usurper, and keep their zealous patrol in the court-yard of his palace; the will, which once inclined to good, is now fierce and greedy after evil; imagination revels in fondest dalliance with sin for its paramour; and conscience, intoxicated with opiate draughts, and in that intoxication smitten with paralysis, gazes hopelessly upon the desolation; or if at times stirred by the spirit within, it breaks out with a paroxysm and terrifies the man with its thunder, he is persuaded to regard it as the incoherence of some meddling drunkard, or the ravings of some frantic madman. Such is the condition to which the usurpation of the evil one has reduced the human soul. It is first earthly, scraping its affluence or its pleasure together; and then, yet more degrading, there is the transformation that happened to Nebuchadnezzar, the heart of a man is taken out, and the heart of a beast is put in; and then, as like grows to like, and as a process of assimilation is constantly going on, it grows into its master's image; the mark of the beast becomes more distinct and palpable, every feature stands confessed of Satan's obscene and loathsome likeness, and there is a living proof of the truth of the scale upon which Scripture has graduated man's increasing degeneracy. First earthly, then sensual, then devilish. This is a fearful picture; is it not? Ah! you see the man, or his bacchanalian orgies, or his midnight prowl, but you do not see the fiend that dogs his steps and goads him to destruction. You see the degradation of the nature that once bore the image of God, but you do not see the jibing, mocking demon that is behind. You trace intelligibly enough the infernal brand, but you cannot hear the peals of infernal laughter as the arch-devil, looking down upon the soul that he has stormed, exults in the extremity of the disgrace and glories in the pollution of the fallen.

The government of Satan over the human soul is not only despotic and degrading, but *destructive.* Sin and punishment are inseparably allied; the powers of darkness, although mysteriously permitted a certain amount of influence, are themselves, in punishment, "reserved in chains under darkness until the judgment of the great day." A man who transgresses, since no coercion comes upon the freedom of his will, must necessarily be regarded as willful; he is under the curses of a violated law, nay, condemned altogether, for "the wrath of God abideth upon him." God will "pour out indignation, and wrath, and tribulation, and anguish upon every soul of man that doeth evil; upon the Jew first, and also upon the Gentile;" for there is no respect of persons with God. I am speaking to unconverted sinners to-night; to some of refined and delicate sensibility, shocked at the ribaldry of the vulgar, and at the licentiousness of the profane. I tell you there is no respect of persons with God. If you flee not to a high and mighty Redeemer, if you repose not in present reliance upon Christ, for you there remaineth nothing but a death whese bitterest ingredient is that it can never die, but that it has eternity about it, eternity beyond it, and eternity within it, and the curse of God, upon it, fretting it and following it forever.

Thank God, there is a promise of a perfect and delightful deliverance from this thralldom under which man has been groaning. Christ has come down on purpose to deliver and ransom him, and he goeth forth conquering and to conquer. In the counsels of the eternal Godhead, in foresight of the temptation of Satan and of the thralldom and depravity of man, Christ was induced to work out a counteracting scheme, by which, in the beautiful language of ancient prophecy, the prey of the mighty should be taken away and the lawful captive delivered. The first initiation of this scheme was given just when the first shadow of sin swept over the world. "The seed of the woman shall bruise the serpent's head." From that time there was a continued series of operations, in the good providence of God perpetuated for thousands of years, all tending to the fulfillment of this original promise, and the achievement of this original plan. At last, in the fullness of time—the time by prophet seers foretold, and by believing saints expected—in the fullness of time, the Son of God was incarnated in the nature that had sinned, and then it was that the battle in earnest began.

II. Look, then, at the Divine Saviour, "stronger than the strong man armed," invested with far higher qualifications, and wielding far mightier power. And how is this? He is the babe in Bethlehem, the rejected wanderer, the arraigned rebel, the scourged and spit upon, the Nazarene, the crucified. But these are only voluntary submissions, and in the deepest humiliation there slumbers Omnipotence within. "All power is given unto Me both in heaven and in earth," and this power is all enlisted upon the side of salvation and of mercy. It is not the power of the lightning, that blasts while it brightens; it is not the power of the whirlwind, whose track is only known by the carnage and desolation that it leaves behind it. It is the power of the water rill, that drops and drops, and in its dropping melts the most stern and difficult of nature's forces. It is the power of the light; it flows in energetic silence, you cannot hear it as it flows, and yet it permeates and illumines all. He is strong, but he is strong to deliver; he is mighty, but, in is own powerful language, he is "mighty to save." It often happens—it used to do so more frequently than it does now—in the history of the strifes of nations, and of the harsh scenes of war, that the interest of spectators was drawn aside from hostile ranks to two courageous champions, who separated themselves from opposing armies for single combat with each other, and the fate of armies appeared to the spectators as nothing compared with who should be the victor in this individual strife. O! conceive, if it were possible, a single combat between the rival princes of light and darkness, the grand, the transcendent, the immeasurable issue of which shall be the ruin or redemption of the human soul! I cannot limn it; I cannot bring it fairly before you; the subject is too mighty: and yet a thought or two may not inaptly illustrate the battle that is now before us.

See, then, the lists are spread; the champions are there. Eager angels crowd around, for they have an interest in the strife, and they are anxious to tune their harps to the anthems of regeneration again. Exulting demons are there, flushed with high hopes they dare not name, that vaunt of a ruined universe and of a peopled hell. This is no gentle passage at arms; this is no gorgeous tournament, or mimic fight, or holiday review; the destinies of a world of souls are trembling in the balance now—depend for weal or woe upon the issue of this mortal strife.

The first grapple seems to have been in the *temptation in the wilderness;* for at the commencement of our Saviour's public ministry the enemy endeavored to tempt the second Adam after the same fashion as he had tempted the first; and when wearied with labor, and exhausted with endurance and suffering from the pangs of hunger and of thirst, he brought before him a similar order of temptation to that which had been successful in the garden of Eden. Ah! but there was a mightier Adam in human flesh this time with whom he had to deal. Grasping the sword of the spirit, with its trenchant blade, he cut asunder the flimsy sophistries of the tempter's weaving, and the discomfited demon went baffled away; and angels came and ministered unto Jesus—fanned with their ambrosial wings his burning brow, and poured their offices of kindness upon his fatigued and sorrowing soul.

Defeated, but not conquered, the enemy returned to the charge; and the next grapple was in the *performance of miracles.* It is customary in ordinary warfare, you know, whenever a fortress is taken, for the conqueror to garrison it with some of his own soldiers, and leave some trusty captain in charge. The enemy appears to have acted upon this plan, and in token of his usurped authority over the human race, he caused certain of his servants to enter into the bodies of men. When Christ came into the world they brought unto him those that were grievously vexed with devils. He sat down before some of their Sebastopols of the evil one, and as speaking by that high exorcism, he at once dislodged the intruders; and as, some in moody silence, and others with piteous cries, they rushed out from the places they had agonized, we can trace in their complaining the confession of their defeat: "What have we to do with thee, Jesus, thou Son of God. Art thou come to torment us before the time?"

The next was the *death grapple*. And was the champion smitten? Did he bend beneath that felon's stroke? Was there victory at last for the powers of hell? Imagine, if you can, how there would be joy is the breast of the evil one when the Saviour expired; how he would exult at that victory which had more than recompensed the struggle of four thousand years. Hours roll on; he makes no sign; day and night succeed each other; there is no break upon the slumber—their victory appears complete and final. Shall no one undeceive them? No; let them enjoy their triumph as they may. It were cruel to disturb a dream like that, which will have so terrible an awaking. But we, brethren, with the light of eighteen hundred years streaming down upon that gory field, understand the matter better. He died, of course, for only thus could death be abolished; he was counted with transgressors, of course, for thus only could sin be forgiven; he was made a curse for us, of course, because thus ouly could he turn the curse into a blessing. O! to faith's enlightened sight there is a surpassing glory upon that cross. He was never so kingly as when girt about with that crown of thorns; there was never so much royalty upon that regal brow as when he said, "It is finished," and he died.

There only remains one more grapple, and that was in *the rising from the dead and ascension into heaven.* It is considered the principal glory of a conqueror, you know, not merely that he repels the aggressive attacks of his enemy, but when he carries the war into that enemy's camp and makes him own himself vanquished in the metropolis of his own empire. This Christ did by concealing himself for a while within the chambers of the grave. We cannot tell you much about the battle, for it was a night attack, it took place in darkness; but we can tell the issue, because on the morning of the third day the sepulchre was empty, and the Redeemer had gone forth into Galilee. This was only like the garnering up of the fruits of the conflict. The cross had settled it. It was finished when he said it was, upon the cross; but this was a sudden surprise in the camp, when the guards were drawn off, and the soldiers carousing in the flush of fancied victory. By death he had abolished death—him that had the power of death. By his resurrection he spoiled principalities and powers; and then he went up that he might "make a show of them openly." You can almost follow him as he goes, and the challenge is given as he rises and nears the gates of the celestial city: "Who is this that cometh from Edom with dyed garments from Bozra? this that is glorious in his apparel travelling in the greatness of his strength?" And then comes the answer: "I that speak in righteousness, mighty to save." "Lift up your heads, O ye gates; and be ye lifted up ye everlasting doors; and the King of glory shall come in. Who is this King of glory? The Lord strong and mighty, the Lord mighty in battle. Lift up your heads, O ye gates; even lift them up ye everlasting doors; and the King of glory shall come in."

> "And through the portals wide outspread
> The vast procession pours."

And on he marches through the shining ranks of the ransomed, until he gets to the throne and points to the captives of his bow and spear, and claims his recompense. And "there is silence in heaven;" and there is given unto him "a name that is above every name; that at the name of Jesus every knee should bow, and every tongue confess that he is Lord, to the glory of God the father." It is finished. Now he rests from his labors, and now he sheathes his sword, and now he wears his crown.

III. Just a word or two upon the victory that he gained. It was complete, it was benevolent, it was unchanging.

The attack which the Saviour made upon the enemy was such as to tear away the very sources and energies of his power. Mark how each fresh onset, whether from earth or hell, has only enhanced his glory and brightened the conqueror's crown. He vanquished in his own person by dying, and in the person of his followers he has continued to manifest that indestructible energy which was always manifest just when it seemed to be overthrown. Why, at the commencement of Christianity would not any one have thought that a breath would annihilate it and exterminate the name of its founder forever? And there they were—Cæsar on the throne, Herod on the bench, Pilate in the judgment-hall, Caiaphas in the temple, priests and soldiers, Jews and Romans, all united together to crush the Galilean, and the Galilean, overcame. And so it has been in all ages until now. Presecution has lifted up her head against the truth; war-wolves have lapped up the blood of God's saints, and for a time silenced the witness of confessors, and the testimony of the faithful has gone upward amid the crackling of fagots, and the ascending flame has been the chariot of fire in which rising Elijahs have mounted to heaven. And not merely is the completeness of this triumph manifested in the aggregate, but in the individual. Not only is every man brought into a salvable state, but every part of every man is redeemed. The poor body is not forgotten: it is taught to cast off the grave clothes and anticipate an everlasting residence in heaven. The mind crouches no longer; it emancipates itself from its vassalage and stands erect in the liberty wherewith Christ made it free. And the whole man, who was a while ago an alien, degraded and desolate, a fitting companion of the beast in his lair, a worthy follower in the serpent's trail, is now "clothed and in his right mind," careering along in the enterprises of godliness, a fellow-citizen with saints and the household of God.

And then the triumphs of the Saviour are *benevolent* too. Tell me not of human glory, it is a prostituted word. Tell me not of Agincourt, and Cressy, and Waterloo, and of the high places of Moloch worship, where men have been alike both priests and victims. One verse of the poet aptly describes them all:

> "Last noon beheld them full of lusty life,
> Last eve in beauty's circle proudly gay.
> The midnight brought the signal sound of strife;
> The morning marshalling in arms; the day
> Battle's magnificently stern array,
> The thunder clouds close o'er it, which when rent,
> The earth is covered quick with other clay,
> Which her own clay shall cover, heaped and pent,
> Rider and horse, friend and foe, in one rude burial blent."

But what is it to be seen in the time of the Lord's victory? Plains covered with traces of recent carnage, and of recent havoc? What is there to be heard in the time of the Lord's victory? Orphans wailing the dead, widows bemoaning those that have departed? No, but a voice breathing down a comfortable word to men: "They shall neither hurt nor destroy in all my holy mountain, saith the Lord." The procession of this conqueror consists of saved souls, and eternity shall consecrate the scene.

And then the triumphs of the Saviour are not only

complete and benevolent, but *unchanging*. The things that are now are very transitory. The sand of the desert is not more unstable; the chaff of the summer threshing-floor is not more helpless on the wind; but the Saviour's triumphs brighten with the lapse of time; their lustre time can tarnish not, nor death itself destroy. O! think of the multitude that have been already saved! think of the multitude who went up in the early ages of the Church with its enrichments of blessings; think of those who had been taken off to heaven before they ever had time to sin after the similitude of Adam's transgression—souls ransomed by the blood of atonement taken from birth under the wing of the quivering cherub right away into the realms of blessedness and rest; think of those from the time of the Saviour's incarnation until now who have passed through death triumphant home; think of the multitudes now upon earth that are working out their salvation with fear and trembling; think of the still greater multitudes that shall yet press into the Church in the times of its millennial glory, when the gates of it shall not be shut day or night, because there shall be no chance of shutting them, the people crowd in so fast. O what a Jubilee in heaven! O gathering of emancipated spirits! Limit the extent of the atonement! Who dares do it? Talk about Christ dying for a few scattered families of the sons of men merely! Why, it is to charge my Saviour with cowardice, and bring a slur upon his conduct in the field. If there be one solitary soul the wide universe through for whom Christ did not die, over that soul death has triumphed, and the conquest of my Saviour is imperfect and incomplete. O! he seems to stand in his triumphal chariot, in the very centre of the universe, with exulting heaven before and with tormented hell behind; and there is not an unconquered rebel there but the glad halleluiahs of the one, and the solemn acquiescences of the other, peal out the universe's anthem, "He is Lord of all."

And now which side are you? Pardon the abruptness of the question, but answer it to your consciences and to your God notwithstanding. Which side are you? There is no neutrality in this war, or if there be one here that intends to preserve a dastardly neutrality, he will get the hottest of the battle, and be exposed to the cross-fire of both sides. Which side are you? Do you belong to the Lord, or the Lord's enemies? Ask yourselves that question in the sight of God. I never knew, until I looked upon it in this aspect, the force and power of a certain question which the Saviour presented in the days of his flesh. I have admired the capacities of the human soul, that it has a memory that can recall the past, imagination that can penetrate the future: that it has a will that no man can tame, that it has immortality as its heritage. But I see all heaven in earnest there, and all hell in earnest yonder, and the prize of the conflict is one poor human soul; and then I see, as I never saw before, what an intensity of emphasis there is in the awful inquiry: "What shall it profit a man if he shall gain the whole world, and lose his own soul?" Brethren, how shall it be with you? "Whosoever therefore will be a friend of the world, is the enemy of God;" and the doom of the enemies of God is brought before us in the Bible: "Bring hither those mine enemies that would not I should reign over them, and slay them before me." On which side are you? There is one passage that I should just like to bring before you, which has always appeared to me to be one of the most fearful in the whole compass of the book of God: "When the unclean spirit is gone out of a man"—mark it, it does not say when he is driven out, it does not say when he is dispossessed by superior powers; but the awful idea, almost too awful to be entertained, is that there are some people in this world of ours of whom Satan is so sure that he can leave them for a while, perfectly certain that they will sweep and garnish his house in his absence, and prepare it for seven other spirits more inveterate and cruel—"When the unclean spirit is gone out of a man he walketh through dry places, seeking rest, and findeth none. Then he saith, I will return unto my house." O mockery of that quiet empire! "To *my* house." The tenancy has not changed; he knows full well there is too much love of the master's service in the heart of the man for that. "I will return into my house from whence I came out; and when he is come he findeth it empty, swept and garnished. Then goeth he, and taketh with himself seven other spirits more wicked than himself, and they enter in and dwell there; and the last state of that man is worse than the first." Oh horrible! horrible! Not merely to have Satan as a guest, but to sweep and garnish the house that he may come in, and that he may bring with him seven other spirits more wicked than himself. And are you doing that? Is there one in the presence of God to-night to whom this awful passage will apply? Oh, I thank God I can preach to you a present salvation in the name Jesus. Be delivered from that bondage of yours, for Christ has come down on purpose that he may deliver, and that he may rescue, and he goeth forth conquering and to conquer. "Ask, and it shall be given you; seek, and ye shall find; knock, and it shall be opened unto you." There is salvation for you from the power of death, and from the thralldom and ascendency of besetting sin, and from the grasp of the destroyer. There is salvation for you in Christ Jesus the Lord. Wherefore he is able to save to the uttermost of human guilt, to the uttermost of human life, to the uttermost of human time. May God help you, for Christ's sake.

IX.

THE CHRISTIAN'S DEATH, LIFE, PROSPECTS, AND DUTY.

"Set your affections on things above, not on things on the earth. For ye are dead, and your life is hid with Christ in God. When Christ, who is our life, shall appear, then shall ye also appear with him in glory."—COLLOSSIANS iii. 2, 3, 4.

IN the former part of this delightful and valuable epistle, the Apostle has been reminding the Colossians of their privileges, and the covenant blessings which they inherited in Christ. He tells them that they have entered upon a new dispensation, that the system of types and shadows has accomplished its purpose, and has been fulfilled, that their circumcision was of the heart, in the spirit, and not in the letter, and that they were "complete in Christ, who is the head of all principality and power." Lest, however, by these considerations, any of them should be exalted above measure, he urges them that they live unto God, tells them that, although freed from the yoke of ceremonial observance, their obligation to obey was as strict and as binding as ever, and though no longer impelled by slavish and spiritless fear, the love of Christ should con strain them to a closer evangelical obedience. There is no antinomianism, brethren, in the Gospel; it tells us that faith without works is dead; that however largely it may talk about its knowledge of the better land, however it may imagine itself to be exalted through the abundance of its revelations, if it do not work by love and purity of heart, if it do not exert a transforming influence upon the character and life, there is no soundness in it, and it is but a specious and delusive mimickry of the faith which saves. The Apostle, in impressing this fact upon their minds, takes hallowed ground; he seems to remind them of their privileges, that he may the more effectually insist upon their duty; and for the grandeur of their blessings, he urges their entire consecration to God. "If ye then be risen with Christ," if ye be merged from the obscurity of the old dispensation unto the strength and beauty of the new, if ye have power over sin, if, by virtue of communion with your Saviour, ye are justified by faith, sanctified by the Spirit, and travelling to heaven, "seek those things that are above;" be at home in heaven; let your desires cluster there, and let there be a gathering of your hopes around the throne; let your affections fasten upon that radiant seat "where Christ sitteth on the right hand of God." He then repeats the exhortation, and assigns reasons for its performance, in the language of the text, "Set your affections on things above, not on things on the earth. For ye are dead, and your life is hid with Christ in God. When Christ, who is our life, shall appear, then shall ye also appear with him in glory."

There are four things presented to us in these words: the Christian's death, the Christian's life, the Christian's prospects, and the Christian's duty; an ineffable blending of precept and promise, upon which, for a few moments, it may profit us to dwell.

I. The first thing that strikes us, is the Christian's death. "For," says the Apostle, "ye are dead." Is not this somewhat of a paradox? Does not Christ say expressly, that he came not to destroy men's lives, but to save them? Was it not one of the purposes of his coming, that we might have life, and that we might have it more abundantly? Was it not one of the designs of his incarnation, that from the fountain of his own underived existence, he might replenish the veins of man, even to life everlasting? And yet, when we enter upon his service, the very first thing we are told to do is to die. Who shall solve the enigma? Only the Scripture, by becoming, as it always does, the authorized and satisfactory interpreter of itself. In St. Paul's Epistle to Timothy, you find this remarkable expression: "She that liveth in pleasure is dead while she liveth." You have no difficulty in understanding that to mean dead in spiritual things. In that pleasure-loving heart there beats no pulse for God; in that spirit, around which the world has flung the spells of its witchery, there is no desire for heaven; the pleasures of sense engross it, and, although compassed by the realities of the other world, its very existence is treated as a question or a fable. Now, just the reverse of this, morally considered, will explain to us the state of the Christian when the Apostle tells us he is dead. The fact is, that between the flesh and the spirit, there is a bitter and irreconcilable enmity; the one cannot exist in the presence and by the side of the other. That which has been garnished for the temple of the Lord, must not be profaned by an idol. Distinct and solemn, and authoritative is the inspired announcement, "Whosoever will be the friend of the world is the enemy of God." Impiety has entered into an unholy compact to amalgamate these two, to adjust their claims, to give them a division of service; but it is a covenant with death—it shall be disannulled; it is an agreement with hell—it shall not stand. Religion peals out her refusal of such reluctant allegiance, lays the grasp of her claim upon the entire nation, and tells us in tones of power, "Ye can not serve God and mammon." The Christian, then, who is a Christian indeed, regards the world as if it were not, and continually endeavors to exemplify that his life and conversation are in heaven. His differences from the world may not, indeed, be apparent to a superficial observer; he goes to and fro among the people like other men; he takes an interest in the ever-shifting concerns that are passing in the world around him; and yet he is dead to the world all the while. How are you to find it out? Try him with some question of difficulty; set his duty before him, and let that duty be painful, and let it involve some considerable deprivation of gain or of pleasure; and with self-sacrificing devotion, he will obey the truth, and glory in the trial. Mark him in the midst of circumstances of discouragement and woe, when waters of a full cup are wrung out to him; he is sustained by an energy of which the world wotteth not, nerved with a principle to which it is an utter stranger; richer blood animates him, loftier inspirations sparkle from his eye, and though surrounded by the things of sense, and of course in some sort influenced by their impressions upon him, he tells you plainly that he seeks a country, nay, that he has already "risen with Christ," and that he lives in the land which is at once his treasury and his home.

We may illustrate the Apostle's meaning again by a reference to another passage; that in which he speaks of "always bearing about in the body the dying of the Lord Jesus." The primary reference of the Apostle is to the sufferings which himself and his compatriots were called upon to undergo in attestation of the resurrection of Christ. The enemies of the cross, those who were doing their utmost to destroy Christianity, were perplexed and baffled by the disappearance of the Saviour from the tomb; and to account for the mystery, they charged the apostles with the felony of their master's body. Thus two statements were put forth directly opposite in character and tendency; the rulers said the body was stolen; the apostles said the body had risen.

The latter could not be disproved; but so intense was their hostility against the Nazarene, that persecution and power were made use of—compendious, but, happily in this case, ineffectual arguments—to silence the proclaimers of the truth. The Apostle refers to this in the words that are now before us, and tells them in effect that though famine might draw the fire from his eye, and long-continued suffering might repress and undermine the buoyancy of his spirit, and though his flesh might creep and quail beneath the pressure of these agonies, and though in all these ways he might bear about in the body the dying of the Lord Jesus, yet, by the patience with which those sufferings were borne, by the consolations which abounded in the midst of them, nay, by the fact of the sufferings themselves, he could point to his marred and shattered body, and say that not the dying only, but the life, the immortal life of Jesus was every moment manifested there. But we are not disposed to limit this bearing about in the body the dying of the Lord Jesus to apostolic times. It is not a thing of one generation merely. We are not now called upon, as were our fathers, to do it in the furnace; the fires of outward persecution have well-nigh forgotten to burn; but it has an existence still as actual and as constant as in days of yore. The Christian does so every moment of his life, because every moment of his life he exercises faith in Christ. And his faith is not only active and appropriating, but realizing in its tendency: it not only unfolds to him the riches and confers on him the blessings of the mighty offering; it paints it as a living vision before the eye of his mind. Darting back through two thousand years of past time, it places him in the midst of the crowd gathered at the crucifixion, aye, at the very foot of the cross. He sees the victim; there is no delusion in the matter; he walks along the thronged and bustling streets; men cross his path in haste, speeding away, the one to his farm and the other to his merchandise; he converses with a thousand beings, he transacts a thousand things; but that scene is ever before him; as the magnet of his highest attractions, his eye always trembles to the cross, and in the midst of evidence fresher every moment he joins in the centurion language, his glad language too, "Truly this man was the Son of God." With such a spectacle as that before him, how can he live unto the world? With the glances of so kind an eye constantly beaming upon him, how can his desires be on earth? Heaven claims him, for his treasure and his heart are there. Nay, so entirely does this death unto sin—for I suppose you have found out that is what we mean—take possession of the Christian, that, as the Apostle in another place expresses it, he is "crucified with Christ." He is not only an anxious spectator, he is something more, he is a living sacrifice. He has his cross. As Christ died for sin, he dies to sin, and they both conquer by dying. As by the dying of the Saviour, the power of death was destroyed, and the world was freed from his dominion, so by the dying of the sinner, the principle of evil is dethroned, the new heart is gained, and the man becomes "a new creature in Christ Jesus."

This is what we imagine the Apostle to mean when he says of Christians, "Ye are dead;" and as it is only when we have thus died that we can be truly said to live, allow us to ask you if you are thus dead unto sin and alive unto God? Have you realized this death unto sin, or this birth unto righteousness? Has this deep, abiding change passed upon you? Or are you still living to the world, the circle of this life your bounded prospect, and its fleeting enjoyments your only reward? Examine yourselves, brethren, and may the Spirit help you to a right decision!

II. We pass upward from the truth of death to the truth of life. "For ye are dead," says the Apostle, "and your life"—a life that you have notwithstanding that seeming death—"is hid with Christ in God." In the creation of God there seems to be nothing absolute or final; everything seems rather in a rudimentary state—a state in which it is susceptive of increase, development, expansion, improvement. It is so in nature. The seed is cast into the earth; years elapse before there are the strength and shadow of the tree. The harvest waves not in its luxuriant beauty at once; "there is first the blade, then the ear, after that the full corn in the ear." And what is thus possible in the ordinary processes of nature is capable of spiritual analogies.

Man ends not in his present condition. The very imperfections with which it is fraught, shadow forth a mightier being. It would seem as if glimpses of this great truth shot across the minds of the sages of ancient Greece and Rome. It is interesting to watch their minds in their various and continual operations, especially when, as it were, brought out of themselves, to see them struggling with some great principle just glowing upon them from the darkness of previous thought, to see them catching occasional glimpses of truth in the distance, and pressing forward, if haply they might comprehend it fully. It must have been in one of those very ecstasies that the idea of immortality first dawned upon them; for, after all, crude and imperfect as their notions were, they must be regarded rather as conjecture than opinion. It was reserved for Christianity, by her complete revelations, to bring life and immortality to light, to unfold this master-purpose of the Eternal Mind, and to give permanence and form to her impressions of the life that dies not. You remember that the inspired writers, when speaking about the present state of being, scarcely dignify it with the name of life, compared with the life to be expected; but they tell us there is provided for us, and awaiting us, a life worthy of our highest approbation, and of our most cordial endeavor; a life solid, constant, and eternal. This is the promise "which he hath promised us"—as if there were no other, as if all others were wrapped up in that great benediction—"this is the promise which he hath promised us, even eternal life;" and of this life they tell us that it is "hid with Christ in God."

It is hidden, in the first place, in the sense of secrecy; it is concealed, partially developed; we do not know much about it. Revelation has not been minute in her discoveries of the better land. Enough has been revealed to confirm our confidence and to exalt our faith. The outlines of the purpose are sketched out before us, but the details are withheld. Hence, of the life to come the Apostle tells us that "we know in part, we see as through a glass darkly;" through a piece of smoked glass like that through which we look at an eclipse of the sun; our senses can give us no information concerning it, for it is beyond their province; reason cannot find it out, for it baffles her proudest endeavors. We may go to the depth in search of this wisdom: "the depth saith, It is not in me." Imagination may plume her finest pinion, and revel in the ideal magnificence she can bring into being; she may so exalt and amplify the images of the life that is, as to picture forth the life that will be; it is a hidden life still, for it hath not entered into the heart of man to conceive it; shadows dense and impervious hang on its approach; clouds and darkness are round about its throne. And we are equally destitute of information from experience. None of those white-robed companies, who have enjoyed this life from the beginning, have been commissioned to explain to us its truths; none of those now venerable ones, who have travelled the road, who have experienced the change, have returned; they come not full fraught with the tidings of eternity to tell to the heedful multitudes tales from beyond the grave. Those dark and silent chambers effectually cut off all communication between the mortal and the changed. We may interrogate the spirits of the departed, but there is no voice, not even the echo of our own. We do not complain of this secrecy, because we believe it to be a secrecy of mercy. The eye of the mind, like the eye of the body, was dazzled with excess of light; and if the full realities of the life to come were to burst upon us, we should be dazzled into blindness; there would be a wreck of reason, and the balance of the mind's powers would be irrecoverably gone. Moreover, we walk by faith, not by sight, and a fuller revelation would neutralize some of the most efficient means for the preservation of spiritual life, and bring anarchy and discord into the beautiful arrangements of God. Thus is this hiding beneficial to believers. Yes, and I will go further than that: to the sinner it is a secrecy of mercy. Wonder not at that. Imagine not that if this vacant area could be filled to-day with a spirit of perdition, with the thunder scar of the Eternal on his brow, and his heart writhing under the blasted immortality of hell, then surely if he could tell the secrets of his prison-house those who are now among the impenitent would be affrighted, and repent and turn. "I tell you nay, for if they hear not Moses and the prophets neither would they be persuaded though one were to rise from the dead."

Just another thought here on this head. Especially is this life hidden in the sense of secrecy, in the hour and the article of death. An awful change passes upon one we love, and who has loved the Lord Jesus Christ. He looks pale and motionless; we see not the glances of his eye, we hear not the music of his voice, and as he lies stretched breathless in his slumbers, it is very difficult to believe that he is not dead. "But he is not dead, but sleepeth." Can you credit it, O ye mourners? Is there no chord in your stricken hearts, ye bereaved ones, that trembles responsive to the tone, "he is not dead, but sleepeth?" His life is with him yet as warm, and as young, and as energetic as in days gone by; only it is hidden "with Christ in God." We mourn you not, ye departed ones that have died in the faith, for ye have entered into life. Natural affection bids us weep, and give your tombs the tribute of a tear, but we dare not recall you. Ye live; we are the dying ones; ye live in the smile and blessing of God. Our life is "hid with Christ in God."

And then it is hidden, secondly, not only in the sense of secrecy, but in the sense of security, laid up, treasured up, kept safely by the power of Christ. The great idea seems to be this: the enemy of God, a lion broken loose, is going round the universe in search of the Christian's life, that he may undermine and destroy it; but he cannot find it; God has hidden it; it is hidden with Christ in God. It is a very uncertain and precarious tenure upon which we hold all our posses sions here; everything connected with the present life is fleeting; plans formed in oversight and executed in wisdom are, by adverse circumstances, rendered abortive and fruitless; gourds grow for our shade, and we sit under them with delight; the mildew comes, and they are withered; friends twine themselves around our affections, and as we come to know them well and love them, they are sure to die; and upon crumbling arch, and ruined wall, and battlemented height, and cheeks all pale that but awhile ago blushed at the praise of their own loveliness, old Time has graven in the word of the preacher, that there is nothing unchangeable in man except his tendency to change. But it is a characteristic of the future life, that it is that which abideth; the lapse of time affects not those who live eternally; theirs is immortal youth; no enemy, however organized and mighty, can avail to deprive them of it; no opposition, however subtile and powerful, can wrest it from him with whom it is secure. Where is it hidden? With Christ; the safest place in the universe, surely, for anything belonging to Christ's people. Where he is, in that land irradiated with his presence, and brightening under the sunshine of his love; on that mountain whose sacred inclosure God's glory pavilions, and within which there shall in nowise enter anything that shall hurt or destroy. Where is this hidden? In God, in the great heart of God, who is never faithless to his promise, and whose perfections are pledged to confer it upon persevering believers. Oh, we will not fear. Unbelief may suggest to us its thoughts of suspicion and warning; fear may shrink back appalled from a way so untried and dangerous; passion may stir our unruly elements in our too carnal minds, and presumptuously fight against our faith; our ancient enemy may do his best to aggravate into intenser force the giant war; but we will not fear; our life shall be given to us, for it is hidden with Christ in God. Even now, in the prospect, we feel a joy of which the world wotteth not—heart-warm, fervent, entrancing, a joy which we may suffer to roam unchecked in its raptures because it is based upon the truth divine.

III. We pass on, thirdly, to the Christian's prospects. "When Christ, who is our life, shall appear, then shall ye also appear with him in glory."

These words imply two things: first, enjoyment; and secondly, manifestation.

They imply, first, enjoyment. We observed before, that revelation has not been minute in her discoveries of the better land; we have the outlines of the purpose before us, but the details are withheld; and yet enough is revealed not merely to fulfill, but to exalt our highest hopes. The similitudes under which the recompense is presented in Scripture cannot fail to fill us with anticipations of the most delightful kind. It is brought before us, you remember, as an inheritance, incorruptible and undefiled; as a paradise ever vernal and blooming; and, best of all, amid those trees of life there lurks no serpent to destroy; as a country through whose vast region we shall traverse with untired footsteps, and every fresh revelation of beauty will augment our knowledge, and holiness, and joy; as a city whose every gate is of jewelry, whose every street is a sun-track, whose wall is an immortal bulwark, and whose ever-spreading splendor is the glory of the Lord; as a temple through which gusts of praise are perpetually sweeping the anthems of undying hosannas; above all, as our Father's house where Christ is, where our elder brother is, making the house ready for the younger ones, where all we love is clustered, where the out-flowings of parental affection thrill and gladden, and where the mind is spell-bound, for aye, amid the sweet sorceries of an everlasting home. Is there no enjoyment in images like these? Does not the very thought of them make the fleet blood rush the fleeter through the veins? And yet these and far more are the prospects of the Christian: knowledge without the shadow of an error, and increasing throughout eternity; friendship that never unclasps its hand, or relaxes from its embraces; holiness without spot or wrinkle, or any such thing; the presence of God in beatific and imperishable vision, combine to make him happy each moment, and to make him happy forever.

Then these words imply manifestation as well as enjoyment. "When Christ, who is our life, shall appear, then shall ye also appear with him in glory." The world says: "You talk about your life being hidden; the fact is, it is lost; it is only a gloss of yours to say it is hidden." But it is not lost, it is only hidden; and when Christ, who has it, shall appear, "then shall ye also appear," to the discomfiture of scoffers and to the admiration of all them that believe; "then shall ye also appear with him in glory. The worldling looks at Christians now, and, in some of his reflective moods, he finds a great difference between them, but it is a difference he can hardly understand. With his usual shortsightedness, and with his usual self-complacency, he imagines the advantage to be altogether upon his own side; he looks at the outside of the man, and judges foolish judgment. Perhaps he glances at his garments, and they are tattered, it may be, and homely, and he turns away with affected disdain. Ah! he knows not that beneath that beggar's robe there throbs a prince's soul. Wait a while; bide your time; stop until the manifestation of the sons of God. With what different feelings will earth's despised ones be regarded at the bar of judgment and before the throne divine! How will they appear when they are confessed, recognized, honored, in the day when he is ashamed of the wicked, and when the hell beneath and the hell within will make them ashamed of themselves? "Beloved," says the rejoicing Apostle, "now are we the sons of God;" that is something, that is no mean gift, that is no small bestowment, to have that in hand; "now are we the sons of God." "Salvation," it is as if the Apostle had said, "is a small thing, a thing unworthy of God;" it is a small thing to take a captive out of a dungeon, and turn him loose upon the cold world's cruel scorn; it is a grand thing to take a captive out of a dungeon, and set him on a throne; and that is done with all those who believe on Jesus: being justified by faith, they have peace with God through our Lord Jesus Christ. "And if children" (for they have received the adoption of sons), "then heirs, heirs of God, and joint-heirs with Christ." Oh! salvation is not to be named in connection with the grand, the august, the stately splendor, the sonship, which is given unto those who put their trust in Christ. "Beloved, now are we the sons of God; but it doth not yet appear what we shall be;" so transcendent, so surpassing is the recompense, that we cannot conceive it now; "it doth not yet appear what we shall be;" it doth not yet appear even to ourselves; we shall be as much astonished at the splendor of the recompense as any one beside. Oh! when we are launched into the boundless, when the attentive ear catches the first tones of heaven's melody, when there burst upon the dazzled eye the earliest glimpse of beatific vision, how shall we be ready almost to doubt our own identity—"Is this I? It cannot be the same. Is this the soul that was racked with anxiety and dimmed with prejudice, and stained with sin? Is this the soul whose every passion was its tempter, and that was harassed with an all-absorbing fear of never reaching heaven? Why, not an enemy molests it now; not a throb shoots across it now; those waters that used to look so angry and so boisterous, how peacefully they ripple upon the everlasting shore; and this body, once so frail and so mortal, is it, can it be, the same? Why, the eye dims not now; the cheek is never blanched with sudden pain; the fingers are not awkward now; but, without a teacher, they strike the harp of gold, and transmit along the echoes of eternity the song of Moses and the Lamb. This is conjecture, you say; not, we hope, unwarranted; but even now, dark as our glimpse is, unworthy as our conceptions are of the promised recompense, there is enough to exalt us into the poet's ecstasy, when, throned upon his own privilege, he sings:

> "On all the kings of earth
> With pity we look down;
> And claim, in virtue of our birth,
> A never-fading crown."

IV. And now, then, you are ready for the duty, I am sure. "For your life is hid with Christ in God. When Christ, who is our life, shall appear, then shall ye also appear with him in glory." "Set your affection on things above." Oh, how solemnly it comes, with all this exceeding weight of privilege to back it! It silences the question urged, it overrides gainsay; it is emphatic and solemn, and to the Christian resistless. "Set your affections on things above." For a Christian to be absorbed in the gainfulness of the world, or fascinated by its pleasures, is at once a grievous infatuation and a sin. It is as if a prince of high estate and regal lineage were to demean himself in the haunts of beggars, to the loss of dignity and imperilling the honor of his crown. What have you, the blood-royal of heaven, to do with this vain and fleeting show? Arise, depart; this is not your rest; it is polluted. And yet how many of you have need of the exhortation this morning, "Set your affections on things above?" Have you not —now let the spirit of searching come unto you—have you not, by your cupidity, avarice, and huckstering lust of gain, distanced the world's devotees in what they had been accustomed to consider their own peculiar walk? Have you not trodden so near the line of demarcation between professor and profane, that you have almost trodden on it, and almost trodden it out? Have you not, strangely enamored of visions of distant joy, postponed as uninfluential and unworthy, the joy that abideth, or, like the man in the allegory, raked up with a perseverance that in aught else might have been laudable, the straws beneath your feet, while above your head there glittered the diadem of glory? Oh, awake! arise! this is not your rest; it is polluted. "Set your affections on things above, and not on things on the earth." If riches be your possession, be thankful for them; do all the good with them you can; if friends make music in your dwelling, regard them as rose-leaves scattered upon life, and by and by to drop from life away. Seek for bags that wax not old, friends that neither weep nor change in the unintermitting reunions of heaven's own glory.

How does this prospect of glory breathe encouragement to the soul in the sad season of bereavement! "He that believeth in Jesus"—this is the promise—"though he were dead, yet shall he live, and whosoever liveth and believeth on Jesus shall never die." Still sounds that great utterance of the Master running along the whole line of being, heard over the graves of the loved, amid rustling leaf and fading flower, and withering grass, and dying man, "He that liveth and believeth in Jesus shall never die." Orphan, believest thou this? Widow, from whom the desire of thine eyes has been taken away with a stroke, believest thou this? Ah! some of us have got friends safe-housed above the regions of the shadow and the storm, but we would not bring them back again. We would sing for them the hallowed pæan:

"By the bright waters now thy lot is cast,
Joy for thee! happy friend; thy bark hath passed
The rough sea's foam.
Now the long yearnings of thy soul are stilled,
Home, home!
Thy peace is won, thy heart is filled!
Thou art gone home."

But we can listen to the voice which they find time to whisper to us in some of the rests of the music: "Be ye therefore followers of us who now, through faith and patience, are inheriting the promises."

Some of you have not got, perhaps, to the realization of this promise yet. There is a misgiving within; there is a yet unsettled controversy between your Maker and yourself. You have not seen Jesus; you have not heard the pardoning voice or felt the power of the reconciling plan. Oh, come to Christ. To-day the Holy Spirit of Christ is here, waiting to take of the precious things of Christ, and to show them unto you; waiting this morning to do honor to Jesus. Hallow the consecration of this house by the consecration of the living temple of your hearts. God is no longer the unknown God, to be viewed with servile apprehension, or followed with slavish dread; he is God in Christ, reconciling the world unto himself. Redemption is no longer a theorem to be demonstrated, a problem to be solved, a riddle to be guessed by the wayward and the wandering; it is the great fact of the universe that Jesus Christ hath, by the grace of God, tasted death once for every man. Mercy is no longer a fitful and capricious exercise of benevolence; it is the very power, and justice, and truth of God. A just God: look that out in the Gospel dictionary, and you will find it means a Saviour. Heaven is no longer a fortress to be besieged, a city to be taken, a high, impregnable elevation to be scaled; it is the grand metropolis of the universe, to which the King, in his bounty, has thrown up a royal high-road for his people, even through the blood of his Son. Oh, come to Jesus with full surrender of heart, and all these blessings shall be yours. Some do not hold this language; they belong to this world, and are not ashamed to confess it. "Bring fresh garlands; let the song be of wine and of beauty; build fresh and greater barns, where I may bestow my fruits and goods." But then cometh the end. "The rich man died and was buried, and in hell lifted up his eyes, being in torment; and seeth Abraham afar off, and Lazarus in his bosom; he cried and said"—the only prayer that I know of, the whole Bible through, to a saint or angel, and that by a damned spirit, and never answered—"I pray thee, father Abraham, that thou wouldst send Lazarus that he may dip the tip of his finger in water, and cool my tongue, for I am tormented in this flame." Listen to it, the song of the lost worldling in hell. Who will set it to music? Which heart is tuning for it now? Sinner, is it thine? Is it thine? Don't put that question away. Ask yourselves and your consciences in the sight of God, and then come, repent of all your sins, flee for refuge to the hope that is laid before you in the Gospel, trusting in serene and child-like reliance upon Christ. Only believe, and yours shall be the heritage in the world to come.

X.

THE APOSTLE'S GROUND OF TRUST.

"But what things were gain to me, those I counted loss for Christ. Yea, doubtless, and I count all things but loss for the excellency of the knowledge of Christ Jesus my Lord; for whom I have suffered the loss of all things, and do count them but dung, that I may win Christ."—PHILIPPIANS iii. 7, 8.

THERE can be no sense of bondage in the soul when the tongue utters words like these. Albeit they flow from the lips of a prisoner, they have the true ring of the inner freedom, of the freedom which cannot be cribbed in dungeons. They are the expressions of a far-sighted trust which yields to no adverse circumstances, which endures, as seeing him who is invisible, in the confidence of quiet power. There was a very tender relationship subsisting between Paul and the Philippian Church. They had sent Epaphroditus to visit him in his prison at Rome, to bear him their sympathies, and to administer their liberality, in his hour of need; and in return for their kindness, and as a token of his unfailing love, he addressed them this epistle. It is remarkable that it contains no solitary word of rebuke, that it recognizes in them the existence of a grateful and earnest piety, and that it aims throughout at their consolation and encouragement. In the commencement of the present chapter he warns them against certain Judaizing teachers, who would fain have recalled them to the oldness of the letter, and who made the commandments of God of none effect by their tradition. "Beware of dogs, beware of evil-workers, beware of the concision." He tells them that the true seed of Abraham, the royal heritors of the covenant, are those who worship God in the spirit, and rejoice in Christ Jesus, and have no confidence in the flesh. He proceeds to remind them that if there were benefit in external trusts, he stood upon a vantage-ground of admitted superiority. "Though I might also have confidence in the flesh. If any other man thinketh that he hath whereof he might trust in the flesh, I more: Circumcised the eighth day, of the stock of Israel, of the tribe of Benjamin, an Hebrew of the Hebrews; as touching the law, a Pharisee; concerning zeal, persecuting the Church; touching the righteousness which is in the law, blameless." But, putting all this aside, renouncing these grounds of confidence as carnal and delusive, resting in sublime reliance upon Christ, he records the noble declaration of the text, at once the enduring testimony of his own faith and the perpetual strength of theirs. "But what things were gain to me, those I counted loss for Christ. Yea, doubtless, and I count all things but loss for the excellency of the knowledge of Christ Jesus my Lord; for whom

I have suffered the loss of all things, and do count them but dung, that I may win Christ." We can conceive of no testimony better calculated than this to cheer the timid, or to confirm the wavering, to silence the misgivings of the doubtful, or cause the inquiring soul to sing for joy. All the conditions which we can possibly desire in order to render testimony accredited and valuable, are to be found here. It is not the utterance of a man of weak mind, infirm of purpose and irresolute in action, whose adhesion would damage rather than further any cause he might espouse. It is Paul, the Apostle, who speaks, the sharp-witted student of Gamaliel, a match for the proudest Epicurean, versed in scholastic subtilties and in all the poetry and philosophy of the day, with a mental glance keen as lightning, and a mental grasp strong as steel. It is not the utterance of youth, impassioned and, therefore, hasty; sanguine of imagined good, and pouring out its prodigal applause. It is Paul, the man, who speaks, with ripened wisdom on his brow, and gathering around him the experience of years. It is not the utterance of the man of hereditary belief, bound in the fetters of the past, strong in the sanctities of early education, who has imbibed a traditional and unintelligent attachment to the profession of his fathers. It is Paul, the some-time persecutor, who speaks, the noble quarry which the arrows of the Almighty struck down when soaring in its pride. It is he who now rests tenderly upon the cause which he so lately labored to destroy. It is not, finally, the utterance of inexperience, which, awed by the abiding impression of one supernatural event, and having briefly realized new hopes and new joys, pronounces prematurely a judgment which it would afterward reverse. It is Paul, the aged, who speaks, who is not ignorant of what he says and whereof he doth affirm, who has rejoiced in the excellent knowledge through all the vicissitudes of a veteran's life; alike amid the misgivings of a Church slow to believe his conversion, and amid the dissipation and perils of his journeys; alike when first worshipped and then stoned at Lystra, in the prison at Philippi, and in the Areopagus at Athens; alike when in the early council it strengthened him, "born out of due time," to withstand to the face of Peter, the elder Apostle, because he was to be blamed, and when, melted into almost womanly tenderness on the sea-shore at Miletus, it nerved him for the heart-breaking of that sad farewell; alike when buffeting the wintry blasts of the Adriatic, and when standing silver-haired and solitary before the bar of Nero. It is he of amplest experience who has tried it under every conceivable circumstance of mortal lot, who, now that his eye has lost its early fire, and the spring and summer are gone from him, feels its genial glow in the kindly winter of his years. Where can we find testimony more conclusive and valuable? Hear it, ye craven spirits, who would dastardly forswear the Master, and let it shame you into Christian manhood! Hear it, ye bruised and tender souls, that dare hardly venture faith on Jesus, and catching inspiration and courage from it, let your voices be heard :

> "Hence, and forever from my heart,
> I bid my doubts and fears depart,
> And to those hands my soul resign,
> Which bear credentials so divine."

In the further exhibition of this passage to-night, we ought to refer, in the first place, to the Apostle's insufficient grounds of trust, and secondly, to the compensating power of the excellency of the knowledge of Christ. I greatly fear, however, that the first part of the subject will be all that I can manage to compass within the time allotted for this evening's service. Our remarks will, therefore, mainly dwell upon the grounds of trust which the Apostle here repudiates: "What things were gain to me, those I counted loss for Christ."

There is something remarkable in the way in which the Apostle refers to the past, and the respectful manner in which he speaks of the faith of his fathers, and of his youth. It is often a sign rather of servility than of independence when men vilify their former selves. The Apostle had not renounced Judaism in any moment of passion, nor in any prejudice of novelty. Strong convictions had forced him out of his old belief. He had emerged into a faith purer and more satisfying far. But there were memories connected with the fulfilled dispensation which he would not willingly let die.

There were phases of his own inner life there. For long years, Judaism had been to him his only interpreter of the divine, the only thing which met a religious instinct, active beyond that of ordinary men. The grounds of trust which he now found to be insufficient, had been the halting-places of his soul in its progress from the delusive to the abiding, from the shadowy to the true. He could not forget that there hung around the system he had abandoned, an ancient and traditional glow: it was of God's own architecture; the pattern and its gorgeous ceremonial had been given by himself in the Mount; all its furniture spoke of him in sensuous manifestation and magnificent appeal. His breath had quivered upon the lips of its prophets, and had lashed its seers into their sacred frenzy He was in its temple service, and in its holy of holies; amid shapes of heavenly sculpture, the light of his presence ever rested in merciful repose. How could the Apostle assail it with wanton outrage or flippant sarcasm? True, it had fulfilled its mission, and now that the age of spirituality and power had come, it was no longer needed; but the halo was yet upon its brow, and like the light which lingers above the horizon long after the setting of the sun, there shone about it a dim but heavenly splendor. While, however, the Apostle was not slow to confess that there was glory in that which was to be done away, he was equally bold in affirming its absolute worthlessness in comparison with the yet greater glory of that which remained. "What things were gain to me, those I counted loss for Christ." It will be found, I think, to be remarkable in the review of the grounds of trust, which the Apostle here repudiates, how much there is kindred to them in the aspects of modern faith, and how multitudes now cling to them with tenacity, and hope to find in them their present and eternal gain. Let us remind you, then, for a few moments, of the catalogue of trusts which the Apostle tried and repudiated.

The first thing he mentions, is sacramental efficacy. "Circumcised on the eighth day." He names circumcision first, because it was the early and indispensable sacrament of the Jewish people, the seal of the Mosaic covenant, the distinguishing badge of the Israelites from all other nations of mankind. Moreover, he tells us he had the advantage of early initiation: "Circumcised the eighth day." The Gentile proselytes could, of course, only observe the rite at the period of conversion, which might be in manhood or in age. But Paul was hallowed from his youth, from the eighth day of his life introduced into the federal arrangement, and solemnly consecrated to the service of the Lord. He was not insensible to this external advantage, but he does not hesitate to proclaim it worthless as a ground of acceptance with God. There are multitudes by whom baptism is regarded in the same reverent light as was circumcision by the Jews of old. If they do not absolutely rejoice in it, as the manner of some is, as the instrument of their regeneration, at least they have a vague notion of a benefit which they deem it to have conferred, and are living on the unexhausted credit of their parents' faith and prayer. If, in adult age, they make any profession of religion, it is by partaking of the Eucharist, whose elements they invest with mystic and transforming power. There is no inward change in them. They are conscious of no painstaking and daily struggle with corruption. They have no conflict for a mastery over evil. No percptible improvement passes upon their conduct and habits from their periodical communions. And yet, absolutely, their only hope for the future, springs from the grace of the baptismal font, and from the efficacy of the sacramental table; for they persuade themselves into the belief that as by the ordinance of baptism there was a mysterious conveyance to them of the title-deeds of an inheritance, so by the excellent mystery of the Lord's Supper, they are as inexplicably ripened into meetness for its possession. Brethren, we would not under-value the ordinances of God's appointing. We are not insensible to the benefit when believing parents dedicate their offspring unto God, when the hand of parental faith rests upon the ark of the covenant, and claims that there should be shed out upon the little ones the spiritual influences of the Holy Ghost. Chiefest among our religious memories, treasured in the soul with a delight which is almost awe, are some of those holy communions, when—the life infused into the bread, the power into the wine—Christ has been evidently set forth before his grateful worshippers, and strong consolations have trooped up to the heavenly festival. But it must not be forgotten that all the graces of ordinances, all the beatific and inspiring comforts which flow through divinely appointed services, are not in the services themselves, but in the fullness of the loving Saviour, the anointed one in the vision of Zechariah, without whom and without whose Spirit they could have neither efficacy nor power. Precious as are the collateral benefits of baptism, and hallowing as are the strength and blessing of the Holy Eucharist, we do solemnly proclaim them worthless as grounds of acceptance before God. Hear it, ye baptized, but unbelieving members of our congregation! Hear it, ye devout and earnest communicants! Sacraments have no *atoning* virtue, no value at all except as avenues to lead the soul to Christ; and if, in a trust like this, you pass your lives, and if, in the exercise of a trust like this, you die, for you there can remain nothing but the agonizing wakening from a deception that will have outlasted life, and the cry wailed from the outside of a door, forever barred, "We were early dedicated unto thee! were accounted as thy followers; we have eaten and drank in thy presence; Lord, Lord, open unto us." That is the first ground of trust which the Apostle here disclaims.

Passing on in the catalogue, we find that the second repudiated confidence is an honored parentage, "Of the stock of Israel, of the tribe of Benjamin, a Hebrew of the Hebrews." To have been circumcised the eighth day, proved that he had been born of parents professing the Jewish faith; but, inasmuch as the Gentile proselytes also observed the rites of circumcision, it did not prove that he had been descended of the family of Israel. He, therefore, shows that in purity of lineal descent, in all those hereditary honors upon which men dwell with pride, he could boast with the proudest of them all. He was of the stock of Israel. But ten of the tribes had revolted from their allegiance to Jehovah, had soiled their nobility by their vices, had entered into degrading companionship with surrounding idolaters. He, therefore, reminds them further, that he was of the tribe of Benjamin; illustrious, because it had given the first king to Israel; more illustrious, because, at the apostasy of Jeroboam it maintained purity of Divine worship, and held itself faithful among the faithlessness of many. Moreover, he had not been introduced into the federal relationship by personal adoption nor by the conversion of his fathers. There had been in his ancestry no Gentile intermarriages; he was "a Hebrew of the Hebrews." His genealogy was pure on both sides. There was no bar sinister in his arms. He was a lineal inheritor of the adoption, and the glory, and the covenant. There was much in all this on which in those times the Apostle might have dwelt with pride; men, generally vaunt those honors which are theirs by birth.

It was no light thing surely, then, to belong to nobility that could trace its far descent from the worthies of the older world, to have for his ancestors those anointed and holy patriarchs who trod the young earth when unwrinkled by sorrow, undimmed by crime, untouched by the wizard wand of time; to have in his veins the same blood that marched proudly over the fallen ramparts of Jericho, or that bade the affrighted sun stand still at Gibeon, or that quailed beneath the dread thunders of the mount that burned. And yet all this accumulated pride of ancestral honor the Apostle counted "loss for Christ." That the Jews prided themselves on their descent from Abraham, you may gather from many passages of Scripture. You remember when our Saviour was conversing with them on the inner freedom, he was rudely interrupted with the words, "We be Abraham's children; we were never in bondage to any man." And that they regarded this descent from Abraham as in some sort a passport to heaven, we may gather from the Saviour's rebuke: "Think not to say within yourselves, we have Abraham to our father, for I say unto you, that of these stones God is able to raise up children unto Abraham." And there are multitudes now, brethren, who have no better hope than this. There are many in this land of ours who are stifling the misgivings of conscience, and the convictions of the Holy Spirit, with the foolish thought that they have been born in a Christian country, surrounded with an atmosphere of privilege, or are the sons "of parents passed into the skies."

Look at that holy patriarch, forsaken of kindred,

bankrupt in property, and slandered in reputation, "Afflicted grievously and tempted sore," and yet holding an integrity as fast in his sackcloth as ever he did in his purple, and amid terrible reverses blessing the goodness which but claimed the gift it gave! Mark that honorable counsellor, pious amid cares of state, and pomps, and pleasure, walking with God amid the tumult and luxury of Babylon, and from the companionship of kings speeding to his chamber that had its lattice open toward Jerusalem! Listen to that preacher of righteousness, as now with earnest exhortation, and now with blameless life, he testifies to the whole world, and warns it of its coming doom, and then, safe in the heaven-shut ark, is borne by the billows of ruin to a mount of safety. What sublime examples of consistency and piety are here! Surely, if a parent's faith can avail for children anything, it will be in the families of Noah, Daniel, and Job!

Now, listen—listen—ye who rest on traditional faith, ye who are making a raft of your parents' piety to float you over the dark, stormy water into church fellowship here, and into heavenly fellowship hereafter—listen to the solemn admonition: "Though these three men, Noah, Daniel, and Job, were in it, as I live they should deliver but their own souls by their righteousness, saith the Lord God." Alas! if the grandson of Moses was an idolatrous priest; if the children of Samuel perverted judgment and took bribes; if David, the man after God's own heart, mourned in hopeless agony over

Absalom dead! how sad the witness that religion is not a hereditary possession! how appalling the danger lest you, children of pious parents, nursed in the lap and surrounded with the atmosphere of godliness, should pass down into a heritage of wrath and sorrow, aggravated into intenser hell for you by the remembrances of the piety of your fathers! That is the second ground of trust which the Apostle disclaims.

Passing on in the catalogue, we find that the next repudiated confidence is religious authority. "As touching the law, a Pharisee." This was not the first time the Apostle had made this affirmation. You remember that before the tribunal of the high priest, he affirmed, with a not unholy pride, "I am a Pharisee, the son of a Pharisee." And, at Agrippa's judgment-seat, he appealed even to the infuriated Jews whether he had not, according to the straightest sect of their religion, lived a Pharisee. And, indeed, there was much in those early times which an honest Pharisee might be excused for counting gain. The word has got in our days, to be regarded as a sort of synonym for all that is hypocritical and crafty; but a Pharisee in the Jewish times, an honest, earnest Pharisee, was a man not to be despised. In an age of prevailing indifference, the Pharisee rallied around him all the godly, religious spirit of the time. In an age of prevailing skepticism, the Pharisee protested nobly against the free-thinking Sadducee, and against the courtly Herodian. In an age of prevailing laxity, the Pharisee inculcated, by precept at all events, austerity of morals and sanctity of life. There might be ostentation in his broad phylacteries; at all events, it showed he was not ashamed of the texts which he had traced out upon the parchment. A love of display might prompt the superb decorations with which he gilded the tombs of the prophets; at all events, and that is no small virtue, he had not ceased to honor the memory of righteousness. There might be self-glory in his fasts, rigidly observed, and in his tithes, paid to the uttermost farthing; at all events, there was recognition of the majesty, and obedience to the letter of the law. I repeat it, in those early times there was much which an honest Pharisee might be excused for counting gain. But this also the Apostle "counted loss for Christ."

There are multitudes now, I need not remind you, whose trust is their orthodoxy, whose zeal is their partisanship, whose munition of rocks is their union with the people of God. There is some danger, believe me, lest even the tender and hallowed associations of the Church should weaken the sense of individual responsibility. We are apt to imagine, amid the round of decorous externalisms, when the sanctuary is attractive and the minister approved, when there is peace in the borders and wealth in the treasury, when numbers do not diminish, and all that is conventionally excellent is seen, that our own piety must necessarily shine in the lustre of the mass, that we are spiritually healthy, and need neither counsel nor warning.

The Church to which we belong, perhaps, has "a name to live;" and we imagine that the life of the aggregate must, in some mysterious manner, imply the life of the individual. And though our conscience reproach us sometimes, and though we are frivolous in our practice, and censorious in our judgment of others, and though, in our struggle with evil, the issue is sometimes compromise and sometimes defeat, although attendances at religious ordinances, an occasional and stifled emotion under a sermon, a spasm of convulsive activity, a hurried and heartless prayer, are really the whole of our religion—we are sitting in our sealed houses, we pass among our fellows for reputable and painstaking Christians, and are dreaming that a joyous entrance will be ministered to us abundantly at last. O, for thunder-pealing words to crash over the souls of formal and careless professors of religion, and startle them into the life of God! I do solemnly believe that there are thousands in our congregations, in different portions of the land, who are thus dead while they are seeming to live; and with all fidelity I would warn you of your danger. It is a ghastly sight when the flowers of religious profession trick out a mortal corpse. It is a sad entombment when the church or chapel is the vault of the coffined spirit, "dead in trespasses and sins." That is the third ground of trust which the Apostle here disclaims.

Passing on in the catalogue, we find that the fourth repudiated confidence is intense earnestness, "Concerning zeal, persecuting the Church." There was much in this that would awake a responsive chord in the heart of a bigoted Jew. The Apostle tells us he was present at the martyrdom of Stephen; and in his zeal for the repression of what he deemed to be a profane mystery, he made havoc of the Church, breathed out threatenings and slaughter, and persecuted unto the death. Often, indeed, did the sad memory press upon him in his after life, bowing him to contrition and tears. "I am less than the least of the apostles, that am not meet to be called an apostle, because I persecuted the Church of God." But there is incontestable evidence in all this of his zeal for the Jewish faith, that he did not hold the truth in unrighteous indolence, but that he exerted himself for its promulgation; that devotion with him was not a surface sentiment, nor an educational necessity, but a principle grasping, in the strong hand of its power, every energy of his nature, and infibered with the deepest affections of his soul. And there was much in all this, which men around him were accustomed to regard as gain; but this also he esteemed "as loss for Christ."

I know no age of the world, brethren, when claim for the gainfulness of zeal, abstract zeal, would be more readily conceded than in the age in which we live. Earnestness, it is the god of this age's reverence. Men do not scrutinize too closely the characters of the heroes they worship. Mad ambition may guide the despotic hand; brain may be fired with dark schemes of tyranny; the man may be a low-souled infidel, or a vile seducer;

he may be a poet stained with licentiousness, or a warrior stained with blood; let him be but earnest, and there is a niche for him in the modern Pantheon. And, as it is an understood principle that the character of the worshippers assimilates to the beings they worship, the devotees have copied their idols, and this is an earnest age. The trade spirit is in earnest; bear witness, those of you who have felt its pressure. Hence the unprecedented competitions of business; hence the gambling, which would rather leap into wealth by speculation, than achieve it by industry; hence the intense, the unflagging, indomitable, almost universal greed of gain. Men are earnest in the pursuit of knowledge. The press teems with cheap, and not always wholesome, literature. Science is no longer the heritage of the illuminati, but of the masses. The common mind has become voracious in its appetite to know; and a cry has gone up from the people which cannot be disregarded, "Give us knowledge, or else we die." It is manifest in all departments and in every walk of life. Men live faster than they used to do. In politics, in science, in pleasure, he is, he must be earnest who succeeds. He must speak loudly and earnestly who would win the heedful multitudes to listen. Such is the impetuosity of the time, that the timid and the vacillating find no foothold on the pavement of life, and are every moment in peril of being overborne and jostled aside, trampled down beneath the rude waves of the rushing and earnest crowd.

While such general homage is paid to earnestness, what wonder if some people should mistake it for religion; and if a man should imagine that, because he is zealous in the activities of benevolence, warmly attached to certain church organizations, and in some measure sympathetic with the spiritual forces which they embody, he is really a partaker of the undefiled religion of the Bible? And I must go further than this. The tolerance—take it to yourselves those who need it—the tolerance with which believers in Christ—those who are really members of the Church, and have "the root of the matter" within them—the tolerance with which they talk about, and apologize for "the zealous but unconverted adjuncts of the Church," tends very greatly to confirm them in their error. Cases throng upon one's memory and conscience as we think upon the subject.

There is a man—he has no settled faith at all in the principles of Christian truth; he is cast forever upon a sea of doubt and darkness; "ever learning, yet never able to come to the knowledge of the truth." He may consider without acting, till he dies. But what says the tolerant spirit of the age? "He is an earnest thinker, let him alone; he has no faith in the Bible; he has no faith in anything certain, settled, and indisputable, but he is an earnest thinker; and, although life may be frittered away without one holy deed to ennoble it, if he live long enough, he will grope his way into conviction by and by."

There is another man; he is not all we would wish him to be; he is unfrequent and irregular in attendance upon the ordinances of God's house; he is not always quite spiritually-minded; we should like to see him less grasping in his bargains; but he is an earnest worker, a zealous partisan, an active committee-man, and we hope all will be right with him in the end.

There is another man, and more chivalrous in his sense of honor; he is known to hold opinions that are dangerous, if not positively fatal, upon some vital subjects of Christian truth. But he is an amiable man; he is very kind to the poor; he has projected several measures of amelioration for their benefit; the widow blesses him when she hears his name. He is an earnest philanthropist; and, thus sheltered in the shadow of his benevolence, his errors pass unchallenged, and have a wider scope for mischief than before.

I do solemnly believe that there are men who are confirmed in their infidelity to Christianity by the tribute thus paid to their zeal. It may be that some infatuated self-deceivers pass out of existence with a lie in their right hand, because earnestness, like charity, has been made to "cover a multitude of sins." Since there is this danger, it is instructive to find out what is the Apostle's opinion of mere earnestness. It may be a good thing—there can be no doubt of that—when it springs from prompting faith, and constraining love, and when the object on behalf of which it exerts its energies is intrinsically excellent. It is a noble thing; we cannot do without it; it is at once the pledge of sincerity and an augury of success. It may be a good thing, but it may be a blasphemy; just the muscle in the arm of a madman, that nerves his frantic hand to scatter firebrands, and arrows, and death; but do not deceive yourselves.

Divers gifts may have been imparted to you; you may have discrimination of the abstruse and the profound; the widow may bless your footsteps, and the orphan's heart may sing for joy at your approach; the lustre of extensive benevolence may be shed over your character; opinions may have rooted themselves so firmly in your nature that you are ready to suffer loss in their behalf, and to covet martyrdom in their attestation, giving your body to be burned. But, with all this earnestness, indisputably earnest as you are, if you have not charity, diviner far—if you have not "faith that works by love and purifies the heart"—earnest, indisputably earnest as you are, it profiteth you nothing; your confidence will fail you in the hour of trial; its root is rottenness, and its blossom will go out as dust. That is the fourth ground of trust that the Apostle here disclaims.

Yet again, and finally. The next ground of trust is ceremonial blamelessness, "Touching the righteousness which is in the law, blameless." The Apostle's zeal for the Jewish faith was rendered more influential by the purity of his life. There are some whose zeal is but a cloak for licentiousness, and who shamefully violate, in daily practice, the rescripts of the religion for which they contend. But the Apostle was not one of those impious fanatics; he had been in sincerity and truth a Jew, so rigid and inflexible in his adhesion to the laws of Moses that he was esteemed a pattern, and rejoiced in as a pillar of the truth. Not that before God the most devout Pharisee had anything whereof to glory, but that, in the eyes of men, who judge in short-sightedness, and who judge in error, he passed for a reputable and blameless man. And this, also, the most ordinary, the most wide-spread ground of false confidence, the Apostle counted "loss for Christ."

I need not remind you, I am sure, how deep in the heart of man, resisting every attempt to dislodge it, self-righteousness lurks and broods; and how men come to regard themselves, in the absence of atrocious crime, and in the presence of much that is humanizing and kindly, as ripening for the kingdom of heaven. And it is no marvel—I do not think it one jot of a marvel—if we consider what the usages of society are, and the verdicts it passes on the virtues and vices of the absent.

There is a tribunal out among men that never suspends its sessions, and that is always estimating themselves by themselves, and comparing themselves among themselves, and so is not wise. From acting as judge in some of these arbitration cases of character, by acting as an arbiter himself, the man comes to know the standard of the world's estimation, and how it is that it comes to its decisions; and, in some reflective mood, possibly, he tries himself by it, and, looking down below him, he sees, far beneath him in the scale, the outcast and the selfish, the perfidious, the trampler upon worldly decencies, and the scandalously sinful. And then he looks into his own case, and he sees his walk through life, greeted with the welcome of many salutations, that his name passes unchallenged, his integrity vouched for among men. Then he looks into his own heart, and finds it is vibrating to every chord of sympathy; friends troop around him with proud fondness; children "climb his knees, the envied kiss to share."

It is no marvel, I say, if a man accustomed to such standards of arbitration, should imagine that the goodness which has been so cheerfully acknowledged on earth, will be as cheerfully acknowledged in heaven, and that he who has passed muster with the world so well, will not be sent abashed and crest-fallen from the judgment-seat of God.

And there is nothing more difficult than to rouse such a one from his dangerous and fatal slumber. There are many, who, thus building on the sand, have no shelter in the hour of the storm. You may thunder over the man's head all those passages which tell of the radical and universal depravity of our race. Yes, and he admires your preaching, and thinks it is wonderfully good for the masses, *but it has no sort of application to him.* He does not feel himself to be the vile and guilty creature you describe; he has an anodyne carried about with him to silence the first misgiving of the uneasy conscience, and he lies down in drugged and desperate repose. And there are many, it may be, who continue in this insidious deception, and are never aroused except by the voice of the last messenger, or by the flashing of the penal fires. That is the last ground of trust which the Apostle disclaims.

And now of the things that we have spoken, what is the sum? Just this. You may be early initiated into the ordinances of the Christian Church; you may have come of a long line of spiritually illustrious ancestry, and be the sons "of parents passed into the skies;" you may give an intellectual assent to the grand harmony of Christian truth; you may be zealous in certain activities of benevolence, and in certain matters connected even with the Church of God itself; you may have passed among your fellows for a reputable and blameless man, against whom no one would utter a word of slander, and in whose presence the elders stand up in reverence, as you pass by; and yet, there may pile upon you—(O God, send the word home!)—there may pile upon you all the accumulation of carnal advantage and carnal endowment; you may gain all this world of honor, and lose your own soul. "And what shall it profit a man if he gain the whole world, and lose his own soul?"

I have no time, as I imagined, to dwell upon the compensating power of the excellency of the knowledge of

Christ. There is this compensation, however, "What things were gain to me," says the Apostle, "those I counted loss for Christ. Yea, doubtless, and I count all things but loss for the excellency of the knowledge of Christ Jesus my Lord." This compensation runs through creation; it seems to be a radical law both in the physical and spiritual government of God. You see it in things around you. A man climbs up to high place, and calumny and care go barking at his heels. There is beauty, dazzling all beholders, and consumption, "like a worm i' the bud, preying upon its damask cheek." There is talent, dazzling and enrapturing, and madness waiting to pounce upon the vacated throne.

Oh, yes, and there is a strange and solemn affinity, too, in the Bible, between crime and punishment. I can only indicate just what I mean. The Jews rejected Christ, perseveringly rejected Christ; and one of their pleas, you remember, was, "If thou let this man go, thou art not Cæsar's friend;" and to conciliate the Roman power, they rejected Christ. That was their crime; what was their punishment? The Romans did come, by and by, and "took away their place and nation." Pharaoh issued his enactment, that all the male children of Israel should be drowned: that was the crime; what was the punishment? Pharaoh and his host were drowned in the waters of the Red Sea by and by. Hezekiah took the ambassadors of Babylon through the treasure-chambers of silver and gold, ostentatiously showing them his wealth: that was the crime; what was the punishment? The treasures of silver and gold went off captive to Babylon by and by. David, in the lust of his power, took the census of the people, and numbered them: that was the crime; what was the punishment? The pestilence fell upon the people whom David had numbered, and dried up the sources of the strength in which he had boasted so fondly.

And, just to remind you of another case, who are those who are represented as standing at the barred gate of heaven, knocking, frantic and disappointed, outside, and crying in tones of agony that mortal lips cannot compass now, thank God! "Lord, Lord, open to us." Who are they? Not the scandalously sinful, not those who on earth were alien altogether—outcast altogether—proscribed altogether from the decencies and decorum of the sanctuary of God. No; those who helped to build the ark, but whose corpses have been strewed in the waters of the deluge; those who brought rafters to the tabernacle, but who, as lepers, were thrust out of the camp, or as transgressors, were stoned beyond the gate; those who, on earth, were almost Christians; those who, in the retributions of eternity, are almost saved; beholding the Church on earth through the chink of the open door, watching the whole family as they are gathered, with the invisible presence and the felt smile of the Father upon them; beholding the family as they are gathered, beatific, and imperishable, in heaven; but the door is shut. Almost Christians! almost saved! Oh strange and sad affinity between crime and punishment! What is your retribution to be? "Every one shall receive according to things he has done in the body, whether they be good, or whether they be bad."

Oh! come to Christ—that is the end of it—come to Christ. Hallow this occasion by dedicating yourselves living temples unto the Lord. He will not refuse to accept you. Mark the zeal with which the Apostle Paul proclaimed the truth: mark the zeal, the love, indomitable and unfailing, with which he clung to the Master—"I determined to know nothing among men but Christ, and him crucified." Oh rare and matchless attachment! fastening upon that which was most in opprobium and in contumely among men. Never did the earnest student of philosophy, as he came away from some Socratic prelection, utter his affirmation, "I am determined to know nothing among men save Socrates, and him poisoned;" never did enraptured youth listen to the persuasive eloquence of Cicero, and utter his affirmation, "I determined to know nothing among men save Cicero, and him proscribed." But Paul takes the very vilest brand of shame, and binds it about his brow, as a diadem of glory: "I determine to know nothing among men but Christ, and him crucified." Yes, that is it, "Christ, and him crucified." "God forbid that I should glory, save in the cross." In the cross is to be our chiefest glory.

Trust that cross for yourselves; take hold of it; it is consecrated. In all circumstances of your history, in all exigencies of your mortal lot, take firm hold of the cross. When the destroying angel rides forth upon the cloud, when his sword is whetted for destruction, clasp the cross; it shall bend over you a shield and a shade; he will relax his frown, and sheathe his sword, and pass quickly, harmlessly by. When you go to the brink of the waters, that you are about to cross, hold up the cross; and by magic power they shall cleave asunder, as did ancient Jordan before the ark of the covenant, and you shall pass over dry-shod, and in peace. When your feet are toiling up the slope, and you arrive at the gate of heaven, hold up the cross; the angels shall know it, and the everlasting doors shall unbar themselves, that you may enter in. When you pass through the ranks of applauding seraphim, that you may pay your first homage to the throne, present the cross, and lower it before the face of the Master, and he, for whose sake you have borne it, will take it from you, and replace it with a crown.

XI.

THE EFFECTS OF PIETY ON A NATION.

"And he said, O, let not the Lord be angry, and I will speak yet but this once: peradventure ten shall be found there. And he said, I will not destroy it for ten's sake."—GENESIS xviii. 32.

MOST remarkable and most encouraging is this instance of prevailing prayer. It might well stimulate us to the exercise of sublimer faith when we behold a mortal thus wrestling with Omnipotence, wrestling with such holy boldness that justice suspends its inflictions, and cannot seal the sinner's doom. Passing over that, however, with all the doctrines it involves, there is another thought couched in the text, to which, at the present time, I want to direct your attention. The history of nations must be regarded, by every enlightened mind, as the history of the providence of God. It is not enough, if we would study history aright, that we follow in the track of battles, that we listen to the wail of the vanquished and to the shout of the conquerors; it is not enough that we excite in ourselves a sort of hero worship of the world's foster-gods, the stalwarth and noble peerage of mankind; it is not enough that we trace upon the page of history the subtile and intricate developments of human character. To study history aright, we must find God in it, we must always recognize the ever-present and the ever-acting Divinity, working all things according to the counsel of his benevolent and holy will. This is the prominent aspect in which history ought to be studied, or grievous dishonor is done to the Universal Ruler, and intense injury is inflicted upon the spirits of men. God, himself, you remember, has impressively announced the guilt and danger of those who regard not the works of the Lord, nor the operations of his hands. The history of ancient Israel, for instance, the chosen people, led by the pillar of cloud by day, and by the pillar of fire by night, through the marching of that perilous wilderness, what was it but the successful development, in a series of wondrous deliverances, of the ever-active providence of God? There were some things in that history which, of course, were incapable either of transfer or repetition; but the history itself included, and was ordained to set forth certain prominent principles for the recognition of all nations; principles which were intended to assert the rights of God, and to assert the obligations of his creatures; principles which are to be consummated in their evolution amid the solemnities of the last day. It was so in the case of Sodom, punished as an example of God's chosen people. Their transgressions had become obduracy, their obduracy had blossomed out into punishment; but a chance in the Divine government yet remained to them; peradventure there might have been ten righteous in the city. If there had been ten righteous in the city, those pious men would have been the substance, the essence, the strength of the devoted nation; for them, on their account, for their sakes, the utter ruin of the land might have been averted, and through them, after the Divine displeasure had passed by, there might have sprung up renewed strength and recovered glory. We may fairly, I think, take this as a general principle, that pious men in all ages of the world's history, are the true strength of the nations in which, in God's providence, they are privileged to live; oftentimes averting calamity, oftentimes restoring strength and blessing, when, but for them, it would have lapsed and gone forever. This is the principle which I purpose, God helping me, to apply for a moment to our own times, and to the land in which we live; and in order to give the subject a great deal of a practical character, I will, in the first place, paint the pious men, and then show the effect which the consistent maintenance of a course of piety may be expected to insure.

I. In the first place, who are the pious men? Who are they whom God, who never judges in short-sightedness, who sees the end from the beginning, and who cannot possibly be deceived or mistaken in his estimate of human character, who are they whom God designates, "the holy seed that shall be the substance thereof"—the pious men that are the strength of the nations in which they live? In order to sustain the honorable appellation which is thus assigned, men must cultivate habits of thought and of practice that are appropriate to such a character. I will just mention two or three particulars.

In the first place, they are pious men who separate themselves avowedly and at the utmost possible distance from surrounding wickedness. Men are placed under the influence of religion, in order that they may separate from sin, in order that they may be governed by the habits of righteousness and true holiness. In times when depravity is especially flagrant, there is a special obligation upon pious men to bring out their virtues into braver and more prominent exercise, regarding that surrounding depravity as in no wise a reason for flinching, or for cowardice, or for compromise, but rather for the augmented firmness of their purity. Now, it cannot for one moment be doubted, that in the times in which we live iniquity does most flagrantly abound. There is not a sin which does not exist, and exists in all rankness and impurity. Because of swearing the land mourns. God's Sabbaths are systematically desecrated, his sanctuaries contumeliously forsaken, his ordinances trampled under foot, his ministers met with the leer oftentimes due to detected conspirators, and regarded as banded traitors, who have conspired against the liberties of the world. The lusts of the flesh scarcely affect to conceal their filthiness, everywhere unveiling their forms, and everywhere diffusing their pestilence. We do not venture upon any sort of comparison, we do not venture to compare the aggregate depravity of this age with the depravity of any age that has preceded. We do not affirm the general fact, that the heart of man is "deceitful and desperately wicked," and that the depravity we see around us, the exhibition of the carnal mind, "which is enmity against God," is most fearfully aggravated by the abundance of privilege by which the people are surrounded. Now, it is the duty, I repeat, of those who would have God's estimate of them as pious men, that they should regard this depravity as invoking them to bear the testimony of unsullied and spotless holiness. Let the exhortations on this matter which are scattered throughout the pages of the Bible be solemnly pondered. "Be not conformed to this world, but be ye transformed according to the renewing of your mind, that ye may prove what is that good and acceptable and perfect will of God." "Abstain from the appearance of evil." In times when depravity is especially flagrant, do not even borrow of the garments of falsehood; do not let there be any meretricious semblance of that which is hateful in the sight of God. Abstain from the appearance of evil. Come out of it so thoroughly that the fellowships and intercourse of social life do not seduce you into a sort of complicity. "Be not partakers of other men's sins. Have no fellowship with the unfruitful works of darkness, but rather reprove." "Be ye not unequally yoked together with unbelievers, for what fellowship hath light with darkness, and what concord hath Christ with Belial, and what part hath he that believeth with an infidel?" "Cleanse yourselves from all filthiness of flesh and spirit; perfecting holiness in the fear of God."

You will not fail to perceive that the whole of these passages have one aim and one summons, and that is holiness; holiness, as spotless in the secrecy of individual consciousness as in the jealous watch of men; holiness shrined in the heart and influencing benignly and transforming the entire character; holiness, that is something more chivalrous than national honor; holiness, something that maintains a higher standard of right than commercial integrity; holiness, something that is more noble-minded than the conventional courtesies of life; holiness which comes out in every-day existence, hallowing each transaction, taking hold of the money as it passes through the hand in ordinary currency, and stamping upon it a more noble image and superscription than Cæsar's; holiness written upon the bells of the horses and upon the frontlet of the forehead, an immaculate and spotless lustre exuding, so to speak, from the man in daily life, so that the world starts back from him, and tells at a glance that he has been with Jesus. Now, brethren, it is to this, to the exercise and maintenance of this unflinching holiness, that you are called. Here is the first prominent obligation of pious men. You are to confront every evil with its exact and diametrical opposite; and he who in circumstances like these in which we stand, ventures to hesitate, or ventures to parley, brand him as a traitor to his country, a traitor to his religion, and a traitor to his God.

Secondly, if you would be what God regards as pious men, you must cultivate firm attachment to the doctrines of Christian truth. There is, brethren, in our day, a very widely-diffused defectiveness of religious profession, a very widely-diffused departure from the faith that was "once delivered to the saints." This is a Christian country. Men call it so, I know; but there is in daily practice a strange and sad departure from the precepts of Christianity—ay, on the part of men by whom the theory of this being a Christian country is most noisily and boisterously maintained.

Are you strangers to the presence in the midst of us of the dark and subtile spirit of unbelief; a venal press and active emissaries poisoning the fresh blood of youth, disheartening the last hope of age, and which, if their own account of the circulation of their pernicious principles is to be relied upon, has already tainted hundreds of thousands with that infectious venom whose poison lies not in the destruction of the body? True, it is for the most part bland, conciliatory, plausible, rather than audacious and braggart, as in former times, veiling its deadly purpose in song or in story. But the dagger is not the less deadly because the haft is jewelled, and infidelity is not the less infidelity, not the less pernicious, not the less accursed, because genius has woven its stories to adorn it, and because fancy has wreathed it into song.

Are you strangers to the avowed denial on the part of some of the divinity and atonement of our Lord Jesus Christ? to the man-exalting opinion which relies for its own salvation upon the piled up fabric of its own righteousness, or which through the flinty rocks of self-righteous morality, would tunnel out a passage to the eternal throne?

Are you strangers to the workings of the grand apostasy darkening the sunlight of the Saviour's love, dislocating the perfection of the Saviour's work, hampering the course of the atonement with the frail entangled frame-work of human merit, restless in its endeavors to regain its ascendency, crafty, and vigilant and formidable as ever?

Are you strangers to the heresy which has made its appearance in the midst of a body once deeming itself the fairest offspring of the Reformation, and which would exclude thousands from covenanted mercies, because they own not priestly pretensions, and conform not to traditional rites?

Are you strangers in the other quarter of the horizon and of the sky, to dark and lowering portents that have come over with rationalistic and German infidelity? Brethren, there is a duty, solemn and authoritative, resting upon the pious men that they hold fast that which was "once delivered to the saints." Let the exhortations, too, on this matter, be carefully pondered. "Be no more children tossed to and fro with every wind of doctrine, by the sleight of man and cunning craftiness whereby they lie in wait to betray." "Stand fast"—not loose, not easily shifted, having a firm foundation—"stand fast in the faith once delivered unto the saints." Be "rooted in the faith;" be "grounded in the faith;" "contend earnestly for the faith." Brethren, here is another invocation, and it is solemnly binding upon you. And while there are some around us that would rob Christ of his grace, and others that would rob Christ of his crown, and others, more royal felons, that would steal both the one and the other, let it be ours to take our stand firm and unswerving by the altars of the truth; let our determination go forth to the universe, "I determine to know nothing among men, save Jesus Christ, and him crucified."

And, then, thirdly, if you would be pious men as God estimates piety, you must cultivate cordial, brotherly love. In times like these, there is a solemn obligation resting upon all "who hold the head" to cultivate the spirit of unity with all "who hold the head." By unity, we do not mean uniformity. There is none, there can be none in the free universe of God. You have it not in nature. You may go out into the waving woodland, when death is on the trees, and you may prune their riotous growth, and mold, and shape, and cut them into something like a decent, a decorous uniformity; but the returning spring, when it comes, will laugh at your aimless labor.

Wherever there is life, there will be found variety of engaging forms which attract and fascinate the eye.

We do not mean uniformity, therefore; the harmony of voices, or the adjustment of actions, the drowsy repetition of one belief, or the harmonious intonation of one liturgy, but we mean "the unity of the spirit in the bond of peace," which we are to intensely labor to maintain and procure. Let the exhortations on this matter also be very solemnly pondered. "A new commandment," so that there are eleven commandments now; the decalogue has been added to by this new commandment, which is, indeed, the substance and essence of all the rest. "A new commandment give I unto you, that ye love one another." "Be kindly affectioned one to another, in brotherly love, in honor preferring one another." Nay, the Apostle does not hesitate to set it down as one of the surest evidences of Christian discipleship. "We know that we have passed from death unto life, because we love the brethren." Compliance with these exhortations is always imperative, especially imperative in seasons of national danger. Everything that is ominous, everything that is solemn, everything that is portentous around us, must be regarded as an earnest call to Christians to live together in love. This love is to be cherished everywhere—to be cherished toward those who are members of the same section of the universal Church. Here, of course, there should be no orphan's heart. Here, all should feel themselves members of a commonwealth. There should be a rejoicing with those that do rejoice, and a weeping with those that weep; and, as by electric fire, the wants and the wishes of the one should be communicated to, and acknowledged by the whole, that it should not only be cherished in our own communion, but toward all who hold "the unity of the spirit in the bond of peace, and in righteousness of life." Wherever Christ is acknowledged, his grace magnified, his crown vindicated, his law made honorable—wherever the service of Christ is the aim, and the glory of Christ is the purpose, there the Church should know as Christian and should hail as brethren. This duty is one that has been scandalously neglected in the times in which we live; and that neglect has darkened the aspect and augmented the perils of the times. Brethren, we must all amend if we would not betray. And when the Church of Christ shall combine in heart as in spirit one, then shall the great building of the universe progress. God shall smile upon the workmen, "the glory of the latter house shall exceed the glory of the former," and the whole "building fitly framed together shall grow up into a holy temple of the Lord."

Then, fourthly, if we would be pious men as God estimates piety, we must be zealous in endeavor for the spread of the Gospel, and for the conversion of the world. The errors and the crimes of which we have spoken, render this essential. We have but to gather into our minds the contemplation of guilt so heinous, so offensive that it rises up in the presence of the Holy One, and calls for vengeance as he is seated upon his throne; then, we have but to remember the consequences of that guilt, everywhere producing misery, everywhere drying up the sources of spiritual affluence, everywhere exposing to the unending perditions of hell. Now, brethren, nothing—and I would speak as one member of the army summoning others to the battle-field—nothing will avail but the combined, and devoted, and persevering exertions of the members of the Church below. How else shall we attempt to grapple with the depravity around us? Parliamentary enactments, what can they do? Threats to affright, or bribes to seduce, what can they do? Patronage in all its prestige, and all its power, all that can be possibly brought out of State treasury or of State influence, what are they? Availless utterly without the power and Spirit of God. No; there must be a band of faithful men who are thus renovated and redeemed going forth in the name of the Lord. They must sustain the ministry in existing pastorates, and spread it wherever it has never been established. They must support institutions for the education of the entire man, institutions based upon the Word of God. They must become themselves preachers of "the truth as it is in Jesus;" by prayer, by influence, by example, by effort, they must display all the grace which has redeemed them; and especially they must all in earnest, repeated, importunate supplications besiege the throne of grace in prayer. There is another summons, the last I shall give you on this matter to-night, and you are now to answer it with intense energy, with intense zeal. Coldness here is irrational. Ardor here is reason. Indifference here is foolishness. Earnestness, or, if you will, enthusiasm here is the highest and sublimest wisdom.

If you would be pious men, therefore, as God estimates piety, you are to come out from the world and to be separated from it; you are to hold fast the doctrines you have received; you are to cultivate to each other the tenderest brotherly love; and you are to be energetic in heart for the conversion of the world.

II. I come now, secondly and briefly, to notice the effects which we are warranted in expecting such conduct as this to insure. This is the doctrine of the text, that Sodom would have been spared if the ten righteous men had been there. Pious men are presented to us, therefore, as the safety of the nation in which they live. This is very beautifully presented in several other parts of Scripture. You have it, for instance, in the prophecy of Isaiah, lxv. 8, 9: "Thus saith the Lord, As the new wine is found in the cluster, and one saith, Destroy it not; for a blessing is in it; so will I do for my servants' sakes, that I may not destroy them all. And I will bring forth a seed out of Jacob, and out of Judah an inheritor of my mountains; and mine elect shall inherit it, and my servants shall dwell there." Then, again, in the prophecy of Malachi, iii. 10, 11: "Bring ye all the tithes into the storehouse, that there may be meat in mine house, and prove me now herewith, saith the Lord of hosts, if I will not open you the windows of heaven, and pour you out a blessing, that there shall not be room enough to receive it. And I will rebuke the devourer for your sakes, and he shall not destroy the fruits of your ground, neither shall your vine cast her fruit before the time in the field, saith the Lord of hosts."

We see here the development of the general principle for which we contend, that God preserves nations for the sake of pious men. The annals of the past show how very frequently he has put to naught statesmanship, fleets, and armies, and has rendered honor to truth, meekness, and righteousness. This I do solemnly believe to be the case in our own land in this crisis of its affairs, and I am bold to affirm my conviction, that the destinies of England and of the British Empire are at this moment in the hands of its pious men. If they be faithful to their high trust and to the vocation to which they are eminently and signally called, nothing can harm us; no weapon that is formed against us shall ever be able to prosper. I think this might be made out from the history of the past, both as to temporal and spiritual matters. I appeal to you whether it is not manifest that the temporal interests of a nation are bound up in its piety? Let pious men prevail in a land, let the population become imbued with the spirit and with the leaven of evangelical godliness, what is the consequence? Order is at once preserved. As their holiness spreads, as their unworldly yet earnest example manifests itself and begins to be felt, sounder views prevail. The moral is felt to exert a supremacy over the secular; the political agitator, the infidel demagogue, the philoosphical theorist, are scouted as physicians of no value; and men everywhere learn to submit to the orderly restraints and the well-regulated government of law.

Let pious men prevail, and they will keep up the freedom of a land. I do not mean that crouching emasculation on the one hand, nor that ribald licentiousness on the other hand, which have both been dignified by the name by extreme political parties; but I mean well-ordered and rational liberty; liberty which respects the rights of other people at the same time that it asserts and vindicates its own; liberty which with one hand renders to Cæsar the things that are Cæsar's, and with the other hand takes care to render to God the things that are God's; liberty which honors men as men, just because the Divine command tells it to "honor all men," and because, all the world over, there is nothing so royal as a man. That liberty will be preserved wherever pious men are found, and wherever the example of these pious men begins to spread itself among people.

And, then, pious men will preserve the prosperity of a land. There is a false prosperity which must be abandoned; there is a false honor which must be speedily forsworn; but that prosperity which is substantial and abiding will remain under the influences of piety. Art will minister then not to luxury but to truth; science will minister then not to infidelity but to truth; com merce will minister then not to selfishness but to benevolence; and other realms shall render to us their unbought and unpurchasable homage, and the sons of our country, in their not unholy pride, may wave their banner to the wind, with the motto on it:

> "He is the freeman whom the truth makes free,
> And all are slaves besides."

Yes, brethren, it is Britain's altar and not Britain's throne, Britain's Bible and not Britain's statute book, that is the great, and deep, and strong source of her national prosperity and renown. Do away with this; suffer that fidelity with which, in some humble measure, we have borne witness for God, to be relaxed; let our Sabbaths be sinned away at the bidding of unholy or mistaken mobs; let us enter into adulterous and unworthy alliance with the man of sin; let us be traitors to the trust with which God has invested us, to take care of the ark of the Lord, and the crown will lose its lustre, the peerage its nobility, and the senate its command; all the phases of social rank and order will be disjointed and disorganized; a lava tide of desolation will overwhelm all that is consecrated and noble, and angels may sing the dirge over a once great, but now hopelessly fallen people: "the glory is departed from Israel, because the ark of God is taken." Keep fast by that ark, hold it—hold your attachment to it as the strongest element of being, and there shall be no bounds to the sacred magnificence of our nation; but the fires of the last day, when they consume all that is perishable and drossy, may see us with the light of the Divine presence gleaming harmlessly around our brow, and in our hand the open law for all the nations of mankind.

Those are temporal benefits. And, then, let there be pious men in the land, and spiritual benefits will also be secured. There will, for instance, be the defeat of erroneous opinions. Truth, when the Spirit inspires it not, abstract truth, is weak and powerless. Truth, with the Spirit in it, is mighty, and will prevail. There can be no fear as to the result, because the world has never been left, and will never be left without the active Spirit of God. Falsehood breaks out impetuously, just like one of those torrents that leap and rattle over the summit of the mountain after the thunder-storm, overwhelming in the first outbreak, but dying away into insignificance and silence by and by; truth is the little spring that rises up imperceptibly and gently, and flows on, unostentatious and noiseless, until at last navies are wafted on its bosom, and it pours its full volume of triumphant waters into the rejoicing sea. So it will be with truth; wealth cannot bribe it, talent cannot dazzle it, sophistry cannot overreach it, authority cannot please it; they all, like Felix, tremble in its majestic presence. Let pious men increase, and each of them will become a centre of holiness; apostates will be brought back to the Church, poor backsliders will be reclaimed into new-found liberty and new created privilege, and there will be a cry like that on the summit of Carmel after the controversy was over, and had issued in the discomfiture of Baal, "The Lord, he is God; the Lord, he is God."

And, then, better than all that, salvation of souls will be secured. The conversion of a soul is an infinitely greater triumph than the eradication of a false opinion. A false opinion may be crushed, and the man that holds it may be in imminent spiritual peril; convert the man's soul, and his opinions will come right by and by. Oh, if as you go from this place to-night, you were to behold the crowds of tempters and temptresses to evil that will cross your path as you travel homeward, if you think of their activity, of their earnestness to proselytize in the grand diabolical army, and to make sevenfold more the children of hell than they are themselves, and if you think of the apathy of the faithful, of the scantiness of effort, of the failure of faith, of the depression of endeavor, of the laxity of attachment on the part of believers in Jesus, surely there is enough to make you abashed and confounded. Brethren, I should like, if I could, to bring before you one solitary soul, to fasten your attention upon that soul, to transfix it as with a lightning glance before you, so that you might trace it in its downward path, see it as habit crusts it over, and selfishness rejoices over it, and the foul fiend gloats upon it in mockery, and disease, prematurely induced, comes upon it, and death waits for his prey, and hell is moved from beneath to meet it at its coming, and that you should follow it down into those dark and dread abodes, which man's pencil painteth not, and of which man's imagination, thank God, cannot conceive! Oh! draw the curtain over that; we cannot bear the sight! But as you think of the real spiritual peril in which not one, not a family—Oh! if there were but a family, all London would be awake for its deliverance—but there is a world in danger—not one, not a family, not an island, not a continent, but a world—if I could only fasten that upon your consciences to-night, each one of you would surely go away with tearful eye and glad heart, glad that you were able to do anything for God, and would not rest without saying, "For Zion's sake I will not hold my peace, and for Jerusalem's sake, I will not rest until the righteousness thereof go forth as the brightness, and the salvation thereof as the lamp that burneth."

Just one parting word. If you would do all this, you must be pious yourselves; but do not be among the number of those who busy themselves in the externalisms of godliness, and are in some measure active in connection with the Church of God, but are out of Christ, aliens themselves from the commonwealth of Israel. If you are not personally pious, you will be accomplices in drawing down the thunderbolt, and chargeable to that extent with your country's ruin, and the ruin of souls. Come to Christ now; let all your past iniquity be forgotten and forgiven as you bow before him in humiliation and in tears; he will not refuse you; he will not cast you out. Then enter upon a life of piety in spite of all that scoffers say. Ah! religion is not so mean a thing as infidels represent it to be! They curl the lip of scorn at us, and we can bear that; they flash the eye of hate at us, and we can bear that, as long as God looks upon us with complacency, as long as he has promised to crown us as conquerors in heaven, for which, by our spiritual conflicts and victories, we shall have come prepared. Oh, it is no mean thing. The saint, the righteous man, the pious believer in Jesus, is a patriot as well as a saint. The worldling may sneer and scorn, but we have a noble revenge, for it is pious men that have kept the conflagrating elements away from this long doomed world up to the present moment of its history; and if the ten righteous had not been in this enormous Sodom, long ere now would the firebrand of destruction have struck it that it might be consumed in its deserved ruin. Thank God, there is hope for the world yet.

When the prophet in depression and in sorrow was saying, "I, even I, only am left, the prophet of the Lord," God pointed him to seven thousand that had never bowed the knee to Baal; and there are faithful ones in the secret places of the world yet, palm-tree Christians growing up in unexpected places, amid sandy soil and with no companionship, who are flourishing in godly vigor and earnest in persevering prayer. There is hope for the world yet. Oh, for the increase of these pious men! Be you of the number of this unostentatious but valiant host. Do you pant for fame? You can find it here. Young men, there are some of you in the presence of God that have ambition high bounding in your hearts, who feel the elasticity of youth within you; who feel that the flight of your soaring spirit is not the flight of the flagging or the breathless; that there is something still within you that pants for a distinction other than you have yet attained; oh come to Christ, enlist yourselves in his service, be soldiers of the cross, fight moral battles, and yours shall be the victory. To you the Church is looking; your fathers, worn out with labor, exhausted with the vicissitudes and the victories of years, are passing rapidly away, and they are wondering where their successors are. They have gone from us; just when we were expecting for them higher fields and wider triumphs, the fiery chariot came and they were not, and nothing was left for us but to cry as we followed the track of the cavalcade, in our hopelessness, almost in our agony, "My father, my father, the chariot of Israel and the horsemen thereof." Oh! thank God, they have flung their mantles down, and it is for you to catch them, to robe yourselves to-day in the garments of the holy departed, and like them, to do and die.

XII.

THE PROPHET OF HOREB—HIS LIFE AND ITS LESSONS.

"Elijah, the Tishbite, who was of the inhabitants of Gilead."—1 KINGS, xvii. 1.

THE mountains of the Bible will well repay the climber. There is a glorious prospect from their summits, and moral bracing in the breathing of their difficult air.

Most of the events in Bible history, which either embody great principles, illustrate Divine perfections, or bear impressively upon the destinies of man, have had the mountains for the pedestals of their achievement. Beneath the arch of the Covenant-rainbow the lone ark rested upon Ararat; Abraham's trial, handing down the high faith of the hero-father, and typing the greater sacrifice of the future time, must be "on one of the mountains" in the land of Moriah; Aaron, climbing heavenward, is "unclothed and clothed upon" amid the solitudes of Hor; and where but on the crest of Nebo could Moses gaze upon the land and die? If there is to be a grand experiment to determine between rival faiths—to defeat Baal—to exalt Jehovah, what spot so fitting as the excellency of Carmel? It was due to the great and dread events of the Saviour's history that they should be enacted where the world's broad eye could light upon them, hence he is transfigured "on the high mountain apart," on Olivet he prays, on Calvary he dies; and, at the close of all, in the splendors of eternal allotment, amid adoring angels and perfected men, we cheerfully "come to Mount Zion."

Precious as is the Scripture in all phases of its appearance, the quality which, above all others, invests it with a richer value, is its exquisite adaptation to every necessity of man. Professing itself to be his infallible and constant instructor, it employs all modes of communicating wisdom. "The Man of our counsel" is always at hand, in every condition and in every peril. But we learn more from living exemplar than from preceptive utterance. The truth, which has not been realized by some man of like passions with ourselves, comes cold and distant like a lunar rainbow. It may furnish us with correct notions and a beautiful system, just as we can learn proportion from a statue, but there needs the touch of life to influence and to transform. Hence, not the least impressive and salutary Bible teaching is by the accurate exhibition of individual character. A man's life is there sketched out to us, not that side of it merely which he presents to the world, which the restraints of society have modified, which intercourse has subdued into decorousness, and which shrouds his meaner self in a conventional hypocrisy; but his inner life, his management of the trifles which give the sum of character, his ordinary and household doings, as well as the rarer seasons of exigency and of trial. The whole man is before us, and we can see him as he is. Partiality cannot blind us, nor prejudice distort our view. Nothing is exaggerated, nothing is concealed. His defects are there—his falterings and depressions—his mistrusts and betrayals—like so many beacons glaring their warning lights upon our path. His excellencies are there—his stern integrity and consistent walking, his intrepid wrestling and heroic endurance—that we may be followers of his patience and faith, and ultimately share his crown. So marked and hallowed is this candor, that we do not wonder at its being alleged as an argument for the book's divinity. The characters are all human in their experience, although divine in their portrayal. They were *men*, those Bible worthies, world-renowned, God-smitten, princely men, towering indeed in moral, as Saul in physical, stature above their fellows, but still men of like passions with ourselves—to the same frailties incident—with the same trials battling—by the same temptations frequently and foully overcome. Their perfect *humanness* is, indeed, their strongest influence and greatest charm. Of what avail to us were the biography of an angel, could you chronicle his joys in the calm round of heaven? There could be no sympathy either of condition or experience.

But the Bible, assuming the essential identity of the race, tells of man, and the "one blood" of all nations leaps up to the thrilling tale. There is the old narrative of lapse and loss; the tidings, ancient and undecaying, of temptation, conflict, mastery, recompense. In ourselves there have been the quiverings of David's sorrow, and the stirrings of David's sin. We, perhaps, like Elijah, have been by turns confessor and coward—fervent as Peter, and as faithless too. The heart answers to the history, and responsive and struggling humanity owns the sympathy, and derives the blessing.

It is a strange history, this history of the Prophet Elijah. Throughout the whole of his career we are attracted almost more by his inspiration than by himself. We are apt to lose sight of the man in the thought of the Divine energy which wielded him at its terrible or gentle will. The unconsciousness of self, which is the distinctive mark of the true seer, is always present with him—in his manliest and in his meekest hours—in his solitary prayer in the loft at Zarephath, in his solemn sarcasm on the summit of Carmel—when he flushes the cheek of a dead child, or pales the brow of a living king. He is surrendered always to the indwelling God. He always seems to regard himself as a chosen and a separated man—lifted, by his consecration, above the love or the fear of his kind—forced, ever and anon, upon difficult and perilous duty—a flying roll, carven with mercy and with judgment—

an echo, rather than an original utterance—"the voice of one," not "one," but "the voice of one crying in the wilderness, Prepare ye the way of the Lord!"

How abruptly he bursts upon the world. We know nothing of his birth, nothing of his parentage, nothing of his training. On all these matters the record is profoundly silent. He is presented to us at once, a full-grown and authoritative man, starting in the path of Ahab sudden as the lightning, energetic and alarming as the thunder. "Elijah the Tishbite, who was of the inhabitants of Gilead." This is all. And it is all we need. What reck we of his ancestry? He is royal in his deeds. Obscure in his origin, springing probably from the herdsmen or vine-dressers of Galilee, regarded by the men of Tishbe as one of themselves—a little reserved and unsocial withal—his person, perhaps, held in contempt by the licentious court, and his intrusions stigmatized as annoying impertinence, he held on his high way notwithstanding, performed stupendous miracles, received large revelations, and at last, tired of the world, went up to heaven in a chariot of fire. How often have we seen the main fact of this story realized in later times! Men have looked at the trappings of the messenger—not at the import of his message. Their faculty of appreciation has been grievously impaired. A prophet has leaped into the day with his burden of reproof and truth-telling, but he has not been clad in silken sheen, nor a speaker of smooth things, and the world has gone on to its merchandise, while the broken-hearted seer has retired into the wilderness to die. A poet has warbled out his soul in secret, and discoursed most exquisite music—but, alas! it has been played among the tombs. A glorious iconoclast has come forth among the peoples, "expecting that they would have understood how that the Lord by him had sent deliverance," but he has been met by the insulting rejoinder, "Who made thee a ruler and a judge?" Thus, in the days of her nonage, because they lacked high estate and lofty lineage, has the world poured contempt upon some of the choicest of her sons. "A heretic!" shouted the furious bigotry of the Inquisition. "And yet it moves," said Galileo—resolute, even in the moment of enforced abjuration, for the immutable truth. A scoffing to Genoese bravos, grandees of Portugal, and the court of England, Columbus spied the log of wood in its eastward drifting, and opened up America—the rich El Dorado of many an ancient dream. "An empiric!" shouted all the Doctor Sangradoes of the time, and the old physiologists hated Harvey with an intensely professional hatred, because he affirmed the circulation of the blood. "A Bedfordshire tinker!" sneered the polite ones, with a whiff of the otto of roses, as if the very mention of his craft was infragrant; "what has he to do to preach, and write books, and set up for a teacher of his fellows?" But glorious John Bunyan, leaving them in their own Cabul-country, dwelt in the land of Beulah, climbed up straight to the presence of the shining ones, and had "all the trumpets sounding for him on the other side." Sidney Smith wrote at, and tried to write down "the consecrated Cobbler," who was to evangelize India; but William Carey shall live embalmed in memories of converted thousands long after the witty canon of St. Paul's is forgotten or is remembered only as a melancholy example of genius perverted and a vocation mistaken. "A Methodist!" jested the godless witlings of Brazennose; "A Jacobin!" reiterated the makers of silver shrines; "A ringleader in the Gordon Riots!" said the Romanists whose errors he had combated; and the formalistic churchmanship of that day gathered up its gentilities, smoothed its ruffled fringes, and with a dowager's stateliness flounced by "on the other side;" and reputable burghers, the "canny bodies" of the time, subsided into their own respectabilities, and shook their heads at every mention of the pestilent fellow; but, calm-browed and high-souled, John Wesley went on until a large portion of his world-parish rejoiced in his light, and wondered at its luminous and ardent flame. And if it be lawful to speak of the Master in the same list as his disciples, who, however excellent, fall immeasurably short of their Divine Pattern, *He* was called a Nazarene, and there was the scorn of a world couched in the contemptuous word.

There are symptoms, however, of returning sanity. Judicial ermine and archiepiscopal lawn robing the sons of tradesmen, and the blood of all the Montmorencies--

fouled by *mésalliance* with crime—cooling itself in a common prison, are remarkable signs of the times. Men are beginning to feel conscious, not, perhaps, that they have committed a crime, but that they have been guilty of what in the diplomacy of Talleyrand was considered worse—that is, a blunder. Whether the chivalry of feudalism be extinct or not, there can be no question that the villenage of feudalism is gone. Common men nowadays question the wisdom of nobilities, correct the errors of cabinets, and do not even listen obsequiously to catch the whispers of kings. That is a strong and growing world-feeling which the poet embodies when he sings:

> "Believe us! noble Vere de Veres,
> From yon blue heavens above us bent,
> The grand old gardener and his wife
> Smile at the claims of long descent.
> Howe'er it be, it seems to me
> 'Tis only noble to be good—
> Kind hearts are more than coronets,
> And simple faith than Norman blood."

Not that rank has lost its prestige, nor royalty its honor. Elevated station is a high trust, and furnishes opportunity for extensive usefulness. The coronet may be honored or despised at the pleasure of the wearer. When the rank is larger than the man, when his individuality is shrouded behind a hundred coats-of-arms, when he has so much of the blood of his ancestors in his veins that there is no room for any generous pulses of his own, why, of course, he must find his own level, and be content to be admired, like any other piece of confectionery, by occasional passers-by; but when the noble remembers his humanity, and has sympathy for the erring and encouragement for the sincere—

> "When, all the trappings freely swept away,
> The man's great nature leaps into the day,"

his nobility men are not slow to acknowledge—the cap and plume bend very gracefully over the sorrow which they succor, and the jewelled hand is blanched into a heavenlier whiteness when it beckons a struggling people into the power and progress of the coming time. The great question which must be asked of any new aspirer who would mold the world's activities to his will, is not, Whence comes he? but, What is he? There may be some semi-fossilized relics of the past who will continue to insinuate, "Has he a grandfather?" But the great world of the earnest and of the workers thunders out, "Has he a *soul?* Has he a lofty purpose, a single eye, a heart of power? Has he the prophet's sanctity and inspiration, as well as his boldness and fervor? Never mind the bar sinister on his escutcheon—has he no bar sinister in his life? Has he a giant's strength, a hero's courage, a child's simplicity, an apostle's love, a martyr's will? Then is he sufficiently ennobled." If I, a Gospel charioteer, meet him as he essays, trembling, to drive into the world, what must be my salutation? Art thou of noble blood?

Is thy retinue large? thy banner richly emblazoned? thy speech plausible? thy purpose fair? No—but "Is thy heart right?" If it be, give me thy hand.

A prominent feature in the Prophet's character, one which cannot fail to impress us at every mention of his name, is *his singular devotion to the object of his great mission.* He was sent upon the earth to be the earth's monitor of God. This was his life-purpose, and faithfully he fulfilled it. Rising above the temptations of sense—ready at the bidding of his Master to crucify natural affection—sternly repressing the sensibility which might interfere with duty; trampling upon worldly interest, and regardless of personal aggrandizement or safety, he held on his course, unswerving and untired, to the end. God was his object in everything; to glorify God, his aim; to vindicate God, his miracles; to speak for God, his message; to exhibit God, his life. As the rod of Moses swallowed up the symbols of Egyptian wizardry, so did this consuming passion in Elijah absorb each meaner impulse, and each low desire. His decision rarely failed him, his consistency never. He "halted not between two opinions." He spurned alike the adulation of a monarch and of a mob. He neither pandered for the favor of a court, nor made unworthy compromise with the idolaters of Baal. Heaven's high remembrancer, he did a true man's work in a true man's way, with one purpose and a "united" heart.

Although many parts of this character cannot, on

account of his peculiar vocation, be presented for our imitation, in his unity of purpose and of effort he furnishes us with a noble example. This oneness of principle—freedom from tortuous policy—the direction of the energies to the attainment of one worthy end—appears to be what is meant in Scripture by the "single eye," ἁπλοῦς—not complex—no obliquity in the vision—looking straight on—taking in one object at one time. And if we look into the lives of the men who have vindicated their right to be held in the world's memory, we shall find that all their actions evolve from one comprehensive principle, and converge to one magnificent achievement. Consider the primitive apostles. There you have twelve men, greatly diverse in character, cherishing each his own taste and mode of working, laboring in different localities, and bringing the one Gospel to bear upon different classes of mind, and yet everywhere—in proud Jerusalem, inquisitive Ephesus, cultured Athens, voluptuous Rome—meeting after many years in that mightiest result, the establishment of the kingdom of Christ. Much of this issue is of course due to the Gospel itself, or rather to the Divine agency which applied it, but something also to the unity of the messengers, their sincere purpose, and sustained endeavor. And so it is in the case of all who have been the benefactors of mankind. They have had some master-purpose, which has molded all others into a beautiful subordination, which they have maintained amid hazard and suffering, and which, shrined sacredly in the heart, has influenced and fashioned the life. If a man allow within him the play of different or contradictory purposes, he may, in a lifetime, pile up a head of gold, a breast of silver, thighs of brass, and feet of clay, but it is but a great image after all. It crumbles at the first touch of the smiting stone, and, like the chaff of the summer threshing-floor, its fragments are helpless on the wind. If, on the other hand, a man's doings grow out of one and the same spirit, and that spirit be consecrated to holy endeavor, they will interpenetrate and combine into beneficent achievement, and stand out a life-giving and harmonious whole. This oneness of design for which we contend, is distinctive of the highest developments of the whole family of genius. A book may run through many editions, and fascinate many reviewers, but it must be informed by one spirit, new correspondences must be revealed to the æsthetic eye, and it must appear "in the serene completeness of artistic unity," ere it can settle down to be a household word in the family, or a hidden treasure in the heart. In whatever department "the beauty-making Power" has wrought—in the bodiless thought, or in the breathing marble; in the *chef-d'œuvres* of the artist, or in the conceptions of the architect; whether Praxiteles chisels, Raffaelle paints, Shakspeare delineates, or Milton sings—there is the same singleness of the animating spirit. Hamlet, Paradise Lost, and Festus; the Greek Slave, and the Madonna; the Coliseum and Westminster Abbey; are they not, each in its kind, creations to which nothing can be added with advantage, and from which, without damage, nothing can be taken away?

And of that other Book—our highest literature, as well as our unerring law—the glorious, world-subduing Bible, do we not feel the same? In its case the experiment has been tried. The Apocryphal has been bound up with the Inspired, like "wood, hay, and stubble," loading the rich fret-work of a stately pile, or the clumsy work of an apprentice superadded to the finish of a master. Doubtless instruction may be gathered from it, but how it "pales its ineffectual fires" before the splendor of the Word! It is unfortunate for it that they have been brought into contact. We might be grateful for the gas-lamp at eventide, but it were grievous folly to light it up at noon. As in science, literature, art, so it is in character. We can wrap up in a word the object of "the world's foster gods;" to bear witness for Jehovah—to extend Christianity—to disinter the truth for Europe—to "spread Scriptural holiness"—to humanize prison discipline—to abolish slavery—these are soon told; but if you unfold each word, you have the life-labor of Elijah, Paul, Luther, Wesley, Howard, Wilberforce—the inner man of each heart laid open, with its hopes, joys, fears, anxieties, ventures, faiths, conflicts, triumphs, in the long round of weary and of wasting years.

Look at this oneness of principle embodied in action. See it in Martin Luther. *He has a purpose, that miner's son.* That purpose is the acquisition of knowledge. He exhausts speedily the resources of Mansfield; reads hard, and devours the lectures at Madgeburg; chants in the hours of recreation, like the old Minnesingers, in streets, for bread; sits at the feet of Trebonius in the college at Eisenach; enters as a student at Erfurt, and at the age of eighteen, has outstripped his fellows, has a University for his admirer, and professors predicting for him the most successful career of the age. *He has a purpose, that Scholar of Erfurt.* That purpose is the discovery of truth, for in the old library he has stumbled on a Bible. Follow him out into the new world which that volume has flashed upon his soul. With Pilate's question on his lip and in his heart, he foregoes his brilliant prospect—parts without a sigh with academical distinction—takes monastic vows in an Augustine convent—becomes the watchman and sweeper of the place—goes a mendicant friar, with the convent's begging-bag, to the houses where he had been welcomed as a friend, or had starred it as a lion—wastes himself with voluntary penances well-nigh to the grave—studies the Fathers intensely, but can get no light—pores over the Book itself, with scales upon his eyes—catches a dim streak of auroral brightness, but leaves Erfurt before the glorious dawn—until at last, in his cell at Wittemberg, on his bed of languishing at Bologna, and finally at Rome—Pilate's question answered upon Pilate's stairs—there comes the thrice-repeated Gospel-whisper, "The just shall live by faith," and the glad Evangel scatters the darkening and shreds off the paralysis, and he rises into moral freedom, a new man unto the Lord! *He has a purpose, that Augustine monk.* That purpose is the Reformation! Waiting with the modesty of the hero, until he is forced into the strife, with the courage of the hero he steps into the breach to do battle for the living truth. Tardy in forming his resolve, he is brave in his adhesion to it. Not like Erasmus, "holding the truth in unrighteousness," with a clear head and a craven heart—not like Carlstadt, hanging upon a grand principle the tatters of a petty vanity—not like Seckingen, a wielder of carnal weapons, clad in glowing mail, instead of the armor of righteousness and the weapon of all prayer—but bold, disinterested, spiritual—he stands before us God-prepared and God-upheld—that valiant Luther, who, in his opening prime, amazed the Cardinal de Vio by his fearless avowal, "Had I five heads I would lose them all rather than retract the testimony which I have borne for Christ"—that incorruptible Luther, whom the Pope's nuncio tried in vain to bribe, and of whom he wrote in his spleen: "This German beast has no regard for gold"—that inflexible Luther, who, when told that the fate of John Huss would probably await him at Worms, said calmly, "Were they to make a fire that would extend from Worms to Wittemberg, and reach even to the sky, I would walk across it in the name of the Lord"—that triumphant Luther, who, in his honored age, sat in the cool shadow and 'mid the purple vintage of the tree himself had planted, and after a stormful sojourn, scaped the toils of the hunters, and died peacefully in his bed—that undying Luther, "who, being dead, yet speaketh," the mention of whose name rouses the ardor of the manly, and quickens the pulses of the free; whose spirit yet stirs, like a clarion, the great heart of Christendom; and whose very bones have so marvellous a virtue, that, like the bones of Elisha, if on them were stretched the corpse of an effete Protestantism, they would surely wake it into life to the honor and glory of God!

But we must not forget, as we are in some danger of doing, that we must draw our illustrations mainly from the life of Elijah. We have before affirmed that unity of purpose and consistency of effort were leading features in his character, but look at them in action, especially as displayed in the great scene of Carmel. Call up that scene before you, with all its adjuncts of grandeur and of power. The summit of the fertile hill, meet theatre for so glorious a tragedy; the idolatrous priests, with all the pompous ensigns of their idol-worship, confronted by that solitary but princely man—the gathered and anxious multitude—the deep silence following on the prophet's question—the appeal to fire—the protracted invocation of Baal—the useless incantations and barbaric rites, "from morning even until noon, and from noon until the time of the offering of the evening sacrifice;" the solemn sarcasm of Elijah; the building of the altar of unfurnished stone—the drenching and surrounding it with water, strangest of all strange preparations for a burnt-sacrifice—the sky reddening as if it blushed at the folly of the priests of Baal—the sun sloping slowly to the west, and falling aslant upon the pale faces of that unweary multitude, rapt in fixed attention, patient, stern, unhungering—the high accents of holy prayer—the solemn pause, agonizing from its depth of feeling—the falling flame, "a fire of intelligence and power"—the consuming of all the materials of the testimony—and that mighty triumph-shout, rolling along the plain of Sharon, waking the echoes of the responsive mountains, and thrilling over the sea with an eloquence grander than its own; there it stands—that scene in its entireness—most wonderful even in a history of wonders, and one of the most magnificent and conclusive forthputtings of Jehovah's power! But abstract your contemplations now from the miraculous interposition, and look at the chief actor in the scene. How calm he is! How still amid that swaying multitude! They, agitated by a thousand emotions—he, self-reliant, patient, brave! Priests mad with malice—people wild in wonder—an ominous frown darkening the royal brow—Elijah alone unmoved! Whence this self-possession? What occult principle so mightily sustains him? There was, of course, unfaltering dependence upon God. But there was also the consciousness of integrity of purpose, and of a heart "at one." There was no recreancy in the soul. He had not been the passive observer, nor the guilty conniver at sin. He had not trodden softly, lest he should shock Ahab's prejudices or disturb his repose. He had not shared in the carnivals of Jezebel's table. He had not preserved a dastardly neütrality. Every one knew him to be "on the Lord's side." His heart was always in tune; like Memnon's harp, it trembled into melody at every breath of heaven.

With these examples before us, it behooves us to ask ourselves, *Have we a purpose?* Elijah and Luther may be marks too high for us. Do not let us affect knight-errantry, couch the lance at wind-mills to prove our valor, or mistake sauciness for sanctity, and impudence for inspiration. It is not probable that our mission is to beard unfaithful royalties, or to pull down the edifices which are festooned with the associations of centuries. But in the sphere of each of us—in the marts of commerce, in the looms of labor—while the sun is climbing hotly up the sky, and the race of human pursuits and competitions is going vigorously on, there is work enough for the sincere and honest workman. The sphere for personal improvement was never so large. To brace the body for service or for suffering—to bring it into subjection to the control of the master-faculty—to acquaint the mind with all wisdom—to hoard, with miser's care, every fragment of beneficial knowledge—to twine the beautiful around the true, as the acanthus leaf around the Corinthian pillar—to quell the sinward propensities of the nature —to evolve the soul into the completeness of its moral manhood—to have the passions in harness, and firmly curb them—"to bear the image of the heavenly"—to strive after "that mind which was also in Christ Jesus" —here is a field of labor wide enough for the most resolute will. The sphere of beneficent activity was never so large. To infuse the leaven of purity into the disordered masses—to thaw the death-frost from the heart of the misanthrope—to make the treacherous one faithful to duty—to open the world's dim eye to the majesty of conscience—to gather and instruct the orphans bereft of a father's blessing and of a mother's prayer—to care for the outcast and abandoned, who have drunk in iniquity with their mother's milk, whom the priest and the Levite have alike passed by, and who have been forced in the hotbed of poverty into premature luxuriance of evil; here is labor, which may employ a man's whole lifetime, and his whole soul. Young men, are you working? Have you gone forth into the harvest-field bearing precious seed? Alas! perhaps some of you are yet resting in the conventional, that painted charnel which has tombed many a manhood; grasping eagerly your own social advantages; gyved by a dishonest expediency; not doing a good lest it should be evil spoken of, nor daring a faith lest the scoffer should frown. With two worlds to work in—the world of the heart, with its many-phased and wondrous life, and the world around, with its problems waiting for solution, and its contradictions panting for the harmonizer—you are, perhaps, enchained in the island of Calypso, thralled by its blandishments, emasculated by its enervating air. O, for some strong-armed Mentor to thrust you over the cliff, and strain with you among the buffeting waves! Brothers, let us be men. Let us bravely fling off our chains. If we can not be commanding, let us at least be sincere. Let our earnestness amend our incapacity. Let ours not be a life of puerile inanities or obsequious Mammon-worship. Let us look through the pliant neutral in his hollowness, and the churlish miser in his greed, and let us go and do otherwise than they. Let us not be ingrates while Heaven is generous, idlers while earth is active, slumberers while eternity is near. Let us have a purpose, and let that purpose be one. Without a central principle all will be in disorder. Ithaca is misgoverned, Penelope beset by clamorous suitors, Telemachus in peril, all because Ulysses is away. Let the Ulysses of the soul return, let the governing principle exert its legitimate authority, and the happy suitors of appetite and sense shall be slain—the heart, married to the truth, shall retain its fidelity to its bridalvow, and the eldest-born, a purpose of valor and of wisdom, shall carve its highway to renown, and achieve its deeds of glory. Aim at this singleness of eye. Abhor a life of self-contradictions, as a grievous wrong done to an immortal nature. And thus, having a purpose—*one* purpose—a worthy purpose—you cannot toil in vain. Work in the inner—it will tell upon the outer world. Purify your own heart

—you will have a reformative power on the neighborhood. Shrine the truth within—it will attract many pilgrims. Kindle the vestal fire—it will ray out a life-giving light. Have the mastery over your own spirit—you will go far to be a world-subduer. Oh, if there be one here whowould up lift himself or advance his fellows, who would do his brother "a good which shall live after him," or enroll himself among the benefactors of mankind, to him we say, Cast out of thyself all that loveth and maketh a lie—hate every false way—set a worthy object before thee—work at it with both hands, an open heart, an earnest will, and a firm faith, and then go on—

"Onward, while a wrong remains
To be conquered by the right,
While Oppression lifts a finger
To affront us by his might.
While an error clouds the reason,
Or a sorrow gnaws the heart,
Or a slave awaits his freedom,
Action is the wise man's part!"

The Prophet's consistency of purpose, his calmness in the time of danger, and his marvellous success, require, however, some further explanation, and that explanation is to be found in the fact that *he was a man of prayer*. Prayer was the forerunner of his every action—the grace of supplication prepared him for his mightiest deeds. Whatever was his object—to seal or to open the fountains of heaven—to evoke the obedient fire on Carmel—to shed joy over the bereft household of the Sareptan widow—to bring down "forks of flame" upon the captains and their fifties—there was always the solemn and the earnest prayer. Tishbe, Zarephath, Carmel, Jezreel, Gilgal—he had his oratory in them all. And herein lay the secret of his strength. The moun tain-closet emboldened him for the mountain-altar. While the winged birds were providing for his body, the winged prayers were strengthening his soul. In answer to his entreaties in secret, the whole armor of God was at his service, and he buckled the breastplate, and braced the girdle, and strapped on the sandals, and stepped forth from his closet a hero, and men knew that he had been in Jehovah's presence-chamber from the glory which lingered on his brow.

Now, as man is to be contemplated, not only in reference to time, but in reference to eternity, this habit of prayer is necessary to the completeness of his character. If the present were his all—if his life were to shape itself only amid surrounding complexities of good or evil—if he had merely to impress his individuality upon his age, and then die and be forgotten, or in the veiled future have no living and conscious concern; then, indeed, self-confidence might be his highest virtue, self-will his absolute law, self-aggrandizement his supremest end. But as, beyond the present, there lies, in all its solemness, eternity; as the world to which we are all hastening is a world of result, discovery, fruition, recompense; as an impartial register chronicles our lives, that a righteous retribution may follow, our dependence upon God must be felt and recognized, and there must be some medium through which to receive the communications of his will. This medium is furnished to us in prayer. It has been ordained by himself as a condition of strength and blessing, and all who are under his authority are under binding obligations to pray.

Young men, you have been exhorted to aspire. Self-reliance has been commended to you as a grand element of character. We would echo these counsels. They are counsels of wisdom. But to be safe and to be perfect, you must connect with them the spirit of prayer. Emulation, unchastened by any higher principle, is to our perverted nature very often a danger and an evil. The love of distinction, not of truth and right, becomes the master-passion of the soul, and instead of high-reaching labor after good, there comes Vanity with its parodies of excellence, or mad Ambition shrinking from no enormity in its cupidity or lust of power. Self-reliance, in a heart unsanctified, often gives place to Self-confidence, its base-born brother. Under its unfriendly rule there rise up in the soul over-weening estimate of self, inveteracy of evil habit, impatience of restraint or control, the disposition to lord it over others, and that dogged and repulsive obstinacy, which, like the dead fly in the ointment, throws an ill savor over the entire character of the man. These are smaller manifestations, but, in congenial soil, and with commensurate opportunities, it blossoms out into some of the worst forms of humanity—the ruffian, who is the terror of his neighborhood; the tyrant, who has an appetite for blood; the atheist, who denies his God. Now, the habit of prayer will afford to these principles the salutary check which they need. It will sanctify emulation, and make it a virtue to aspire. It will curb the excesses of ambition, and keep down the vauntings of unholy pride. The man will aim at the highest, but in the spirit of the lowest, and prompted by the thought of immortality—not the loose immortality of the poet's dream, but the substantial immortality of the Christian's hope—he will travel on to his reward. In like manner will the habit of prayer chasten and consecrate the principle of self-reliance. It will preserve, intact, all its enterprise and bravery. It will bate not a jot of its original strength and freedom, but, when it would wanton out into insolence and pride, it will restrain it by the consciousness of a higher power; it will shed over the man the meekness and gentleness of Christ, and it will show, existing in the same nature and in completest harmony, indomitable courage in the arena of the world, and loyal submission to the authority of Heaven. Many noble examples have attested how this inner life of heaven—combining the heroic and the gentle, softening without enfeebling the character, preparing either for action or endurance—has shed its power over the outer life of earth. How commanding is the attitude of Paul from the time of his conversion to the truth! What courage he has, encountering the Epicurean and Stoical philosophers, revealing the unknown God to the multitude at Athens, making the false-hearted Felix tremble, and almost constraining the pliable Agrippa to decision; standing, silver-haired and solitary, before the bar of Nero; dying a martyr for the loved name of Jesus!—that heroism was born in the solitude where he importunately "besought the Lord." "In Luther's closet," says D'Aubigné, "we have the secret of the Reformation." The Puritans—those "men of whom the world was not worthy"—to whom we owe immense, but scantily-acknowledged, obligations—how kept they their fidelity? Tracked through wood and wild, the baying of the fierce sleuth-hound breaking often upon their sequestered worship, their prayer was the talisman which "stopped the mouths of lions, and quenched the violence of fire." You cannot have forgotten how exquisitely the efficacy of prayer is presented in our second book of Proverbs:

"Behold that fragile form of delicate, transparent beauty,
Whose light-blue eye and hectic cheek are lit by the bale-fires of decline;
Hath not thy heart said of her, Alas! poor child of weakness!
Thou hast erred; Goliath of Gath stood not in half her strength:
For the serried ranks of evil are routed by the lightning of her eye;
Seraphim rally at her side, and the captain of that host is God,
For that weak, fluttering heart is strong in faith assured—
Dependence is her might, and behold—she prayeth." *

Desolate, indeed, is the spirit, like the hills of Gilboa,

* Tupper's "Proverbial Philosophy," of Prayer, p. 109.

reft of the precious things of heaven, if it never prays. Do *you* pray? Is the fire burning upon that secret altar? Do you go to the closet as a duty? linger in it as a privilege? What is that you say? There is a scoffer in the same place of business with you, and he tells you it is cowardly to bow the knee, and he jeers you about being kept in leading-strings, and urges you to avow your manliness, and as he is your room-mate, you have been ashamed to pray before him; and, moreover, he seems so cheerful, and resolute, and brave, that his words have made some impression? What! he brave? He who gave up the journey the other day because he lucklessly discovered it was Friday; he who lost his self-possession at the party because "the salt was spilt—to him it fell;" he who, whenever friends solicit and the tempter plies, is afraid to say no; he who dares not for his life look into his own heart, for he fancies it a haunted house, with goblins perched on every landing to pale the cheek and blench the courage; he a brave man? Oh! to your knees, young man; to your knees, that the cowardice may be forgiven and forgotten. There is no bravery in blasphemy, there is no dastardliness in godly fear. It is prayer which strengthens the weak, and makes the strong man stronger. Happy are you, if it is your habit and your privilege. You can offer it anywhere. In the crowded mart or busy street; flying along the gleaming line; sailing upon the wide waters; out in the broad world; in the strife of sentiment and passion; in the whirlwind of battle; at the festival and at the funeral; if the frost braces the spirit or the fog depresses it; if the clouds are heavy on the earth, or the sunshine fills it with laughter; when the dew is damp upon the grass, or when the lightning flashes in the sky; in the matins of sunrise or the vespers of nightfall; let but the occasion demand it, let the need be felt, let the soul be imperilled, let the enemy threaten, happy are you, for you can pray.

We learn from the prophet's history that *God's discipline for usefulness is frequently a discipline of trouble.* His enforced banishment to the brook Cherith; his struggles in that solitude, with the unbelief which would fear for the daily sustenance, and with the selfishness which would fret and pine for the activities of life; Ahab's bloodthirsty and eager search for him, of which he would not fail to hear; Jezebel's subsequent and bitterer persecution; the apparent failure of his endeavors for the reformation of Israel; the forty days' fasting in the wilderness of Horeb—all these were parts of one grand disciplinary process, by which he was made ready for the Lord, fitted for the triumph on Carmel, for the still voice on the mountain, and for the ultimate occupancy of the chariot of fire. It is a beneficent arrangement of Providence, that "the divinity which shapes our ends" weaves our sorrows into elements of character, and that all the disappointments and conflicts to which the living are subject—the afflictions, physical and mental, personal and relative, which are the common lot—may, rightly used, become means of improvement, and create in us sinews of strength. Trouble is a marvellous mortifier of pride, and an effectual restrainer of self-will. Difficulties string up the energies to loftier effort, and intensity is gained from repression. By sorrow the temper is mellowed, and the feeling is refined. When suffering has broken up the soil, and made the furrows soft, there can be implanted the hardy virtues which out-brave the storm. In short, trial is God's glorious alchemistry, by which the dross is left in the crucible, the baser metals are transmuted, and the character is riched with the gold. It would be easy to multiply examples of the singular efficacy of trouble as a course of discipline. Look at the history of God's chosen people. A king arose in Egypt "which knew not Joseph," and his harsh tyranny drove the Hebrews from their land of Goshen, and made them the serfs of an oppressive bondage. The iron entered into their souls. For years they remained in slavery, until in his own good time God arose to their help, and brought them out "with a high hand and with a stretched-out arm." We do not mean, of all things, to make apologies for Pharaoh and his task-masters, but we *do* mean to say that that bondage was, in many of its results, a blessing; and that the Israelite, building the treasure-cities, and, perhaps, the Pyramids, was a very different and a very superior being to the Israelite, inexperienced and ease-loving, who fed his flocks in Goshen. God overruled that captivity, and made it the teacher of many important lessons. They had been hitherto a host of families; they were to be exalted into a nation. There was to be a transition effected from the simplicity of the patriarchal government and clanship to the superb theocracy of the Levitical economy. Egypt was the school in which they were to be trained for Canaan, and in Egypt they were taught, although reluctant and indocile learners, the forms of civil government, the theory of subordination and order, and the arts and habits of civilized life. Hence, when God gave his laws on Sinai, those laws fell upon the ears of a prepared people; even in the desert they could fabricate the trappings of the temple service, and engrave the mystic characters upon the "gems oracular" which flashed upon the breastplate of the High Priest of God. The long exile in the wilderness of Midian was the chastening by which Moses was instructed, and the impetuosity of his temper mellowed and subdued, so that he who, in his youthful hatred of oppression, slew the Egyptian, became in his age the meekest man, the much-enduring and patient lawgiver. A very notable instance of the influence of difficulty and failure in rousing the energies and carrying them on to success, has been furnished in our own times. Of course we refer to this case in this one aspect only, altogether excluding any expression as to the merit or demerit of the man. There will probably be two opinions about him, and those widely differing, in this assembly. We are not presenting him as an example, but as an illustration—save in the matter of steady and persevering purpose—and in this, if he be even an opponent, *Fas est ab hoste doceri.*

In the year 1837, a young member, oriental alike in his lineage and in his fancy, entered Parliament, chivalrously panting for distinction in that intellectual arena. He was already known as a successful three-volumer, and his party were ready to hail him as a promising auxiliary. Under these auspices he rose to make his maiden speech. But he had made a grand mistake. He had forgotten that the figures of St. Stephen's are generally arithmetical, and that superfluity of words, except in certain cases, is regarded as superfluity of naughtiness. He set out with the intention to dazzle, but country gentlemen object to be dazzled, save on certain conditions. They must be allowed to prepare themselves for the shock, they must have due notice beforehand, and the operation must be performed by an established parliamentary favorite. In this case all these conditions were wanting. The speaker was a *parvenu.* He took them by surprise, and he pelted them with tropes like hail. Hence he had not gone far before there were signs of impatience; by and by the ominous cry of "Question," then came some parliamentary extravagance, met by derisive cheers; cachinnatory symptoms began to develop themselves, until, at last, in the midst of an imposing sentence, in which he had carried his audience to the Vatican, and invested Lord John Russell with the temporary custody of the keys of St. Peter, the mirth grew fast and furious; somnolent squires woke up and joined in sympathy, and the house resounded with irrepressible peals of laughter. Mortified and indignant, the orator sat down, closing with these memorable words: "I sit down now, but the time will come when you will hear me!" In the mortification of that night, we doubt not, was born a resolute working for the fulfillment of those words. It was an arduous struggle. There were titled claimants for renown among his competitors, and he had to break down the exclusivism. There was a suspicion of political adventuring at work, and broadly circulated, and he had this to overcome. Above all, he had to live down the remembrance of his failure. But there was the consciousness of power, and the fall which would have crushed the coward made the brave man braver. Warily walking, and steadily toiling, through the chance of years, seizing the opportunity as it came, and always biding his time, he climbed upward to the distant summit, prejudice melted like snow beneath his feet, and in 1852, fifteen short years after his apparent annihilation, he was in her Majesty's Privy Council, styling himself Right Honorable, Chancellor of the Exchequer, and leader of the British House of Commons.

Sirs, are there difficulties in your path, hindering your pursuit of knowledge, restraining your benevolent endeavor, making your spiritual life a contest and a toil? Be thankful for them. They will test your capabilities of resistance. You will be impelled to persevere from the very energy of the opposition. If there be any might in your soul, like the avalanche of snow, it will require additional momentum from the obstacles which threaten to impede it. Many a man has thus robed himself in the spoils of a vanquished difficulty, and his conquests have accumulated at every onward and upward step, until he has rested from his labor—the successful athlete who has thrown the world. "An unfortunate illustration," you are ready to say, "for all cannot win the Olympic crown, nor wear the Isthmian laurel. What of him who fails? How is he recompensed? What does he gain?" What? Why, STRENGTH FOR LIFE. His training has insured him *that*. He will never forget the gymnasium and its lessons. He will always be a stalwart man, a man of muscle and of sinew. THE REAL MERIT IS NOT IN THE SUCCESS, BUT IN THE ENDEAVOR, and, win or lose, he will be honored and crowned.

It may be that the sphere of some of you is that of endurance rather than of enterprise. You are not called to aggress, but to resist. The power to work has reached its limit for a while; the power to *wait* must be exerted. There are periods in our history when Providence shuts us up to the exercise of faith, when patience and fortitude are more valuable than valor and courage, and when any "further struggle would but defeat our prospects and embarrass our aims." To resist the powerful temptation; to overcome the besetting sin; to restrain the sudden impulse of anger; to keep sentinel over the door of the lips, and turn back the biting sarcasm, and the word unkind; to be patient under unmerited censure; amid opposing friends, and a scoffing world, to keep the faith high and the purpose firm; to watch through murky night and howling storm for the coming day; in these cases, to be still is to be brave; what Burke has called a "masterly inactivity" is our highest prowess, and quietude is the part of heroism. There is a young man in business, battling with some strong temptation, by which he is vigorously assailed; he is solicited to engage in some unlawful undertaking, with the prospect of immediate and lucrative returns. Custom pleads prescription: "It is done every day." Partiality suggests that so small a deviation will never be regarded—"Is it not a little one?" Interest reminds him that by his refusal his "craft will be in danger." Compromise is sure that "when he bows himself in the house of Rimmon, the Lord will pardon his servant in this thing." All these fearful voices are urging his compliance. But the Abdiel-conscience triumphs—help is invoked where it can never be invoked in vain, and he spurns the temptation away. Is he not a hero? Earth may despise such a victory, but he can afford that scorning when, on account of him, "there is joy in heaven." Oh, there are, day by day, vanishing from the world's presence, those of whom she wotteth not; whose heritage has been a heritage of suffering; who, in the squalors of poverty, have gleaned a hallowed chastening; from whom the fires of sickness have scaled their earthliness away, and they have grown up into such transcendent and archangel beauty, that Death, God's eagle, sweeps them into heaven. Murmur not, then, if, in the inscrutable allotments of Providence, you are called to suffer, rather than to do. There is a time to labor, and there is a time to refrain. The completeness of the Christian character consists in energetic working, when working is practicable, and in submissive waiting, when waiting is necessary. You believe that beyond the waste of waters there is a rich land to be discovered, and, like Columbus, you have manned the vessel and hopefully set sail. But your difficulties are increasing. The men's hearts are failing them for fear; they wept when you got out of sight of land; the distance is greater than you thought: there is a weary and unvaried prospect of only sky and sea; you have not spoken a ship nor exchanged a greeting; your crew are becoming mutinous, and brand you mad; officers and men crowd round you, savagely demanding return. Move not a hair's breadth. Command the craven spirits to their duty. Bow them before the grandeur of your courage, and the triumph of your faith:

"Hushing every muttered murmur,
Let your fortitude the firmer
Gird your soul with strength;
While, no treason near her lurking,
Patience in her perfect working,
Shall be queen at length."

Ha! What is it? What says the watcher? LAND in the distance! No; not yet—but there's a hopeful fragrance in the breeze; the sounding-line gives shallower and yet shallower water; the tiny land-birds flutter round, venturing on timid wing to give their joyous welcome. Spread the canvas to the wind; by and by there shall be the surf-wave on the strand; the summits of the land of promise visible; the flag flying at the harbor's mouth, and echoing from grateful hearts and manly voices, the swelling spirit-hymn, "So he bringeth us to our desired haven."

We are taught by the Prophet's history *the evil of undue disquietude about the aspect of the times.* The followers of Baal had been stung to madness by their defeat on Carmel, and Jezebel, their patroness, mourning over her slaughtered priests, swore by her idol-gods that she would have the Prophet's life for theirs. On this being reported to Elijah, he seems to be paralyzed with fear, all his former confidence in God appears to be forgotten, and the remembrance of the mighty deliverances of the past fails to sustain him under the pressure of this new trial. Such is poor human nature. He before whom the tyrant Ahab had quailed—he whose prayer had suspended the course of nature, and sealed up the fountains of heaven; he who, in the face of all Israel, had confronted and conquered eight hundred and fifty men—terrified at the threat of an angry woman, flees in precipitation and in terror, and, hopeless for the time of his own safety, and of the success of his endeavors for the good of Israel, wanders off into the wilderness, and sighs forth his feelings in the peevish and melancholy utterance: Let me die. "It is enough —now, O Lord God, take away my life, for I am no better than my fathers." This desertion of duty, failure of faith, sudden cowardice, unwarranted despondency, petulance, and murmuring, are characteristics of modern no less than ancient days. There is one class of observers, indeed, who are not troubled with any disquietude; to whom all wears the tint of the rose-light, and who are disposed to regard the apprehensions of their soberer neighbors as dyspeptic symptoms, or as incipient hypochondriacism. Whenever the age is mentioned, they go off in an ecstasy. They are like the Malvern patients, of whom Sir Lytton Bulwer tells, who, after having made themselves extempore mummies in the "pack," and otherwise undergone their matutinal course of hydropathy, are so intensely exhilarated, and have such an exuberance of animal spirits, that they are obliged to run a considerable distance for the sake of working themselves off. Their volubility of praise is extraordinary, and it is only when they are thoroughly out of breath, that you have the chance to edge in a syllable. They tell us that the age is "golden," auriferous in all its developments, transcending all others in immediate advantage and in auguries of future good. We are pointed to the kindling love of freedom, to the quickened onset of inquiry, to the stream of legislation broadening as it flows, to the increase of hereditary mind, to the setting further and further back of the old landmarks of improvement, and to the inclosure of whole acres of intellectual and moral waste, thought formerly not worth the tillage. We would not for one moment be understood to undervalue these and other signs, equally and yet more encouraging. On the other hand, though no alarmists, we would not be insensible to the fears of those who tell us that we are in danger; that our liberty, of which we boast ourselves, is strangely like licentiousness; that our intellectual eminence may prove practical folly; that our liberality verges on indifferentism; and that our chiefest dignity is our yet-unhumbled pride, that *φρόνημα σαρκὸς*, which, in all its varieties, and in all its conditions, is "enmity against God." A very cursory glance at the state of things around us will suffice to show that with the dawn of a brighter day there are blent some gathering clouds.

Amid those who have named the Master's name, there is much which calls for caution and for warning. Political strife, fierce and absorbing, leading the mind off from the realities of its own condition; a current of worldly conformity setting in strongly upon the churches of the land; the ostentation and publicity of religious enterprises prompting to the neglect of meditation and of secret prayer; sectarian bitterness in its sad and angry developments; the multiform and lamentable exhibitions of practical Antinomianism which abound among us—all these have, in their measure, prevented the fulfillment of the Church's mission in the world.

If you look outside the pale of the churches, viewed from a Christian stand-point, the aspect is somewhat alarming. Crime does not diminish. The records of our offices of police and of our courts of justice are perfectly appalling. Intemperance, like a mighty gulf-stream, drowns its thousands. The Sabbath is systematically desecrated, and profligacy yet exerts its power to fascinate and to ruin souls. And then, deny it as we will, there is the engrossing power of Mammon. Covetousness—the sin of the heart, of the Church, of the world—is found everywhere; lurking in the guise of frugality, in the poor man's dwelling; dancing in the shape of gold-fields and Australia before the flattered eye of youth; shrined in the marts of the busy world, receiving the incense and worship of the traders in vanity; arrayed in purple, and faring sumptuously every day, in the mansion of Dives; twining itself round the pillars of the sanctuary of God; it is the great world-emperor still, swaying an absolute authority, with legions of subordinate vices to watch its nod, and to perform its bidding.

Then, besides this iniquity of practical ungodliness, there is also the iniquity of theoretical opinion. There is Popery, that antiquated superstition, which is coming forth in its decrepitude, rouging over its wrinkles, and flaunting itself, as it used to do in its well-remembered youth. There are the various ramifications of the subtile spirit of Unbelief: *Atheism*, discarding its former audacity of blasphemy, assuming now a modest garb and mendicant whine, asking our pity for its idiosyncrasy, bewailing its misfortune in not being able to believe that there is a God; *Rationalism*, whether in the transcendentalism of Hegel, or in the allegorizing impiety of Strauss, or in the pantheistic philosophy of Fichté, eating out the heart of the Gospel, into which its vampire-fangs have fastened; *Latitudinarianism* on a sentimental journey in search of the religious instinct, doling out its equal and niggard praise to it wherever it is found, in Fetichism, Thuggism, Mohammedanism, or Christianity; that species of active and high-sounding skepticism, which, for want of a better name, we may call a *Credophobia*, which selects the confessions and catechisms as the objects of its especial hostility, and which, knowing right well that if the banner is down, the courage fails, and the army will be routed or slain, "furious as a wounded bull, runs tearing at the creeds;" these, with all their off-shots and dependencies (for their name is Legion) grouped under the generic style of Infidelity, have girt themselves for the combat, and are asserting and endeavoring to establish their empire over the intellects and consciences of men. And as this spirit of Unbelief has many sympathies with the spirit of Superstition, they have entered into unholy alliance —"Herod and Pilate have been made friends together"—and hand joined in hand, they are arrayed against the truth of God. Oh, rare John Bunyan! Was he not among the prophets? Listen to his description of the last army of Diabolus before the final triumph of Immanuel: "Ten thousand DOUBTERS, and fifteen thousand BLOODMEN, and old *Incredulity* was again made general of the army."

In this aspect of the age its tendencies are not always upward, nor its prospects encouraging, and we can understand the feeling which bids the Elis of our Israel "sit by the wayside, watching, for their hearts tremble for the ark of God." We seem to be in the mysterious twilight of which the prophet speaks, "The light shall not be clear nor dark, but one day *known unto the Lord,* not day nor night." Ah! here is our consolation. It is "known unto the Lord;" then our faith must not be weakened by distrust, nor our labor interrupted by fear. "It is known unto the Lord;" and from the mount of Horeb he tells us that in the secret places of the heritage there are seven thousand that have not bowed the knee to Baal. It is "known unto the Lord;" and while we pity the Prophet in the wilderness asking for a solitary death, death under a cloud, death in judgment, death in sorrow, he draws aside the veil, and shows us heaven preparing to do him honor, the celestial escort making ready to attend him, the horses being harnessed into the chariot of fire.

Sirs, if there be this opposition, be it ours to "contend" the more "earnestly for the faith once delivered to the saints." Many are persuading us to give up and abandon our creeds. We ought rather to hold them with a firmer grasp, and infuse into them a holier life. We can imagine how the infidel would accost an intelligent and hearty believer. "Be independent; don't continue any longer in leading strings, taking your faith from the *ipse dixit* of another; use your senses, which are the only means of knowledge; cast your confessions and rituals away; a strong man needs no crutches." And we can imagine the reply. "Brother, the simile is not a happy one—my creed is not a crutch—it is a highway thrown up by former travellers to the land that is afar off. 'Other men have labored,' and of my own free will I 'enter into their labor.' If thou art disposed to clear the path with thy own hatchet, with lurking serpents underneath and knotted branches overhead, God speed thee, my brother, for thy work is of the roughest, and while thou art resting—fatigued and '*considering*'—thou mayest die before thou hast come upon the truth. I am grateful to the modern Macadamizers who have toiled for the coming time. Commend me to the King's highway. I am not bound in it with fetters of iron. I can climb the hill for the sake of a wider landscape. I can cross the stile, that I may slake my thirst at the old moss-covered well in the field. I can saunter down the woodland glade, and gather the wild heart's-ease that peeps from among the tangled fern; but I go back to the good old path where the pilgrim's tracks are visible, and, like the shining light, 'it grows brighter and brighter unto the perfect day.'" Sirs, this is not the time for us to be done with creeds. They are, in the various churches, their individual embodiments of what they believe to be truth, and their individual protests against what they deem to be error. "Give up our theology!" says Mr. James of Birmingham; "then farewell to our piety. Give up our theology! then dissolve our churches; for our churches are founded upon truth. Give up our theology! then next vote our Bibles to be myths. And this is clearly the aim of many, the destruction of all these together; our piety, our churches, our Bibles." This testimony is true. There cannot be an attack upon the one without damage and mischief to the other.

> "Just as in old mythology,
> What time the woodman slew
> Each poet-worshipped forest-tree—
> He killed its Dryad too."

So as the assault upon these expressions of Christianity is successful, the spiritual presence enshrined in them will languish and die. "Hold fast," then, "the form of sound words." Amid the war of sentiment and the jangling of false philosophy, though the sophist may denounce, and though the fool may laugh, let your high resolve go forth to the moral universe; "I am determined to know nothing among men save Christ and him crucified."

There is another matter to which, if you would successfully join in resistance to the works of evil, you must give earnest heed, and that is the desirableness, I had almost said the necessity—I will say it, for it is my solemn conviction, and why should it not be manfully out-spoken?—the *necessity* of public dedication to the service of your Master—Christ. You will readily admit that confession is requisite for the completeness of discipleship; and you cannot have forgotten how the Apostle has linked it to faith. "Confess with thy mouth, and believe with thine heart." To such confession, in the present day, at all events, *church-fellowship* is necessary. You cannot adequately make it in social intercourse, nor by a consistent example, nor even by a decorous attendance with outer-court worshippers. There must be public and solemn union with the Church of Christ. The influence of this avowed adhesion ought not to be forgotten. A solitary "witness" of obedience or faith is lost, like an invisible atom in the air; it is the union of each particle, in itself insignificant, which makes up the "cloud of witnesses" which the world can see. Your own admirable Society exemplifies the advantage of association in benevolent and Christian enterprise, and the Churches of the land, maligned as they have been by infidel slanderers, and imperfectly—very imperfectly—as they have borne witness for God, have yet been the great breakwaters against error and sin, the blest Elims to the desert wayfarer, the tower of strength in the days of siege and strife. Permit us to urge this matter upon you. Of course we do not pretend to specify—that were treason against the noble catholicity of this Society—though each of your lecturers has the Church of his intelligent preference, and we are none of us ashamed of our own;

but we do mean to say, that you ought to join yourselves to that Church which appears to your prayerful judgment to be most in accordance with the New Testament, there to render whatever you possess of talent, and influence, and labor. This is my testimony, sincerely and faithfully given; and if, in its utterance, it shall, by God's blessing, recall one wanderer to allegiance, or constrain one waverer to decision, it will not have been spoken in vain.

Yet once more upon this head. There must be deeper piety, more influential and transforming godliness. An orthodox creed, valuable Church privileges—what are these without personal devotedness? They must be faithful laborers—men of consecrated hearts—who are to do the work of the Lord. Believe me, the depth of apostolic piety, and the fervor of apostolic prayer, are required for the exigencies of the present and coming time. That Church of the future, which is to absorb into itself the regenerated race, must be a living and a holy Church. Scriptural principles must be enunciated by us all, with John the Baptist's fearlessness, and with John the Evangelist's love. It is a mistake to suppose that fidelity and affection are unfriendly. The highest achievements in knowledge, the most splendid revelations of God, are reserved in his wisdom for the man of perfect love. Who but the beloved disciple could worm out of the Master's heart the foul betrayer's name? Whose heart but his was large enough to hold the Apocalypse, which was flung into it in the island of Patmos? There must be this union of deepest faithfulness and deepest love to fit us for the coming age; and to get it, we must just do as John did: we must lie upon the Master's bosom until the smile of the Master has burned out of our hearts all earthlier and coarser passion, and has chastened the bravery of the hero by the meekness of the child.

The great lesson which is taught us in the Prophet's history, is that which was taught to him by the revelation on Horeb, that *the Word is God's chosen instrumentality for the Church's progress, and for the world's recovery.* There were other lessons, doubtless, for his personal benefit. He had deserted its duty and was rebuked; he had become impatient and exasperated, and was calmed down; craven-hearted and unbelieving, he was fortified by the display of God's power; dispirited and wishing angrily for death, he was consoled with promise, and prepared for future usefulness and duty. But the grand lesson of all was, that Jehovah, when he works, works not with the turbulence and passion of a man, but with the stillness and grandeur of a God. "He was not in the whirlwind, nor in the earthquake, nor in the fire, but in the still, small voice." And so it is still. "The whirlwind" of battle, "the earthquake" of political convulsion and change, "the fire" of the loftiest intellect, or of the most burning eloquence, are valueless to uplift and to regenerate the world. They may be, they very often are, the forerunners of the moral triumph, but God's power is in his Gospel, God's presence is in his Word. Here it is that we are at issue, at deep and deadly issue, with the pseudo-philosophers and benevolent "considerers" who profess to be toiling in the same cause as ourselves. They discrown Christ; they ignore the influence of the Holy Spirit; they proclaim the perfectibility of their nature in itself; they have superseded the Word as an instrument of progress; and, of their own masonry, are piling up a tower, if haply it may reach unto heaven. This is the great problem of the age. Do not let us deceive ourselves. There are men, earnest, thoughtful, working, clever men, intent upon the question. Statesmanship has gathered up its political appliances; civilization has exhibited her humanizing art; philanthropy has reared educational, and mechanics', and all other sorts of institutes; amiable dreamers of the Pantheistic school have mapped out in cloud-land man's progress, from the transcendental up to the divine; communism has flung over all the mantle of its apparent charity, in the folds of which it has darkly hidden the dagger of its terrible purpose—nay, every man, now-a-days, stands out a ready-made and self-confident artificer, each having a psalm, or a doctrine, or a theory, which is to recreate society and stir the pulses of the world. And yet the world is not regenerated, nor will it ever be, by such visionary projects as these. Call up History. She will bear impartial witness. She will tell you that, before Christ came with his Evangel of purity and freedom, the finer the culture, the baser the character; that the untamed inhabitant of the old Hercynian Forest, and the Scythian and Slavonic tribes, who lived north of the Danube and the Rhine, destitute entirely of literary and artistic skill, were, in morals, far superior to the classic Greek and all-accomplished Roman. Call up Experience; she shall speak on the matter. You have increased in knowledge; have you, *therefore*, increased in piety? You have acquired a keener æsthetic susceptibility; have you gotten with it a keener relish for the spiritually true? Your mind has been led out into higher and yet higher education; have you, by its nurture, been brought nearer to God? Experience throws emphasis into the testimony of History, and both combine to assure us that there may be a sad divorce between Intellect and Piety, and that the training of the mind is not necessarily inclusive of the culture and discipline of the heart. Science may lead us to the loftiest heights which her inductive philosophy has scaled; art may suspend before us her beautiful creations; nature may rouse a "fine turbulence" in heroic souls; the strength of the hills may nerve the patriot's arm, as the Swiss felt the inspiration of their mountains on the Mortgarten battle-field; but they cannot, any or all of them, instate a man in sovereignty over his mastering corruptions, or invest a race with moral purity and power. If the grand old demon, who has the world so long in his thrall, is, by these means, ever disturbed in his possession, it is only that he may wander into desert places, and then return fresher for the exercise, and bringing seven of his kindred more inveterate and cruel. No! if the world is to be regenerated at all, it will be by the "still, small voice;" that clear and marvellous whisper, which is heard high above the din of striving peoples, and the tumult of sentiment and passion; which runs along the whole line of being, stretching its spiritual telegraph into every heart, that it may link them all with God. All human speculations have alloy about them; that Word is perfect. All human speculations fail; that Word abideth. The Jew hated it; but it lived on, while the veil was torn away from the shrine which Shekinah had forsaken, and while Jerusalem itself was destroyed. The Greek derided it, but it has seen his philosophy effete, and his Acropolis in ruins. The Roman threw it to the flames, but it rose from its ashes, and swooped down upon the falling eagle. The reasoner cast it into the furnace, which his own malignity had heated "seven times hotter than its wont;" but it came out without the smell of fire. The Papist fastened serpents around it to poison it, but it shook them off and felt no harm. The infidel cast it overboard in a tempest of sophistry and sarcasm, but it rode gallantly upon the crest of the proud waters; and it is living still, yet heard in the loudest swelling of the storm; it has been speaking all the while; it is speaking now. The world gets higher at its every tone, and it shall ultimately speak in power, until it has spoken this dismantled planet up again into the smiling brotherhood of worlds which kept their first estate, and God, welcoming the prodigal, shall look at it as he did in the beginning, and pronounce it to be very good.

It is as they abide by his Word, and guard sacredly this precious treasure, that nations stand or fall. The empires of old, where are they? Their power is dwarfed or gone. Their glory is only known by tradition. Their deeds are only chronicled in song. But, amid surrounding ruin, the Ark of God blesses the house of Obed-Edom. We dwell not now on our national greatness. That is the orator's eulogy and the poet's theme. We remember our religious advantages —God recognized in our Senate, his name stamped on our currency, his blessing invoked upon our Queen, our Gospel ministry, our religious freedom, our unfettered privilege, our precious Sabbath, our unsealed, entire, wide-open Bible. "God hath not dealt with any nation as he hath dealt with us," and for this same purpose our possessions are extensive, and our privileges secure— that we may maintain among ourselves, and diffuse amid the peoples, the Gospel of the blessed God. Alas! that our country has not been true to her responsibility, nor lavish of her strength for God. It would be well for us, and it is a startling alternative, if the curse of Meroz were our *only* heritage of wrath—if our only guilt were that we "came not up to the help of the Lord against the mighty." But we have not merely been indifferent—we have been hostile. The cupidity of our merchants, the profligacy of our soldiers and sailors, the impiety of our travellers, have hindered the work of the Lord. Our Government has patronized paganism; our soldiery have saluted an idol; our cannon have roared in homage to a senseless stone—nay, we have even pandered to the prostitution of a continent, and to the murder of thousands of her sons, debauched and slain by the barbarities of their religion—and, less conscientious than the priests of old, we have flung into the national treasury the hire of that adultery and blood. Oh! if the righteous God were to make inquisition for blood, upon the testimony of how many slaughtered witnesses might he convict pampered and lordly Britain! There is need—strong need—for our national humiliation and prayer. He who girt us with power can dry up the sinews of our strength. Let but his anger be kindled by our repeated infidelities, and our country shall fall. More magnificent than Babylon in the profusion of her opulence, she shall be more sudden than Babylon in her ruin; more renowned than Carthage for her military triumphs, shall be more desolate than Carthage in her mourning; princelier than Tyre in her commercial greatness, shall be more signal than Tyre in her fall; wider than Rome in her extent of territorial dominion, shall be more prostrate than Rome in her enslavement; prouder than Greece in her eminence of intellectual culture, shall be more degraded than Greece in her darkening; more exalted than Capernaum in the fullness of her religious privi lege, shall be more appalling than Capernaum in the deep damnations of her doom.

Young men, it is for you to redeem your country from this terrible curse. "The holy seed shall be the substance thereof." As you, and those like you, are impure or holy, you may draw down the destruction, or conduct it harmlessly away. You cannot live to yourselves. Every word you utter makes its impression; every deed you do is fraught with influences—successive, concentric, imparted—which may be felt for ages. This is a terrible power which you have, and it clings to you; you cannot shake it off. How will you exert it? We place two characters before you. Here is one—he is decided in his devotedness to God; painstaking in his search for truth; strong in benevolent purpose and holy endeavor; wielding a blessed influence; failing oft, but ceasing never; ripening with the lapse of years; the spirit mounting upon the breath of its parting prayer; the last enemy destroyed; his memory green for ages; and grateful thousands chiselling on his tomb: "HE, BEING DEAD, YET SPEAKETH." There is another—he resists religious impressions; outgrows the necessity for prayer; forgets the lessons of his youth, and the admonitions of his godly home; forsakes the sanctuary; sits in the seat of the scorner; laughs at religion as a foolish dream; influences many for evil; runs to excess of wickedness; sends, in some instances, his victims down before him; is stricken with premature old age; has hopeless prospects, and a terrible death-bed; rots from the remembrance of his fellows; and angel-hands burning upon his gloomy sepulchre the epitaph of his blasted life: "AND THAT MAN PERISHED NOT ALONE IN HIS INIQUITY."

Young men, which will you choose? I affectionately press this question. Oh, choose for God! "Seek first the kingdom of God and his righteousness, and all things"—science, art, poetry, friendship—"shall be added unto you." I do unfeignedly rejoice that so goodly a number of you have already decided.

I have only one fitness to address you—but it is one which many of your lecturers cannot claim—and that is, a fitness of sympathy. Your hopes are mine; with your joys, at their keenest, I can sympathize. I have not forgotten the glad hours of opening morning, when the zephyr has a balmier breath, and through the richly-painted windows of the fancy, the sunlight streams in upon the soul. I come to you as one of yourselves. Take my counsel. "My heart's desire and prayer for you is that you may be saved."

There is hope for the future. The world is moving on. The great and common mind of Humanity has caught the charm of hallowed Labor. Worthy and toil-worn laborers fall ever and anon in the march, and their fellows weep their loss, and then, dashing away the tears which had blinded them, they struggle and labor on. There has been an upward spirit evoked, which men will not willingly let die. Young in its love of the beautiful, young in its quenchless thirst after the true, we see that buoyant presence:

> "In hand it bears, 'mid snow and ice,
> The banner with the strange device:
> EXCELSIOR!"

The one note of high music struck from the great harp of the world's heart-strings is graven on that banner The student breathes it at his midnight lamp—the poet groans it forth in those spasms of his soul, when he cannot fling his heart's beauty upon language. Fair fingers have wrought in secret at that banner. Many a child of poverty has felt its motto in his soul, like the last vestige of lingering divinity. The Christian longs it when his faith, piercing the invisible, "desires a better country, that is, an heavenly." Excelsior! Excelsior! Brothers, let us speed onward the youth who holds that banner. Up, up, brave spirit!

> "Climb the steep and starry road
> To the Infinite's abode."

Up, up, brave spirit! Spite of Alpine steep and frowning brow, roaring blast and crashing flood, up! Science has many a glowing secret to reveal thee! Faith has many a Tabor-pleasure to inspire. Ha! does the cloud stop thy progress? Pierce through it to the sacred morning. Fear not to approach the divinity; it is his own longing which impels thee. Thou art speeding to thy coronation, brave spirit! Up, up, brave spirit! till, as thou pantest on the crest of thy loftiest achievement, God's glory shall burst upon thy face, and God's voice, blessing thee from his throne, in tones of approval and of welcome, shall deliver thy guerdon: "I have made thee a little lower than the angels, and crowned thee with glory and honor!"

THE END.

LIBRARY OF SACRED CLASSICS.

PRINTED FROM NEW AND BEAUTIFUL LARGE (PICA) TYPE.

BUNYAN'S PILGRIM'S PROGRESS, 12mo., $1 00
The Same—full gilt sides and edges, ... 1 50
The Same—half calf antique, ... 2 00

DODDRIDGE'S RISE & PROGRESS, 12mo., 1 00
The Same—full gilt sides and edges, ... 1 50
The Same—half calf, antique, ... 2 00

BAXTER'S SAINTS' REST, 12mo., ... 1 00
The Same—full gilt sides and edges, ... 1 50
The Same—half calf, antique, ... 2 00

TAYLOR'S HOLY LIVING, 12mo., ... 1 00
The Same—full gilt sides and edges, ... 1 50
The Same—half calf, antique, ... 2 00

Other volumes of a similar character to follow.

John Bunyan! Philip Doddridge! Richard Baxter! Jeremy Taylor! "*Pilgrim's Progress,*" "*Rise and Progress,*" "*Saints' Rest,*" *and* "*Holy Living.*" What Authors! What Subjects! What Books! Writers for immortality on immortal subjects, familiar to every reader from early infancy—household names and words and books for our maturer years. They will live forever, and do good to all. Old and young alike can drink at this well, "pure and undefiled," certain of refreshing draughts of pure and wholesome literature.

*** The above will be sent by mail, post-paid, on receipt of price.

W. H. Tinson, Printer and Stereotyper, 43 & 45 Centre St., N. Y.

"To the list of John Milton and other 'blind men eloquent,' must be added the name of WILLIAM HENRY MILBURN."—*London Athenæum.*

AN AUTOBIOGRAPHY OF DEEP INTEREST!

For Sale by Booksellers, Preachers, Colporteurs, and Book Agents generally.

TEN YEARS OF PREACHER LIFE;

OR, CHAPTERS FROM AN AUTOBIOGRAPHY.

BY WILLIAM HENRY MILBURN

AUTHOR OF "THE RIFLE AXE, AND SADDLE-BAGS."

One neat 12mo. volume. Price, One Dollar.

"There was a time when meadow, grove and stream,
The earth, and every common sight,
To me did seem
Apparelled in celestial light,
The glory and the freshness of a dream."

LIST OF THE CONTENTS (IN PART).

Early Reminiscence. The Accident.
The Sick Chamber. Surgical Consultation.
Two Years' Imprisonment.
Land of the Setting Sun.
"There were Giants in those days."
The Backwoods Preacher.
The Saddle-bags taken up.
Let no Man Despise thy Youth.
A Western Wedding.
A Western Camp-Meeting.
An Exhorter in a Dilemma.
Liberality of Methodists.
The Last Scene of Conference.
Walking the Hospital.
Cry Aloud and Spare not. A Sermon on Deck.
Its unexpected Rewards.
Heavy Purse and Congressional Chaplain.
Necessities for Extempore Speaking.
A Stump Speech Described.
Value of the Eye in an Orator.
Congress and two of its Young Men.
Congressional Eloquence.
Stephen A. Douglas.
Alexander H. Stephens.
Entering the Senate Chamber.
Memories of the Great Departed.
Author's First Prayer in Congress.
Henry Clay. John C. Calhoun. Daniel Webster.
Social Life in Washington.
Attractions of the Capital.
Power of Memory. Influence of Women.
A Death-bed Summons. Marriage of the Author.
Chicago in 1841, 1846, and 1855.
A Night Ride in a Deluge. Narrow Escape.
The Dying Preacher.
Grace in "Spots." Life on Wheels.
Life on the Mississippi. A Boat Race.
Passengers excited. S. S. Prentiss.
Phelps the Desperado. Riding the Circuit.
Sojourn in New Orleans.
Alabama Scenery. A Southern Home.
Tribute to the South.
Author Charged with Heresy.
Stage Coach Diálogue. A Fearful Spectacle.
Strange Superstition. The Anxious Moment.
Homage to Ladies. Southern Hospitality.
Southern Matron. Southern Literature.
Old Friends and Pleasant Faces.
The Pioneer Preacher. Western Cookery.
A Night Scene in a Village Store.
Indisposition of the Author.
Returns to New York. The Infant's Cry.

***** The above will be sent by mail, post-paid, on receipt of price**

DERBY & JACKSON, PUBLISHERS,
119 NASSAU ST., NEW YORK.

"Miss Evans may well be called the Charlotte Bronte of America."—*Troy Whig.*
"We place 'BEULAH' beside 'John Halifax.'"—*Baltimore Advocate.*

BEULAH.

BY AUGUSTA J. EVANS.

One neat 12mo. Price $1 25.

From MARION HARLAND, *herself, the writer of the most popular series of Novels ever published in this country.*

"TO MESSRS. DERBY & JACKSON:

"I speak my honest sentiments when I pronounce 'Beulah' the best work of fiction ever published by a Southern writer. To my mind, no American authoress has ever produced a greater book. Can it be true that Miss Evans is young? There is a life-time of thought and research, of struggles of mind and heart, in 'Beulah.' I have read every word with intense interest. The character-painting is fine, the description of passing events and scenery graphic and striking; but to me the chief charm of the book lies in the vivid portraiture of the doubts, the conflicts, the yearnings and the final triumph of a great soul seeking for truth. If the public can appreciate a thoroughly good work, they will thank you for having given them 'Beulah.'"

From Rev. Wm. H. Milburn (the Blind Preacher Eloquent).

"I have no hesitation in saying that few books have ever interested me more. The plot, the delineation of character, and the action, I think, are all admirable. It would be an extraordinary work from the hand of any woman, but it is peculiarly so from one so young. The reading of it cannot but do great good."

From Frederic S. Cozzens, author of the "Sparrowgrass Papers."

"I have been greatly interested by this story of the Mobile heroine, and I am convinced that the story will produce a sympathetic impression on the public mind. There is not a word in it, nor a phrase in it, that I have not meted and measured. Over and above the method of telling the story, the story itself wins, commands, controls the sympaties of the reader. This, I take it, is the highest test of excellence."

From the Home Journal.

"Since the appearance of 'Jane Eyre,' no volume has fallen from the pen of a lady writer evincing more power and learning than the novel 'Beulah,' and we do not hesitate to say that in the production of this volume, Miss Evans has achieved the highest rank among novelists of her sex in this country."

From the New York Evening Post.

"She has, at any rate, established a rank among the best novelists of her sex whom our country can boast, and we do not remember any work of fiction which has been produced in this country for years, which is written with more power and is more full of promise than 'Beulah.' She has achieved a decided literary success, a success which will at least be as cordially recognized at the North as at the South."

From the Boston Post.

"'Beulah' is a book of great merit, and one which will bear critical and close inspection. * * * The volume is one deserving the attraction of the reading public. It is healthy in sentiment, pure in its influences, and *grand in its treatment of great moral questions.* As a literary work, 'Beulah' will rank with any issue of the day."

***** The above will be sent by mail, post-paid, on receipt of price**

W. H TINSON, Printer and Stereotyper, 43 & 45 Centre St., N. Y.

THE WORKS OF CHARLOTTE BRONTE

(CURRER BELL.)

Comprising "Jane Eyre," "Shirley," and "Villette." Complete in 3 Vols., 12mo.

Price in Cloth,		$3 00
"	Sheep, library style,	3 75
"	Half calf, gilt or antique,	6 00

EVELINA;

OR,

The History of a Young Lady's Introduction to the World.

BY FRANCES BURNEY, (*MADAME D'ARBLAY.*)

With a Life of the Author by T. B. Macaulay. 12*mo.*

Price in Cloth,		$1 00
"	Sheep, library style,	1 25
"	Half calf, gilt or antique,	2 00

"Frances Burney was the wonder and delight of the generation of novel readers succeeding that of Fielding and Smollett, and she has maintained her popularity better than most secondary writers of fiction. In painting the characters in a drawing-room, or catching the follies and absurdities that float on the surface of fashionable society, she has rarely been equalled."—*Cyclo. of English Literature.*

CORINNE; or, Italy.

BY MADAME DE STAEL.

TRANSLATED BY ISABEL HILL.

With Metrical Versions of the Odes by L. E. Landon. 12mo.

Price in Cloth,		$1 00
"	Sheep, library style,	1 25
"	Half calf, gilt or antique,	2 00

"It (Corinne) possesses the highest merit as a work delineating character, and descriptive of scenery, and inculcates a pure morality. Its eloquent rhapsodies upon love, religion, virtue, nature, history, and poetry, have given it an enduring place in literature."—*Goodrich.*

* * The above will be sent by mail, post-paid, on receipt of price.

W. H. Tinson, Printer and Stereotyper, 43 & 45 Centre St., N. Y.

THE WORKS OF ANNE RADCLIFFE.

Two vols., now ready.

Comprising "The Mysteries of Udolpho," and "Romance of the Forest" With steel portrait. 12mo.

Price in Cloth,	. . . .	$2 00
"	Sheep, library style, . .	2 50
"	Half calf, gilt or antique, .	4 00

Like the great painter with whom she has been compared, Mrs. Radcliffe loved to sport with the romantic and terrible—with the striking images of the mountain forests, the cloud and storm, wild banditti, ruined castles, half-discovered glimpses of visionary shadows of the invisible world which seem at times to cross our path, and which still haunt and thrill the imagination.

THE WORKS OF JANE PORTER.

Two vols., now ready.

Comprising "The Scottish Chiefs," and "Thaddeus of Warsaw." With steel portrait. 12mo.

Price in Cloth,	. . . .	$2 00
"	Sheep, library style, . .	2 50
"	Half calf, gilt or antique, .	4 00

"'Thaddeus of Warsaw,' 'which in our youth beguiled us of our tears,' is a favorite. It is to Miss Porter's fame that she began the system of historical novel-writing, which attained the climax of its renown in the hands of Sir Walter Scott. And no light praise it is that she has thus pioneered the way for the greatest exhibition of the greatest genius of our time. She may parody Bishop Hall, and tell Sir Walter:

'I first adventured—follow me who list,
And be *second* Scottish novelist.'"

Frazer's Magazine.

*** The above will be sent by mail, post-paid, on receipt of price.

THE WORKS OF JANE AUSTEN.

Comprising "Pride and Prejudice," "Sense and Sensibility," "Mansfield Park," "Northanger Abbey," "Emma," and "Persuasion." First American Edition, with steel vignettes, complete in 4 vols., 12mo.

Price in Cloth,	. . . .	$4 00
" Sheep, library style,	. . .	5 00
" Half calf, gilt or antique,	. .	8 00

Miss Austen is emphatically the novelist of Home. The truth, spirit, ease, and refined humor of her style, have rarely been equalled. She will always retain a leading position in literature, as the representative of the domestic school of novels, of which she was the founder, the great charm of which is truth and simplicity; and notwithstanding the brilliant successes of many recent imitators, she still remains undisputed mistress of this class of composition.

THE WORKS OF HANNAH MORE.

Two vols. now ready.

Comprising "Cœlebs in Search of a Wife," her Tales and Allegories. With portrait on steel. 12mo.

Price in Cloth,	. . . .	$2 00
" Sheep, library style,	. . .	2 50
" Half calf, gilt or antique,	. .	4 00

"How many have thanked God for the hour that first made them acquainted with the writings of Hannah More. She did, perhaps, as much real good in her generation as any woman that ever held the pen. It would be idle for us to dwell here on works so well known. They have established her name as a great moral writer, possessing a masterly command over the resources of our language, and devoting a keen wit and a lively fancy to the best and noblest of purposes."—*Quarterly Review.*

*** The above will be sent by mail, post-paid, on receipt of price.

W. H. Tinson, Printer and Stereotyper, 43 & 45 Centre St., N. Y.

THE

WORKS OF LEIGH HUNT,

Comprising his "Italian and English Poets," "Wit and Humor," "Essays," "Miscellanies," and "English Authors," 4 vols.

Price in Cloth, ...	$5 00
" Sheep, library style, ...	6 00
" Half calf, extra, ...	9 00
" Half calf, antique, ...	9 00

"We ought to say that nothing can be less formal than the style of Mr. Hunt's Essays. It reminds us of the manner of some of Steele's best papers. Indeed, since the death of Southey, we think Leigh Hunt the pleasantest writer we have. * * * An account was given in this Journal by an admirer of the only surviving member of a group of which Lamb was the central figure; it is probable that of this group Hazlitt was the man of highest intellectual powers—Lamb the person who sought to see everything in the point of view in which it could be most favorably seen—and Hunt, combining in a great measure both their powers, seems to have looked on life and books in a spirit of more thoughtful appreciation than either, and in a feeling more thoroughly genial."—*Dublin University Magazine.*

THE WORKS OF LORD CHESTERFIELD.

Comprising his "Letters to his Son." Complete in 1 *vol.*, 12*mo.*

Price in Cloth, ...	$1 25
" Sheep, library style, ...	1 50
" Half calf, extra, ...	2 25
" Half calf, antique, ...	2 25
" Full tree calf, ...	3 00

*** * The above will be sent by mail, post-paid, on receipt of price**

W. H. Tinson, Printer and Stereotyper, 43 & 45 Centre St., N. Y.

THE LADY'S GUIDE

TO

PERFECT GENTILITY

IN MANNERS, DRESS, AND CONVERSATION,

IN THE FAMILY, IN COMPANY, AT THE PIANO FORTE, THE TABLE, IN THE STREET, AND IN GENTLEMEN'S SOCIETY.

ALSO,

A USEFUL INSTRUCTOR IN LETTER-WRITING, TOILET PREPARATIONS, FANCY NEEDLE-WORK, MILLINERY, DRESSMAKING, CARE OF WARDROBE, THE HAIR, TEETH, HANDS, LIPS, COMPLEXION, ETC.

BY EMILY THORNWELL,

AUTHOR OF "THE YOUNG LADIES' OWN BOOK," ETC.

One Handsome 12mo. Volume, with Steel Plate. Price 75 cents.

CONTENTS.

Agreeableness and Beauty of Person—Requisites to Female Beauty—Pimples and Wrinkles—Choice Cosmetics for Beautifying the Skin—Treatment of the Hair—How to Preserve the Teeth Sound and White—Choice Dentifrice—Means of securing a Beautiful Tint to the Lips—Means of Improving the Appearance of the Hands—Ornamental effect of neatly kept Nails—How to have a Sweet Breath—Gentility and Refinement—Taste with Regard to Manners—Low and Vulgar Associations—Gait and Carriage—Gentlemen's Attendance—Kind of Cards and Manner of Carrying them—Length of Calls—Receiving Visitors—Introductions—Giving Invitations—Who may be Invited—Taking Leave—Dancing Occasions—Invitation to Sing or Play—Conversation at the Table—The Ceremony—After Congratulations and Festivities—Invitations to Ride on Horseback—Polite, Easy, and Graceful Deportment—Female Dress—How to combine Elegance, Style and Economy—Ladies' Morning Attire—Street Dress—Young Ladies' Attire—The Apparel of Older Ladies—Gloves, Handkerchiefs, Stockings, etc.—The Relation of Colors—Effect of Tight Lacing, etc.—Cleaning and Washing Dresses—To Perfume Linen—To Extract Grease Spots—To Prevent Moths—The Art of Conversing with Fluency and Propriety—How to Treat Flattery—How to Address Young Gentlemen—Speaking of One's Self—Things, Words, and Sayings to be Avoided—Art of Correct and Elegant Letter-Writing—Useful Hints and Rules for Letter-Writers—Style of Addressing Different Persons—Models or Plans for Various Letters—Elegant Fancy Needle-work—Bracelets—A Pretty Lace Collar—Embroidery in its Various Modes—Stitches on Muslin and Lace—Composition for Drawing Patterns—The Art of Millinery and Dressmaking—Effect of Bonnets on the general appearance—Facts and Rules in Dressmaking, etc. etc. etc.

***** The above will be sent by mail, post-paid, on receipt of price**

W. H. TINSON Printer and Stereotyper, 43 & 45 Centre St. N. Y.

GOOD AND POPULAR BOOKS,

PUBLISHED BY DERBY & JACKSON.

TEN YEARS OF PREACHER LIFE. By Rev. W. H. Milburn. 12mo. $1 00
RIFLE, AXE AND SADDLEBAGS. " " " 12mo. 1 00
GREECE AND THE GOLDEN HORN. By Rev. Stephen Olin. 12mo. 1 00
TRAVELS IN EGYPT AND THE HOLY LAND. By Stephens. 8vo. 2 00
CAPTAIN COOK'S VOYAGES ROUND THE WORLD. 12mo....... 1 00
PICTORIAL LIFE OF BENJAMIN FRANKLIN. 8vo.............. 2 00
RANDALL'S LIFE OF THOMAS JEFFERSON. 3 vols. 8vo. 7 50
BUNYAN'S PILGRIM'S PROGRESS. 12mo.......................... 1 00
BUNYAN'S HOLY WAR. 12mo.. 1 00
FOX'S BOOK OF MARTYRS. 12mo..................................... 1 00
DODDRIDGE'S RISE AND PROGRESS OF RELIGION. 12mo.... 1 00
BAXTER'S SAINTS' REST. 12mo.................................... 1 00
TAYLOR'S HOLY LIVING. 12mo.................................... [illegible]
THE SCOTTISH CHIEFS. By Jane Porter. 12mo.......... ... ... [illegible]
THADDEUS OF WARSAW. " " 12mo.................... 1 00
ADVENTURES OF DON QUIXOTE. 12mo.......................... 1 00
ARABIAN NIGHTS' ENTERTAINMENTS. 12mo..................... 1 00
ADVENTURES OF ROBINSON CRUSOE. 12mo..................... 1 00
SWISS FAMILY ROBINSON. 12mo.................................. 1 00
ÆSOP'S FABLES, with the Morals attached. 12mo. 1 00
VICAR OF WAKEFIELD and *RASSELAS.* (Two in one.) 1 00
PAUL AND VIRGINIA and *EXILES OF SIBERIA.* (Two in one.).. 1 00
RELIGIOUS COURTSHIP and *GREAT PLAGUE.* By De Foe. 1 00
CŒLEBS IN SEARCH OF A WIFE. 12mo........................... 1 00
HANNAH MORE'S TALES AND ALLEGORIES. 12mo............ 1 00
THOUGHTS AND ESSAYS OF JOHN FORSTER. 12mo. 1 00
THE ESSAYS OF ELIA. By Charles Lamb. 12mo. 1 00
JOHNSON'S LIVES OF THE POETS. 2 vols. 12mo.................. 2 50
THE SPECTATOR. By Joseph Addison. 2 vols. 12mo. 2 50
THE TATTLER AND GUARDIAN. By Addison and Steele..... .... 2 00
WIRT'S LIFE OF PATRICK HENRY. 12mo........................ 1 00
SIMMS' LIFE OF GENERAL MARION. 12mo........................ 1 00
WALKER'S LIFE OF GENERAL JACKSON. 12mo..... .... 1 00
LIFE AND CHOICE WORKS OF ISAAC WATTS. 12mo............ 1 25
LAYARD'S POPULAR DISCOVERIES AT NINEVEH. 12mo....... 1 00
FROST'S INDIAN BATTLES AND CAPTIVITIES. 12mo.......... 1 00
WORKS OF OLIVER GOLDSMITH. 4 vols. 12mo. 5 00
WORKS OF CHARLES LAMB. 5 vols. 12mo......................... 6 25
BOSWELL'S LIFE OF DR. JOHNSON. 4 vols. 12mo. 5 00
ROLLIN'S ANCIENT HISTORY. 2 vols. 8vo.................. ..... 4 00
PLUTARCH'S LIVES OF THE ANCIENTS. 8vo..................... 2 00

Either of the above sent by mail, post-paid, on receipt of Price. A liberal Discount to Preachers and Agents. Address

DERBY & JACKSON,
119 Nassau Street, New York.

www.ingramcontent.com/pod-product-compliance
Lightning Source LLC
LaVergne TN
LVHW010148110826
845151LV00002B/460

* 9 7 8 1 4 2 5 5 3 7 5 1 7 *